Ken Newton

Richard Calvert Williamson was born in Devon in 1935, the fifth child of Henry Williamson (author of *Tarka the Otter*), but spent his childhood on the north Norfolk coast where his father farmed during the Second World War.

He was interested in nature from his earliest years. Not being academic, he preferred to roam around the country-side looking at nature, watching birds, butterflies and plants.

On leaving school Richard spent five years in the RAF with two tours in the Middle East, including Cyprus during the Suez Crisis in 1956. He then took on a variety of jobs in forestry and farming before obtaining a post with Nature Conservancy (now Natural England). In 1963 he became the warden of Kingley Vale National Nature Reserve on the South Downs. Richard married Anne in 1964, and they lived in an old gamekeeper's cottage which was totally isolated in the middle of a hazel coppice wood.

He remained as warden until his official retirement in 1995, but then continued with scientific recording work, with a total of over 50 years of records of breeding bird and butterfly populations.

Richard also wrote a weekly column in his local press covering more than 56 years without a break, and published several books. He died in 2022.

A Shadow in the Clouds tells the story of Richard's extraordinary journey to the Wakhan area of eastern Afghanistan in 1972.

Books by Richard Calvert Williamson

The Dawn is My Brother, Faber & Faber, 1969
Capreol, the Story of a Roebuck, Macdonald, 1973
The Great Yew Forest, Macmillan, 1978
Nature Trails, Yew Tree Publishing, 1995
52 Favourite West Sussex Walks, Summersdale, 2012
The Birdwatcher's Year, Summersdale, 2013
Flights of the Mind, Yew Tree Publishing, 2022

Books awaiting publication

Posted to Cyprus (a young airman's view of the Suez Crisis)

Yew, Ewe, and You (an update of *The Great Yew Forest*)

With Love from Russia (a story set around a young Russian girl and an English pilot living on the south coast of England – with a brent goose go-between)

The Star Swan (a love story between a local girl and a German youth set just before and during the Second World War on the north Norfolk coast with a tragic outcome)

A Shadow in the Clouds

The author mounted on his yak in the Sargass Pass

A
SHADOW
IN THE
CLOUDS

Looking for the snow
leopard in Afghanistan

Richard Calvert
Williamson

Skirr Books

Published by
Skirr Books
An imprint of the Henry Williamson Society
14, Nether Grove, Longstanton, CB24 3EL

First published 2023

A CIP catalogue record for this book is available from the
British Library

ISBN 978-1-873507-78-0

Cover photograph: Vince Burton/Alamy Stock Photo
Design by John Gregory

Printed and bound by Page Bros (Norwich) Ltd

Contents

1

It was half-past two on a Tuesday afternoon in September when the telephone rang. Nothing much had been happening in my home, high up on the Sussex Downs. I had been up since dawn and out working, and had come back at lunchtime to sort out some urgent office work. Wood pigeons crooned in the big beech trees outside the office door, and my eye, playing truant from the official letter I was typing, followed the flight of one pigeon after another as they flipped like paper darts over the wood. The leaves out there were beginning to look tired and dusty. Bunches of small green grapes planted by a previous tenant were beginning to ripen in the sun on the wall of my workplace, but I had told myself I must not touch them until mid-October at the earliest – and they were marked for making a gallon of wine anyway.

There were some apples too, over in the little orchard outside the front door, and a handful of plums on one old tree. We had gathered raspberries off the stand of canes growing in the garden of a derelict house hidden even further into this wild wood nature reserve than ours, including a few of what the children had called 'golden drops'. The old larder was full of bottles of fruit, jars of jam and demi-johns of home-made wine. The blackberries were ripening fast and would increase this store two-fold.

On these hot afternoons the house would stretch itself like a dog, creaking as the sun caught under the gables. It had been doing this for over seventy years, according to a small carved oak panel bearing the date 1899 attached to the red tile shingles hanging above the front door. The house had been built for the head game-keeper of the local estate in the glorious days when King Edward VII had attended the shoot on his frequent visits during the season. A large wooden luncheon hut had been built next to the house. Its timber walls had been hung with red, white, and blue silk drapes to make the King feel at home. They had still been there after the Second World War when, rumour had it, the estate staff had finally removed them and made them into silk underwear. The shed was now my garage.

The walls of the house were a foot thick. The chequered red and yellow earthenware floor tiles had been scraped and roughened by the many years of hob-nailed boots. By day the sun might rage outside, trapped by the tall beech trees. But milk stood cold all day in the jug by the north window. There was no electricity in the house and no mains water, although the previous tenants had installed a telephone. The kitchen contained an old iron stove and a huge brick copper in one corner. We (myself, wife, two small children and a Labrador dog) had moved in exactly one year before and were waiting for work to begin on modernisation. Meanwhile we had a routine of lamp cleaning, water carrying and wood collecting.

In winter the moon had wandered across the small glass window-panes, bulging or shrinking, often splintering at the edges as the Victorian glass distorted her image. In spring the bats had silently emerged from under the eaves outside the bedroom window, and we lay awake listening to the song of the nightingale hidden among the woodland shrub. The cherry tree outside the bedroom window was a delight of blossom soon turning to the promise of a huge crop of fruit. But in early June, awake while still in our cloudy sheets, we watched as the jays and blackbirds slipped like brigands among the branches to steal the still unripe green baubles. They didn't leave even one.

We were very happy with our life in this isolated domain: so much to see, so much for our two young children to learn. It was never monotonous but nothing ever changed and we didn't want it to. Then the telephone rang.

'This is Lavinia Swift speaking,' a female voice announced, in somewhat clipped tones. 'I am speaking on behalf of David Cobham, the film producer and director. You will remember him.'

We had met David when he had made a landmark film with my father the previous year for the BBC about the problem of vanishing hedgerows and their effect on the wild-life of this country. I knew he was wanting to make a film of my father's book *Tarka the Otter* and immediately thought that this call was going to be about that. But the voice continued with something rather startling.

'Could you go to Afghanistan on Saturday? We need a writer at once, to do a script for a film about the Marco Polo sheep and the snow leopards in the Pamir Mountains.'

I twigged immediately – this was my wife Anne, having me on. She liked playing these sorts of clever jokes. Well, I would go along with it.

'Yes, of course.' I replied.

'Oh, good,' the voice said after a slight pause. 'Excellent. It was a long shot. The person who was to make the film has been taken ill and can't go. David thought of you. You will be joining a small hunting party, who pay a large amount of money to take one prize head of the Marco Polo. The money goes to the local tribes so that they protect the animals instead of shooting them to extinction. David thought this was a good chance to get into the terrain. It is a very difficult area, the Wakhan Corridor, very cold, all that sort of thing.' The clipped tones continued, 'You will need to be very fit, you will be going up to twenty thousand feet. Is that all right?'

Struggling not to laugh I answered: 'Yes! No problem! Um,

what about money? Are you going to pay me?'

'Of course. There will be a cheque from the BBC for three hundred pounds, but I will also meet you here at the office and hand over some dollars and your airline ticket. You travel to Tehran and then there are connection flights to Kabul. You'll be away about three to four weeks. Oh – is your passport up to date? Fine. I will telephone you tomorrow morning with further details. Thank you. Goodbye.'

The phone went dead. Well, that was all very clever, I thought, not a slip in the delivery and not the hint of the giggle that was usually my wife's Achilles heel. But I felt a bit uneasy. Could it actually have been genuine? No, it was definitely Anne playing a joke. Next Saturday? Afghanistan? I didn't even know where the country was, or what a Marco Polo sheep was, though to see a fabled snow leopard was a dream from my childhood.

My curiosity aroused I went into the house and looked at the old globe we had bought for our son. I must know where Afghanistan is, I thought, but I didn't. At that time no one knew anything about that remote country. That was to change: a year later the Russians invaded, and it has been in the news ever since. In September 1972 it might have been on Mars as far as I was concerned.

Then I remembered that the voice on the telephone had mentioned Tehran. Well, I knew where that was and turned the globe and found Persia (Iran, as it is now called). Then my finger traced around, finding Kashmir and Soviet Baluchistan, and then the Gobi Desert – surely too far, so back west and then there it was. Land-locked, barren, mountainous, and a long way away. How had Anne known about this? Something to do with her work had started it off, I supposed. I could imagine her sitting with her workmates, laughing their heads off. Well, she would soon be home with the children. I went back out to my office and finished the job I was doing.

It was not long before I heard the car and Anne arrived, having collected the children from school on the way as usual.

'That was brilliant!' I exclaimed as she came through the door. 'You should have taken up acting as a career.'

She stared at me. 'What on earth are you talking about?' she asked rather crossly. The children were grizzling a bit. They were hungry and wanted her attention and their tea.

'Going to Afghanistan on Saturday. You really had me fooled. When did you think up a story like that? Marco Polo sheep! What on earth are they?'

'Oh, for goodness' sake, let me get these children settled.'

'Is Daddy being silly, Mummy?' five-year-old Bryony asked in her serious voice.

'Well, one of his funny stories, I expect. You'd better ask him.'

'What are you talking about, Daddy?' asked Brent, grinning, his seven-year-old mouth full of bread and jam.

'Yes, what are you talking about?' echoed Bryony.

'Your mother played a very clever trick on me this afternoon over the telephone. She pretended she is going to send me to somewhere a very long way away to look at some very odd sheep and make a film about snow leopards.' They are stared at me in silence.

'Oh really, Rikky dear, I've got better things to do than to play tricks over the telephone. You know how busy I am, not even a lunch hour so I can leave off early. Besides I don't even have a phone anywhere near my desk.'

'Oh! What? You mean —?'

'It certainly wasn't me who phoned you – or is this your joke on me? No? Well, if someone phoned you then it was real. What did they say?'

'Well, she said that David Cobham was going to make a film for the BBC, and the chap who was supposed to go is taken ill and could I go instead – this Saturday. I thought it was you – so I said "Yes" – oh, glory be, what have I done?'

'Well, that certainly sounds real. Saturday – there's only three days. Afghanistan!'

Anne sounded a bit worried. When I eventually got back from that terrible place, she told me that as I left she had wondered if she would ever see me again. She knew a bit about Afghanistan and the Wakhan Corridor. She had done A-level Geography, and as her teacher had been the sister of the Himalayan explorer Eric Shipton, had chosen that area to study. She knew the Wakhan was a long hostile pan-handle gap between mountains that even Marco Polo had travelled in trepidation. It was the link between Persia and China, a very tenuous living space, almost as a vacuum to human life, a thread of existence still living a more or less medieval life. It was the rift that kept Russia and India apart. Very few westerners had explored it: a few military personnel of the Raj, and the occasional hunter.

The second phone call the next morning proved it was all rather too real. It was also all rather exciting. But panic set in; three days in which to get organised. I had a job – I had no suitable clothes for rugged mountain trekking. Urgent phone-calls were made to my official employers to get permission to have special leave of absence from my work for a month. Fortunately they co-operated, seeing it as useful training for me and perhaps publicity for themselves. It was all in the name of nature conservation after all. Anne went off to the shops to try and find suitable clothes. The local yachting shop had just had its winter supplies delivered, and so I became the owner of a thickly padded nylon coat complete with hood, new padded boots – and thick warm thermal underwear. I already had plenty of rough country wear, woolly hat, mitts, socks, and waterproof leggings.

Everything was packed into my old RAF kitbag, still with

its Cyprus Draft numbers painted on for the 1956 Suez Crisis, the 'Challenger' expedition of Anthony Eden's confrontation with President Nasser of Egypt. I added notebooks, camera, binoculars, some basic first aid, and for some reason decided to take a small silver thermometer which I had bought in Sweden on a trip a few years previously – but no RAF uniform this time. Also missing was the security of others in the pack, no mates: I was on my own.

On the Saturday I took the train to London, and made my way to David Cobham's office, meeting up with the lady who had telephoned and who now handed over some dollars, the air tickets, and a pile of official papers about the conservation of endangered species together with a couple of books borrowed from the Nature Conservancy library on the area. She told me to report to the British Embassy and the Afghan Tourist Office on arrival. They had been informed about my visit and everything was arranged. David appeared, his usual genial self, to wish me well. I spent the night at my sister's London home, and early next morning she drove me to Heathrow Airport. I bought a Sunday newspaper complete with expensive weekend coloured comic and clutched it like a rag-doll all the way to Beirut. In the departure lounge I felt very alone, a westerner among a crowd of dark-skinned bearded foreigners all cheerfully and noisily going back to their own country.

Soon the jumbo jet was trembling above the brown and green countries of Europe showing occasional patches of white snow; rivers became tinsel strips far below, reminding me of the aluminium strips known to British Intelligence in the Second World War as 'window'. A lot of it got dropped around the area of our farm on the Norfolk coast by the German Luftwaffe, a treasured prize to all the local boys scrambling through barbed-wire fences to collect it up.

An American lady with a dry brown face announced to me

15

after a second glass of wine that this travelling was old stuff to her. She was going onwards to China after Beirut. It was just too dull in Europe. She had seen Blenheim Palace, but not the Downs. She had seen Versailles but not the Auvergne. She had been to Vienna but had not seen Beethoven's statue, or the grave of Schubert. She had never heard of Mahler or the Steinbach Hauschen on Lake Attersee where he had written his second and third symphonies. Actually she had not heard of the composer at all. No wonder she had found Europe boring: it was all just 'ticks' on the tourist list. Where was I going? Surely there was nothing in Afghanistan – rather a god-forsaken sort of a place.

I thought of my last travel adventure – to Cyprus at the time of the Suez Crisis. At least there wasn't going to be a welcome from machine guns and land-mines directed at me, which is what Cyprus welcomed us with. I thought again of the snow leopards, the huge sheep, the local tribes, the grand mountains, and camping out. This trip was going to be pretty wonderful, I told myself.

I started to read the brief about the conservation efforts in Afghanistan by the World Wildlife Fund. A man called Petocz, a Canadian biologist, who had studied moose and bighorn sheep, had made some safaris into the Hindu Kush and reported on his sightings of one of the rarest goats in the world, the Markhor, whose numbers were down to less than a thousand in the world. He had made a proposal via UNICEF to the Afghan authorities for the conservation of the Marco Polo sheep in its highest mountain ranges in the Pamir Mountains. The BBC wanted to make a film around this story. From what I read, he was playing a crucial and daring role with the government and the Afghan king, insisting that large reserves be set up at once, where none had ever been before. Money from special hunting licences was to help fund this project.

Beautiful girls brought food and drink. Outside the window the sun shone very bright. It had been raining when I left. When a wing dipped I could see the shadow sliding across the remote and constantly moving clouds. Nobody else looked out of the window at the Bosphorus moving slowly below. I seemed to be the only person who saw the beauty of it, spread out as we hung far above it all. The American lady, obviously also finding me boring, had reclined herself over the only three empty seats on the plane and gone to sleep. A group of Jews with sensuous eyes and lips were whispering excitedly over a large book they were sharing. They looked cultured, the only ones on board who did. Most of the others were asleep.

I wished my wife was with me: she loved the same things that I did. I wondered what she was doing. I did not know until sometime later that the following morning the builders had arrived without warning to begin the work that had been promised for the past year. She went off to work leaving the dog in their care – and when she returned with the children later in the day there was a huge hole where the kitchen wall had been, covered only with a large canvas sheet, so a lobby and bathroom could be built on the far side, and the vegetable garden was a large hole ready for a septic tank to be built there. It rained and froze and the wind flapped that canvas sheet every night I was away. The wall was rebuilt just before I returned. She told me the workmen had thought she had been abandoned and they felt quite sorry for her!

Meanwhile, to stop my own gloomy thoughts, I opened my Sunday newspaper, and saw reports of the last night of the Proms, with pictures of long queues of happy youths in sleeping bags along the pavements. I felt very homesick, like being hopelessly in love for the first time. But I also felt like an adventurer, a Crusader, setting forth on a momentous adventure to conquer the vast mountains ahead of me.

Our stop at Ankara made the jumbo's retarding devices roar and shake, for the runway was short. Now a new curved moon hung in the sky, and on flags. The bitter smell of the desert came through the pores of the aircraft, a smell that was familiar to me from my service in the Middle East, that exhilarating stink of ammonia, burning camel dung, and aromatic desert plants blooming and dying into brittle skeletons. Dawn brought the hot bare light of the East, which reminded me of the desert in Syria where I had slept in the tents of Bedouins. Suddenly excited, I thought – I am back! Back here in the East, and those distant moments of youth in the land of El Laurens, and Doughty, and Burton: back to the dry and shimmering plains where camels sometimes seemed to walk on lakes of water.

Men mooched about the airfield with brooms, sweeping the runway when planes were not landing. They were thin, showing cheek bones and sun-scorched brows. A herd of goats grazed the plant skeletons a few feet from us as we floated on our dozens of fat tyres clustered under us like an over-burdened life-raft. We were a whale, beached reluctantly, ready to roar a huge spout of gas and hang again in the oceans of the sky. I wanted to stop here and explore beyond the flags, take a caravan to the darker side of the moon.

But the hunting group I was to join was leaving Kabul soon, and I had to be there. The plane taking off again gave an urgency to my mind, but also a high thin whine of doubt. Not an actual sound but a thinning of air and sustenance. I felt aware of the transition between Western affluence and Eastern existence. Twenty years before, the East had meant danger, an old memory that the senses had not forgotten, and which had quietly been exhuming themselves unknown to my conscious mind, and were now warning me. I was committed: I had to go; but let's get it over quickly and hopefully I'll get out in one piece.

There was another stop in the darkness in Beirut. The American lady with whom I had nothing in common got off, and I immediately missed her company. The hills reared up to meet us, strewn with lights, and then dropped away and went out. I peered past window reflections, seeing the horned moon low and yellow, but revealing nothing of the desert below. I had flown over this desert before, in the RAF days. A journey had been made at some eight thousand feet aboard a Vickers Valetta, successor of the Wellington. It was a stubby transport plane affectionately called the Pig, because of its fat body. It was hardly more shapely than a barrage balloon, but reliable. It had two growling Hercules engines whose cylinder explosions could be heard separately.

On that journey we had run into a series of thunderstorms whose peaks rose eight miles into the skies; that is six and a half miles above our own height. It was day-time, but so dark the cabin lights were on. Somebody had just said it was time the galley-boy poured out the tea, when the kite lurched with a kick under the port wing, lifting it sixty degrees. Then we hurled down like a boulder over a cliff, bouncing off some black rocks of air at the bottom of a cloud canyon. The wings had bowed down and flapped up. The aircraft had been thrown on its side several times through ninety degrees of roll. Lightning had flickered around us and had fissured its clouds like the seams in cracked marble, and St Elmo's fire had burned with blue and purple flames all over the wings. Our pilot, whose credentials were as long as his handlebar moustaches, said this had been his most interesting flight of all, including bombing raids over Germany. 'Interesting' was not the word the rest of us RAF 'erks' used to describe that flight.

Now, as we crossed this same desert twenty years later, there was a strange coincidence. There was another storm, but this time it was well below us and the jumbo scarcely trembled. Pale blue strobes of light dashed back and forth, searchlight like floods of light whitened the clouds, showing them for a second, hiding them again, driving bright daggers into billows, creating networks of white-hot veins, turning pitch black to the pearly gleam of oyster shells. Only in the let down to Tehran did the bumping remind me of the old days with its alarming taste of sickness in the mouth. But this time there were reassuring beautiful women between us and danger, wearing grey and blue uniforms, with soft hands and necks, and a magical ability to ward off any evil, not with muscles and machines but with a power of their own, not possessed by men.

'Is your seat-belt fixed sir?' A white smile, a dark eye, a close bosom, and a scent holding all together, like the sweet ascending violin in the Brahms' violin concerto. It was still the Shah's enlightened Persia then. Persian women did not have to wear purdah. They showed their thick, black, glistening hair in the airport and they showed natural happiness and confidence at being free and equal.

I had not the faintest idea where to go, because I had been looking at the women instead of the airport directions. I stood behind one of these Persian girls who was in a queue moving towards a gate. Such long, thick hair, such fine dark skin! She turned and smiled; somebody had called out to her from behind me. Now there was a tongue and pink mouth to add, with every tooth crater as white as fresh snow, untouched, like the dimples in a high mountain snowfield.

No other nation's women have such eyes. They are not the cold blue eyes of Finland, nor the soft but suffering eyes of India, certainly not the half-closed, calculating, sundew traps of America, whose false lashes lay as wide as spring traps. My Persian beauty said something: I tried to record it in my mind but when I later tried to remember its cadence it eluded me totally. All I could hear was my wife's voice saying faintly:

'Goodbye Rikky dear, safe journey.'

Before I got any further a man was gabbling at me about a visa, and his hard yellow teeth cut off my glimpsed dream-way to the soft black nights of Tehran. He sent me off to the internal holding lounge. It was small, with a curve of padded seats and a glass case or two filled with local jewellery. There was no food, no drink, no other airliner, and no more travellers except me. Even RAF desert airfields had been better equipped twenty years previously. I studied the bracelets made of that familiar fine silver filigree which were only thirty per cent silver and the rest copper, lead, or whatever else was surplus after remodelling scrapped cars into steel trunks, kitchen ware, house security gates, parts for other cars, or bits for guns. There are several ways to mine metal, and only the West does it expensively.

I bought one for my wife. Twenty years before, the moment I landed in Egypt I had bought a carved ivory figure for my mother, carrying it everywhere, just as my father had worn his mother's letters next to the skin in the trenches of 1914, together with the cigarettes a German soldier had given him on Christmas Eve.

In the early hours of the morning, when the black earth was shuffling with unseen people and donkeys, I boarded the next airline. There were just two passengers, myself and a large Persian business-man with a crater zone of old pimples on his neck. The gazelle who served coffee, just after the jet became airborne into a molten green dawn, fussed continually round His Fatness, dazzled, I supposed, by the gold on his fingers and his teeth. Power, Kissinger said, is the ultimate aphrodisiac. I felt better: the gazelle was welcome to him if that was what impressed her.

The jet's skin was hammered pink by the metal sky of the desert, and was as clean and oven-baked as the flawless paint on Elvis Presley's Cadillac. But it was changing its colours by the minute until it was hard silvery blue. Below on the ground was not the desert of Arabia with the crisp white linen of the princes; nor was it the Shah's Persia of the picture books, or even the civilisation of Jordan or Iraq that I had once known.

2

There was a burst of gabbling noise and a lot of heat when the plane doors were opened. Men with tousled hair and slop buckets were waiting to come aboard to clean the already immaculate interior. Outside a hot desert wind was blowing, but in the distance there was snow on the tops of biscuit-coloured mountains. Black shapes that could have been men or donkeys or camels made of jelly wobbled on the runway a mile away. A faint haze and smell lay in the air coming from the city, and I noticed a man holding a rag across his mouth.

In the airport lounge stood a stuffed ram. It was as tall as a New Forest pony and its head held two curling crowns of horn, each of which cork-screwed out to twice the width of its body. Its glass eyes stared past me up into the distant mountains and its eye-lashes were those of the Persian girl's. It did not look anything like an English sheep. Its fleece was as short as the hair on a Labrador. A label announced it was an '*Ovis poli*' – a Marco Polo. I stood and stared. My first sighting of what I was here for. Here was an animal which had once bounded around the roof of the world with the grace and fluid ease of a porpoise. How could it have survived up there?

I felt a sense of purpose and belonging when the customs and immigration officials asked me how long I was staying and where was I going. They exchanged glances and whispered something to each other when I said: 'Pamir Mountains and the Wakhan Corridor – to see your wild animals.' But no comment was made openly, and returning my passport duly stamped they waved me past, explaining in answer to my question that a taxi outside would take me into Kabul.

As I left the airport building one of them called me and came running out.

'Sir! Mr Wilson!'

I felt important. The vulnerability of being so far from home and on my own in a very foreign country was rather unsettling. But already they knew me, even if they had got my name slightly wrong.

'Please! Did you leaf your bag in airport? Please to come at once and identify, please.'

With a start I realised that indeed I had left the black plastic brief-case behind. Now feeling embarrassed and foolish I turned back. They now stood a little more stiffly and stared hard at me, and one said softly, 'Please to say what you carry in the bag.'

'Papers, about wild life, in this country. I said, that is why I am here.'

'We open, please?' Said with a smile, but the question was a formality as I realised the bag was already open. He carefully slid out the airline sugar packets and paper towels and spread them with his hands. They were all looking at me.

'And sugars too?' his voice icily soft. 'And small paper towels?' A slight movement ran through the other men, like a breeze through young poplar trees. I felt like a small boy again in front of the headmaster. But for goodness' sake, I was a grown man, English, and it was hardly a crime.

'Well, you never know, up in the mountains.'

'Of course.' The items were swept back into the bag and it was handed over to me with a very superior look.

My heart was pounding slightly and I decided to go to the lavatory to get out of their sight. When I came out, they were involved with a small group of Japanese tourists who were obviously on their way out of the country on the jet that had just brought me in. Voices were raised and I could see there was some confusion going on. I stood and pretended to read a notice. Their cases were being searched by the customs. One case was wide open revealing a pair of ancient horns, which I recognised from the papers and books I had been reading on the flight over as from a Markhor goat, and so knew was one of the species that was endangered in the area. I had read that they were down to one thousand individuals. The horns were two huge corkscrews each a metre long, attached to the skull, and only just fitting in the case. (In those days the restrictions on luggage size were not so tight.)

'I am sorry. Is not possible to take horns.' said the official who had found my sugar packets. 'Is endangered species. You must leave in Afghanistan.'

The Japanese gentleman showed signs of agitation.

'But I have paid one hundred dollars for these! I must have them. You cannot take them. I bought them in the bazaar. The man said it was all right to take them out of the country.'

'I am sorry, pleas' belief' me. In bazaar they do not know these things. You must not take away from Afghanistan. I haf' to remove. This is law here, is endangered specie.'

He spread his arms wide and smiled like a tiger. In vain the Japanese man asked for his money back. In vain he set his face against all bazaar owners. In vain he protested the antiquity of the horns which were obviously old and dirty with the detritus of the bazaar. Watching, I was impressed that the Convention of Endangered Species, which forbade the export or import of Red Data species including any bit of any species for any country that was a signatory of that law, was being held up so vigorously in Afghanistan.

'They will be destroyed now and bazaar man punished.'

The official closed the case and the Japanese party sullenly continued. I now also left the building and stood for a moment to get accustomed to the glare and heat. To my surprise, I saw the official come out of a side door and hand the Markhor goat horns to a young lad on a bicycle, who stuck them over the handlebars and sped off with them towards the city. Later I was to see those same horns back up for sale in a shop in the bazaar. It was quite a neat little racket!

A line of what appeared to be universally dark green Mercedes, all rather battered but with a broad identifying stripe of red along their flanks, marked the taxi rank. Kabul airport is about four kilometres from the city along a straight road. Today, seeing television footage of Kabul is like residents of London or Dresden seeing their fair cities in 1945 after the war-time bombing raids. But in 1972, although a little stark, it was still all in one piece, in the better areas anyway; and although deeply Muslim, its colonial past was still very much in evidence. The driver of the taxi taking me to my hotel talked of the reigning monarch in a hushed voice. This was His Majesty King Mohammed Zahir Shah. As we came towards the palace the driver stared out of his window, obviously hoping to catch a glimpse of His Majesty. And took no notice of anything that was happening on the actual road. Several drivers in other cars hooted frantically at him: he automatically hooted back. Then he stopped.

'I tell you story,' he said and proceeded to do so. His English was good enough for me to follow his tale. The palace was called the arg, which he explained was a Turkish word and meant citadel. The old palace had apparently been destroyed by the British army during the Second Anglo-Afghan War of 1878–1880 but that was a long time ago and no one was very interested in that now. The driver waved his arms in dismissal. Since then, there had been much else to talk about especially the assassination of the present king's father, King Nadir

Shah, but that was many years ago too, 'before your war, 1933'. It was obviously a tale that he had by heart and rolled out for all visitors who used his taxi: he knew it was worth an extra tip.

The palace was set behind a high wall, but the roof could be seen. Opposite was the Kabul Hotel where I was to stay. The Kabul Hilton was too expensive. I was glad of that, as mine was redolent of the 1930s, only two stories high and with a long ochre-coloured frontage with tall old windows divided by wooden frames and small panes of glass. It looked like a smaller, soft-cheese version of Petworth House in Sussex near where I lived, where Turner had painted the fallow deer herd in the evening sunlight with their trailing cobwebs of shadow stretching far across the closely cropped parkland. There was a similar hazy look in the air.

The taxi swung dangerously across the road and deposited me at my destination. There was a high roofed doorway and a young Afghani in starched white coat and creased black trousers came forward to open the door for an obvious European. At that moment a Land Rover hummed busily by on the tarmac with that familiar pitching on its old-fashioned springs. I had noticed as we drove along that the traffic was composed mainly of the beaten-up red-striped Mercedes taxis with a few Ladas and several lorries laden with an assortment of goods.

Next to the hotel, across an intersection, I saw there was a mosque with a squashed onion dome on its roof and four small minarets facing the four quarters of the compass. Pergola-style lower roofs were sheathed in zinc. There was a wide verandah over the front door. Palm trees grew around it, and beyond, a grove of eucalyptus and willow. But noticing the taxi driver was holding a rag over his mouth and nose as dust streamed past like smoke from a bonfire of rubbish, that had created the hazy air – and now also a pungent smell –

I scurried quickly into the hotel.

Kabul Hotel had been the home of Europeans, clearly enough. The reception desk was tall, made of hardwood and shiny with age, unlike, as I discovered, the unpolished, dusty, softwood from willow or poplar faded to a pale creamy-green, as found in the rest of Kabul. No one was in sight, but a small bronze bell sat on the desk, and when I rang it a man toddled out of the gloom to greet me, wearing glasses too small for his round fat face, which showed that he had never had to worry about his next meal, as did everyone else I had seen so far. Yes, I was expected. A booking had been made, Sir. All was arranged, Sir. I was to have a room overlooking the Royal Palace, and beyond that a view to the foothills of the Hindu Kush. I handed over my passport with an apprehensive feeling that it would never be seen again.

'But of course, Sir, it will be returned to you at dinner this evening. Your details have to be recorded but it is important you have it on you all the time, Sir. That is our rule here.'

My room also, of course, overlooked the main road. Even with the windows shut it was noisy. I felt slightly breathless, which I put down to being 5,000 feet above sea level. Someone had once told me a tale about some secret signs they had seen in the bedrooms of Egyptian hotels in the Thirties. They were apparently to do with requests for night-time comforts available for residents. I wondered if there would be any here. But it was probably all an old wives' tale anyway. The notices had probably been to do with local customs. Certainly, the only notices here were the usual official ones to be found in most hotels. Anyway, these people had nothing to do with the Egyptian Pharaohs and the thousands of years of sensuality that had reigned along the banks of the Nile, where sex had once been a religious experience. There was nothing here worshipped like the exquisite boy kings and girl queens, doe-eyed and gentle-lipped, reaching paradise through sexual feelings. Life here was obviously hard. Their land over millennia had supplied the crushed rock which was carried as silt a thousand miles down the rivers, draining away the fertility of the land to the plains of India. I hadn't seen the face of a woman, in fact hadn't actually seen a woman at all, I realised, but the men were hard-lipped and deep brown, looking hard-bodied and lithe when young but soon ageing. They were clean shaven, except the mullahs who I knew had full beards of black curly hair like my own. I had already noticed that the few people I had met had kept looking at my beard and pursing their lips. Well, I had survived the Middle East. It couldn't be any worse here.

The next day I visited, as instructed by 'The Voice', as I called her to myself, the British Embassy, a place set delicately in a small green garden. The iron railings surrounding the property were bright white, and someone was even painting more bright white over the top of this. The orange-tiled roof and white walls were hung with wisteria. Mulberry trees made pools of shadows across the green well-watered lawn. Fig trees were holding delights and promise for those within its walls. The feeling was of enchantment and the comfort of the Victorian Empire – and very English. Part of me felt at home: the other part felt that it was very alien, totally out of keeping with its setting and rather unsettling.

The men within were very British, very Public School, working hard to show they were keeping the Empire on its rails. They were so typical of the type that I had to been to school with that I smiled wryly to myself. I felt a little more confident. But it was immediately evident that they had not been told of my visit and proposed trek. They made me wait for some time before I was ushered into an office where there were two officials. They were polite, but distant and a little dubious about me. I wasn't wearing a suit and probably looked little different from the usual English nationals they dealt

29

with, who were of the age and inclination of hippies, although I was not wearing the ubiquitous jeans. But when I mentioned the BBC, they relaxed and smiled and said, well that was jolly good, and offered me coffee. But they both seemed a little uneasy; they kept glancing sideways at each other as if concerned about something that was not being mentioned. That made me uneasy in turn. What did they know that they were not telling me?

After a few minutes of social talk about England and its weather, one of these minor diplomats got up and left the room. His companion continued to ask questions, but then hardly seemed to be listening to my replies, though when I said I would be going up into the Pamir Mountains and on along the Wakhan Corridor towards the Chinese and Russian borders, he became suddenly alert.

'Good grief! I hope you come back! It's practically unheard of. It's a long way there and a long way back again. All pretty rough going, you know. You'll only be about the hundredth British person to go there this century. Good lord! King George the Fifth shot a Marco Polo sheep up there sometime in the Twenties. Of course, there were a lot of skirmishes there in the Afghan Wars in the Victorian days, and we lost a lot of troops one way and another.'

He stopped abruptly, his eyes continually going to the door the other man had gone out of. I began to feel quite nervous. What was going on? Surely not some sort of coup. I started to imagine all sorts of things.

'Is something wrong?'

'What? Oh no, of course not, oh excuse me.' He got up and left the room; as the door opened I could hear the sound of running water, and then the other man returned. He did not sit down again, and indicated the interview was over by holding out his hand and wishing me well.

'You'll need a visa for the journey out of this province and into the next. You get that from the police station. Well, all the best, old chap. Let us know when you are back, just for the records, you know.'

A smartly dressed Afghani opened the door as I left. It was only later that I realised the reason for their strangely unsettling behaviour: that night, in fact. Meanwhile I made my way to the Afghan Tourist Office as instructed by The Voice. Introducing myself, it was again immediately obvious that they had no knowledge of my existence, or of the proposal that I was to join the American hunting party.

'But, sir, you have missed them. They have already left.'

That rather shook me. What on earth was I to do now? I had come all this way to do a job and it was a total disaster.

'Can I catch them up?'

'Sir, I am afraid not possible. But there is more hunters later. You can join them?'

'Really? You are sure? How much later?'

And so it was arranged that I would return and meet up with two American hunters in three weeks' time. That created its own problems. I only had one month's leave of absence: that would now be up before I even started on the actual trip. I returned to the hotel. Could I make an urgent phone call to England? They would arrange it. After a short while I was telling my wife of the problem. She said she would contact my bosses and get it sorted – meanwhile not to worry. There was nothing that could be done about it. She would also contact David Cobham's office. There was no time for personal chat; we said that we would write to each other, and then the time was up.

I went into the dining room for dinner, and then still having jet-lag and after a difficult day, I suddenly felt very tired and went off to bed. And soon after I got there it struck: the Kabul Trots. It was then that I realised that that was what the trouble had been at the Embassy that morning. The two officials had dysentery and were worrying about the lavatory being free for their next urgent visit. No wonder they were thin. I was up and down all night, and felt pretty rotten. My stomach had the unreal flickering tense feeling that I had once felt when my brother John took me flying in his glider and did a loop. But now the loop was continuous throughout the night; and I went on feeling upside-down for several days.

Eventually my system got accustomed to the situation, and I decided to take a look around the city. I went down side streets, into gardens, and small parks. The main roads were wide, and tarmac had been spread like blackberry jam: thick, uneven, and pippy with gravel. There were traffic lights on each intersection. They went amber, red, and back to green as all traffic lights do. The Russians had put them there and they were working as they should. The trouble was – nobody took any notice of them. Cars sped through them during vague lulls in the traffic whatever colour they happened to be. When traffic was heavy, a tuneless cacophony like a brass band of non-players brayed endlessly during these suicidal merges.

There is a national sport in Afghanistan called 'buzkashi', originating, no doubt, back in the mists of time, from training in horse and survival skills of nomadic tribes, but supposedly invented by Attila and enthusiastically followed by Genghis Khan and Tamerlane. Rather like primitive polo, and surely its forerunner, I was soon to see this game, played thirty a side, on horseback, the ball being a headless goat. Meanwhile the city car drivers thought they were on a buzkashi pitch as they drove through the streets. One day I saw the inevitable happen.

After a screech and a thud, glass spouted like a fountain, two cars slewed, one began to roll, and an arm flailed out of the window like a dead winter branch in a gale. Long red marks of paint showed all down the road and bits of rusty metal lay among the traffic which carried on as though nothing had happened. Pools of shining oil, water and petrol spread out from the wrecked cars into the cratered tarmac. I couldn't get near to help. In any case, both drivers extricated themselves, and clutching wrists, holding arms into their bodies and with bloody heads, ran away in opposite directions among the traffic, like frightened rabbits dazzled by headlights at night. One scuttled down a side street, the other behind some bushes at the edge of a park. They tried to hide by crouching low. One of them was moaning. By our standards they were quite badly injured, but no one was taking any notice. I felt a bit alarmed, but I had seen this kind of incident and injury when in the RAF in Cyprus, when EOKA was active. Greek Cypriot patriots, known to us at the time as terrorists, ambushed our vehicles on country lanes by laying mines to stop the vehicle, then opening fire with machine guns and shotguns. One had got used to that sort of thing.

I went on watching, curious to see what would happen next. After a few minutes, one of the men stood up and shouted to the other. He held up an arm which was hanging at an odd angle and pointed to it with the other. His face was ashen from shock. The other driver limped slowly across the road, hanging grimly on to a hand that appeared to be about to fall off. As they got close to each other they began to speak excitedly, once or twice forgetting their wounds and waving their arms, only to wince and double up with pain. The traffic still swerved itself around the two wrecked cars without slowing. I expected further accidents at any moment.

A policeman, looking to be about seventeen, wearing faded blue denim fatigues, forage cap, and wooden truncheon fixed to his leather body-belt, arrived in a truck and placed a red cross on the road by each car. The two drivers sheepishly approached and there was a great deal of talking, after which they left the scene in opposite directions. Later in the day I saw that both cars had been removed.

I related this incident to a local doctor I met, curious about, to me, the strange behaviour of the drivers. He explained that among the less educated classes it was the custom going back to very early times, that if a person was wounded, justice would be meted out upon the assailant by the victim's family, when an identical wound would be given. Since both these men had received broken arms, they would consider that they were equal and no further justice was needed.

'But you would not have seen them again in that place. They did not reclaim their own car. That would have been too risky. The first one to do so would then have been the assailant. No, even a car is not worth being killed in retribution. No, certain other men take away such vehicles and make their own living that way. That is the system here.'

There were other ways to die in Kabul. One could smell it in certain areas. But the sweet yellow of autumn, the fine silty dust which never stopped its insane hurrying to nowhere and hung like cornflour on the streets, the smell of apples and apricots and the soft red juice of loganberries masked this underlying hint of death, as did the smiles and abstracted inner expressions on the faces of its victims. The youth of France, England, Germany, and America, escaping from rich indulgent parents, had tracked across the deserts and the plains to find the beginning of the world and its end, the source of the sun's arousal and its consummation, the explanation for why they lived and who had planned it all. They were looking for paradise and thought they had found it. They had found opium and cannabis and each other, and were loath to leave this gentle cradle. There were queues of them at the banks, drawing out cash sent by bewildered parents, to keep themselves in this state of happy well-being. It was not a life that had ever tempted me. Father had told us life was hard work and set an example, whether it was writing or running a farm. He had experienced the First World War, and then the Second. His comrades had given their lives. Their sacrifice must not be wasted. Mother's role of holding the family together confirmed this. It was drilled into me that I had to earn my living. Like my father, I combined that with writing. I liked the job I now had in nature conservation and worked hard at it, and wrote in what spare time I had.

One day I went to the British Council, a small, whitewashed concrete bungalow with a fig tree in its muddy garden, to borrow a book from its library. I found that this was where the English hippies gathered to read *Country Life*, last week's *Times*, and perhaps wonder whether life did not begin back in civilised London after all. In Kabul they were living in slums and were despised by the devout Muslims who rented out rooms to them. Curious about their lives, I talked to them and they invited me to visit them. I found them, a mile from the palace, in an upstairs room in a house of pale mud set in a street of filth. A faintly lovely girl lay on a bed, her arms behind her neck showing rich blossom of shining pale hair in her armpits. A sweet smile of welcome, dusty as though with pollen, greeted me. Her cheeks were faintly golden too, with delicate down that glowed in the warm light. There was a shine of something damp on her lips and an opened pomegranate in her outstretched hand, its red seeds dripping juice. The small window of the medieval house directed a beam of sunlight like a searchlight over her body. Other shapes lounged in semi-darkness on beds and chairs, or on dirty coloured rugs across the floor.

'Sit down, man,' a voice suggested slowly as though talking in its sleep. 'Have you got hash?'

I sat on the floor, wondering why I was there and what I should do next. I was not used to this kind of encounter. They did nothing. The room was full of the cloyingly sweet smell of their drugs.

'You've got nice eyes,' the girl on the bed said.

There was a long silence, as if all life and even existence was suspended; that we in this room would not move again, would not grow any older; that we were in an everlasting state of benign existence. A man like a pirate, with curly black hair and gold ear rings, handed me a loose, limp cigarette like an ear of barley. It was horrible. I pretended to take a few puffs then left it to smoulder, and after a while it went out. It was a badge of entry to the clan, just like the bowler hat on the early morning suburban train into the City. Another man was puffing on a small pipe in a corner of the room, letting forth loose small signals of white smoke. They seemed to come from a long way away, as on a far-away hilltop in a desert. He also had black hair, drawn into a tail behind. His arms were scrawny, brown and quite hairless. I could now see that there were about twelve men in the room, all moving very slightly, sighing, all thin and sunburnt, all rather like the Italian prisoners of war who came to work on our farm when I was still a child, to produce food for the towns. But these men were useless, nothing more than time-wasters, producing nothing.

Among them were some young women, also very thin, the bones in their arms like thin tree branches. They were all smiling dreamily, no longer wondering when or where or how or why they were there. Time in that place was stilled. Nothing more was needed. Any vision of the future had obviously vanished: time was here, now, and forever. The glazed look in their eyes showed they were in their own eternity. The beautiful girl on the bed fingered the pomegranate and put some seeds in her mouth, smiling secretly to herself. The sun had moved on: the hair in her armpits was now a dull brown colour.

A man sitting next to me said: 'Perhaps we should go for a walk.'

The girl on the bed slowly turned her head to where the voice had come from, then stayed looking at me, her eyes even wider. But no one moved, and there was silence again for a long while. At last came a far-away voice, crooning to itself like the driver of a camel-train crossing the desert, and saying for reasons known only to itself, 'The consequences of dianism leads to irrational thinking.'

'There is nothing that is irrational; concepts are constrained by circumstances,' answered another far-away voice after an interval. 'Ergo, present fashion and dominant leader patterns condition us to think we know what the world is. But the world is further away than we've been told.'

Another man roused himself off the floor on his elbow and added more thoughts. 'This is cosmos, man, now, here, present time and place. It's all here. Here we're seeing. I can see into the black hole, the black hole of time. The meaning of life is there.'

'Seeing, man, seeing,' another voice added.

It was loose and meaningless. It had been just the same on piss-up nights in the services. And it was no different from the meaningless management-speak that later crossed the Atlantic and at great cost infiltrated and drugged practically every organisation into thinking it held the answers. It promised solutions to everything but there was no real action. It was a way of controlling the horror of not actually knowing the answer to 'the meaning of life'.

I left, wondering what 'dianism' meant to the person who had uttered it. It was all rather sad. They seemed to be intelligent, but were wasting away in their fairy-land world. I saw these groups of hippies wandering around the city every day I was there. The local Afghanis tended to ignore them. They were too busy with the realities of life, which was as much as they could cope with. Their eyes were on the ground, thinking of survival.

Onc incident caused me a great deal of interest. I watched a big young American wearing a sort of Stetson buy a young wolf in the bazaar. I could see that he handed over quite a lot of notes. The animal seemed tame and loped erratically behind him on a rope tied round its neck. Having nothing better to do, I followed at a slight distance. Knowing a bit about wild animals from my work, and having once kept a tame fox cub, I noticed that the wolf kept its nose high into the wind, and is grey eyes were taking in everything along the way: I knew it was biding its time. It would escape the moment the chance arose. The look-alike cowboy was boasting in a loud voice to his group of friends that he might take it back to the States, or he might take it out to the Hindu Kush and let it go. He had no idea of the reality of looking after such an animal. I also thought that by the next morning the wolf would have disappeared – though no doubt only to get killed in the mad Kabul traffic.

The next day in the park I saw another incident which showed how out of place these young people were in this third world country. I came upon an excited group of men running around the grass in pursuit of a dog. Two hippies were in the lead. The dog was covered in soap suds. I asked another group, who were just watching, what was going on. Apparently, the hippies had bought the dog in the bazaar. It was dirty and no doubt riddled with fleas, so they had decided to give it a shampoo. They had begun by placing it in one of the open concrete drains running alongside the streets. In those days such water-courses were used for everything, including water to make tea. The mongrel was well lathered, but not being used to such treatment it became terrified, suddenly snapped at its new owners and escaped. Although it had probably been beaten by its previous owners, that was normal 'pack behaviour', and merely made it subservient.

Now it rushed off, but kept stopping to shake itself, to rid itself of whatever strange thing was covering its body, with the two hippies running after it calling loudly; which only made it run on again. They had been joined by every local man loafing in the area, and there was a gang of about thirty men, shrieking with laughter at this sudden game. They had never seen anything like it. But suddenly the dog squeezed through the fence and disappeared up the road. The fun was over, the hippies walked disconsolately away; but the local crowd buzzed for half an hour afterwards, obviously telling and retelling the tale to each other, roaring with laughter, slapping each other on the back.

Normally, dogs padded silently through the streets, mainly in early morning or late evening; during the heat of the day they slept in doorways or in the middle of side-alleys. If run over their bodies vanished quickly; I thought probably to be barbecued. Later, I was to see how they were used in the mountains.

People had enough trouble finding water to wash themselves to ever worry about washing animals. That network of open drains drew its water from the river Kabul, which flowed eastwards through Kabul gorge, between the Ashmai and Sherdarwaza hills. The city's water may have been sweeter than the notorious 'Sweet-water Canal' in Egypt, against which we had been warned in my RAF days – but I doubted it. Frequently it petered out among its many arteries into a slimy filth of rubbish. Often it lay beneath the sky in a false tranquillity of blue. Donkeys drank it, and so did people. Sometimes dogs lay down in it during the hottest part of the day, and then peed into it as well. Many times I saw men washing in it, stripped naked except for a kind of shawl draped round their shoulders, throwing water up around their private parts and up into their behinds to clean them, then scrubbing their teeth with their fingers and washing out their mouths.

In all the side streets the poor had their own communal lavatories. These were piles of excrement seven feet high and often four times as long, on to which men crawled and undid their belts. I questioned one of the men at the hotel about this. They shrugged. The Afghan Tourist Authority did not like to mention the problem, other than to suggest every year that this should all be cleared away. Apparently the Russians had supplied a lorry or two for the purpose, the filth to be taken out of the city and dumped downstream. But the lorries had gone astray. The Afghan Tourist Authority went tut-tut to tourists and said it was a disgrace, and that His Majesty's government would soon solve all these problems.

They told me proudly that my English Princess Alexandra had been to Kabul, as if that was the answer to all the problems. All I saw, apart from the hippies, was a scattering of Japanese, Germans, and some from communist countries. And, of course, then there were the hardy, rich American big-game hunters.

3

The Voice had given me a telephone number to contact, a Dr Nogge, a German zoologist who helped run Kabul Zoo. I telephoned him, and on being invited to meet, took a taxi out to his house. The poor fellow had hepatitis and was in great discomfort. His face wore the look of woeful suffering that could be seen on most of the Europeans I had met in this country.

He told me that the zoo had been opened in 1967 by His Highness Price Nadir, son of the king, and that a previous monarch, King Amanullah, had erected a decorated stone pillar, known as the Minar-i-elm-wa-jahil, which meant the column of knowledge and ignorance. When it was built in 1925 it had been a symbol of modernisation over the dark ages of fundamentalism, but, to me, it gave the hope of recognition for a more enlightened view of wildlife in this primitive country. There was grave concern for much of the Afghan fauna, especially the Marco Polo sheep, Markhor goat, wild ass, otter, Bactrian camel, the snow leopard and the grizzly bear. Dr Nogge said that there was also talk of a sub-species of Bactrian tiger, but that it was probably already extinct.

The next day I went to the zoo. There were primitive texts and panels describing the country's wildlife. But the inmates were not happy ambassadors of their cause. In deep pits with high mud walls, the animals prowled desperately, looking up at their chattering human enemies. The guide book described how the otter playfully entertained the public with his antics, but all I saw it doing during my late September visit was bite its penis in frustration. The lion had died, the tiger was continually snarling and slinking round the bare walls of its prison. There was a tired-looking leopard, a civet, a leopard cat, a red fox, a desert fox, a wolf, a wild boar, a porcupine and a coypu, which looked like a beaver. It was all very depressing to look at.

The list advertised a snow leopard, brought up as a cub by the zoo's founder, E. Kullman. That was the animal I was most hoping to see on this journey: the face behind the mask, the breath unheard, the reason for being on the mountains. It was the spirit that made the shadows move, all unseen; itself all seeing. Snow leopards lived high up, where most humans never went, on secluded ledges, on the lower steps of invisible ladders that could take them higher to safety in an instant, almost to oblivion as far as the human race was concerned. Little was known about how they lived or where they roamed. They were in a permanent moon darkness, one of the few animals that could deal with the killing cold and depleted oxygen.

Dr Nogge had told me that here and there, now and then, people had captured one, dragging them out of bouldered lairs into the sun, when they sometimes became quite tame, almost kittenish. Stories were told of the extraordinarily long tail sweeping everything off tables on to which they would bound. But for me such a role was untenable and without that honour of being the only creature that could survive the edges of the world. To tame them was like the Chinese forcing musicians and ballet dancers to become farm workers in their so-called Cultural Revolution. Every cat can play and amuse humans. Only the snow leopard can live on the highest mountains.

But when I came to its enclosure a notice said the animal had been removed. I was glad that Mr Kullman's example had gone and that I had not seen it. My first glimpse of this superb animal should – would – be unadulterated, I told myself. (But unhappily, that is not quite how it happened.)

So instead, I looked at the wolf that September day, because I was soon going to see them in their natural habitat. The wolf was the substance of the hills, while the snow leopard was the shadow of the clouds. Dr Nogge had said there was talk of wolves attacking and eating elderly people and small babies in the severe winters around the suburbs of Kabul, even in the recent past. The wolf in the zoo turned its pale face towards me, lifted its nose just a fraction, and narrowed its eyes, as it considered. Not once did its attention leave me. Even when it looked to one side at a noise, its eyes came back, and the ears were continually pricked. What was it seeing; what was it considering? I felt it must sense my own thoughts, my sympathy, my admiration. Thousands must have hung over the wall, shouted at it and stoned it; but it showed no fear or apprehension of me at all.

I thought back to the last time I had seen these creatures: in London Zoo, in the severe winter of 1963, when around midnight I had slipped away for a few minutes from a party celebrating the launch of *Animals Magazine*, to walk in the moonlit snow of Regent's Park, and had come across half a dozen timber wolves just imported from Canada. They were only a foot from me and although they were of course behind a substantial wire fence, they seemed not to be. Silently the pack ran up and down next to me, and for those few minutes London seemed to vanish, to be replaced by the forest wilderness. Now, the mud walls of the dingy pit of Kabul Zoo vanished too. The wolf had its own space that went with it everywhere. Though it was a prisoner, the space around it belonged only to itself. That was visible in the eyes that watched me all the time I stood there looking at the creature. There was a wild pride that would never submit, and it was waiting and watching for the chance to escape.

The foxes slept while I was there. They had buried food in the dust and accepted their fate. An ibex stood with its forefeet on a small boulder, its beard more masculine that the mandarins of China. Its eyes had the glaze of goat's eyes, as though their retinas had become detached from head-butting. It stood on guard, patiently comprehending the rock's three-foot drop as its brothers in the mountains looked at an empty mile-drop into space beneath them. It was not planning, like the wolf; just poised, like a mascot on a sports car, as eager in the garage as on the road. The ibex stood so still and calm, it might have been a statue made of bronze. (Although, if it had been, in Kabul it would have been melted down to make car parts.) I was soon to see the ibex in the wild, and then I would see them at the impossible apogee of their ability, where they lived on the edge of possibility, almost in flight like the eagles around them. As the eagle its perch, so the ibex its crag, both foot-rests could be used by either. Only the word was different.

I never saw the zoo bears, either brown or black, though there were slumbering noises coming from a dark shed. *Ursus horribilis* was to appear on the mountain though, and we were even to camp in its winter cave. As for the golden eagle, the lanner falcon, or the eagle owl, they were in such a sorry state that I passed hurriedly by. They would have been better stuffed.

The zoo's water birds were expected to live, somehow or other, with less water than even the humans had in the city. To me it was worse seeing the greasy unkempt feathers, dirty and spattered barbs and barbicels tangled and uncombed by the bird's beak, than it was to see the matted fur of the animals. I wasn't sure how they stayed alive. I saw pochard, shelduck, ruddy shelduck, teal, coot, pelican, heron, egret, flamingo, and demoiselle crane: all in the same state. I did stop and look closely at a bar-headed goose, because I was hoping to see them in the wild. They bred at their most northerly station in Mongolia but also in the Pamirs where I was waiting to go. The thought of seeing these wild geese migrating at twenty thousand feet, something that usually only the very occasional airline pilot saw at first hand, or radar operators at second hand on their screens, was thrilling. Just a couple of weeks previously I could never have imagined that I could possibly actually see them for myself while standing on the ground itself. The ground surface of the earth in mountains is as remote, as cold, as rarefied, as exhilarating, as dangerous as being airborne without support. One flies on the mountains when walking – it takes that sort of effort.

Because we were near China, we were near the true and natural habitats of wild pheasants. I knew quite a lot about these birds, as the man who owned the estate we lived on kept them as pets; my wife had helped look after them and had even managed to breed some of the rarer species. The zoo had several species: Lady Amherst, golden, Reeve's, silver, and Chinese ring-neck. I had read about vast coveys of rock partridges being seen and hunted by the occasional westerner in the nineteenth century. There was also talk of rarities such as Himalayan monals and snowcock. The pheasants were the only birds in the zoo that seemed to be thriving. They were pecking up corn and mincing about in the dust, even enjoying a dust-bath.

I left, feeling disturbed and depressed. The zoo was a very poor example of its kind and the creatures it contained should never have been living in such conditions. Life in the wild was hard, but it was where they were meant to be. Every living thing, whether human, bird, mammal, plant, insect, or even spider could only just manage to live in this strange country, embattled in mind and mountain, but how magnificently they lived: primitive and extreme. It was a thread back to that very distant mythical invisible halo in the sky that has given rise to every religion that there has ever been: from ancient pagan beliefs to the certainty of one God (though in many forms), from Mayans, Romans, Greeks, Pharaohs, Crusaders and the mysticism of the east. I thought of Chekhov and the magnificent speech beginning 'All living things . . .'. Chekhov had felt as I was feeling.

I was impatient to get on and out into the wild and natural countryside, and do the job I had been sent here to do. But I had to wait. Luckily the Kabul Trots had improved, though still lingering on. I spent my time reading a book borrowed from the British Council library (*Tess of the D'Urbervilles*, the selection was very limited) and exploring more of this medieval city.

One afternoon, in the city park of the mausoleum of Amir Abdur Rahman, a story-teller was at work beneath the willows. His white turban was wound loosely round his head, making shadows and folds like the snowy peaks of the Hindu Kush that I could see from my hotel room window. His baggy black trousers hung loosely. He had a stick with which he drew circles in the dust and in the air about him, his voice never stopping as he recounted the legend (as I learned later) of the holy hermit of Qhandahar Baba Farid. A circle of thirty-five men in similar dress, the workers of Kabul, whose clothes were as formally charcoal in colour as the suits of London business men, but which had been flailed clean in the Kabul River, were listening intently. I stood in the shade with them, and recorded on my very basic tape-recorder what the old man told the small crowd. It was a scene that had its origins in earliest time. The story-teller had once been one of the most important people in primitive society, and I felt part of an age-old tradition.

While he was talking, with many gestures of his stick and what seemed like dramatic pauses, I watched a boy of about

46

sixteen years of age take off his clothes and, completely naked, stand in the drain, splashing its grey water over his shaven head. It was all very natural, and his youthful body was beautiful in its innocent task. I was glad that women did not wash openly in the streets as well, as it would have been difficult to ignore their bodies: I had been warned by The Voice that even the merest glance at a woman was considered bad manners, an insult, and could cause an outrage, with possibly dire consequences.

When he had finished, the story-teller held out a tin, and the listeners without exception put a coin or two in it, myself included. The old man stared hard at me. I smiled and bowed a greeting. He turned away and spat. His audience spoke among themselves for a time, perhaps retelling the story, and then dispersed. Later, back at the hotel, I asked the manager if he could tell me what the story had been. He listened to my tape and translated, and I wrote down what he said.

'Ah! It is the famous story of Baba Farid of Qhandahar!' he exclaimed. Evidently he knew the story well.

'You wish to know? There was once a holy man. I think you might call him a hermit? His name was Baba Farid, and he lived by himself in the hills of Qhandahar called Safid Koh. This is the place of treacherous and difficult weather. The snows lay deep there for half the year, and the melting water in spring can sweep men to their deaths. Few places can be used to grow barley or any fruit, the plum and the apple tree cannot easily set its seed, nor the peach or the apricot bear fruit, neither pomegranate grows, or the loganberry. Only the grass and small herbs grow, and the animals are wild. But Baba Farid had no need of these, nor yet of the small fish in the mountain streams, for he had magic. This magic is the greatest of all gifts. It is the means by which a man may travel between heaven and earth. Baba Farid could find grapes to eat where no other man could find grapes. He ate walnuts where no

47

other man could find walnuts, nor any fruit of any trees. Baba Farid kept his magic to himself. For there was no need, he thought, to share it with the people of Qhandahar for they had everything already of the fruit of the trees, all vegetables of the gardens, all animal flesh and animal milk, both the horse and the goat, as well as the sheep, and the wild birds which they could take. So Baba Farid lived alone, and kept his magic to take what only he himself wanted.

'One day a traveller, a holy man on his way to Herat, met Baba Farid on the mountains. He complained that the Qhandahari had left him hungry and without any sustenance, not even tea, not even the smallest crumb of bread. This made Baba Farid very angry, for it is the custom always to feed and help the traveller, and especially a holy man, on a pilgrimage to a holy place. All are guests for as long as they require. Baba Farid did his duty, produced nuts and fruit for the holy man, who went on his way, showering blessings on the hermit.

'Baba Farid was still very angry. He went down the mountain to Qhandahar and begged for a small piece of bread. All day he prostrated himself before the people but they would give him nothing. The next day, as the sun came to its height in the sky, Baba Farid went down to the river bank and shouted to the people, and drew a great crowd. Then, jumping into the river, he caught a great fish, and held it high in the air. The people wondered what he was going to do. Then the sun came down, lower and lower, until it became so hot that it was unbearable, and it cooked the fish that Baba Farid was holding in his hands so that it became very sweet smelling and succulent, and as crisp as if it had been roasted in the fire of an oven. But the sun was too hot for the people and the water in their vessels all boiled away, and the river was too hot to stand in and the road too hot for their feet to touch. The people were very afraid of what was to become of them.

'Then Baba Farid said unto them:

48

"Now the sun will always descend low into Qhandahar and make the life of its people hard and uncomfortable but they shall be able to survive even so. But let the people remember always to respect the traveller and the visitor and especially those that are the holy men and give them what they need. If you do not, I shall cause the sun to come even lower, and Qhandahar shall become a town that shall be shown no mercy."

'And today, any traveller will know that Qhandahar is hotter than any other place, and this is the reason.'

I thanked the manager for his help. 'I can see why everyone put money in the story-teller's tin,' I said, laughing. 'But also, the story is very like a parable from our own Christian Bible. That is interesting.'

On another day I wandered through the streets and found a tailor and outfitter's shop. The hotel manager had told me that one could buy a hand-made suit for just a few pounds. (He must have thought that I was very poorly dressed.) The narrow wooden door, painted dull green at some time back in the last century it seemed, had heavy clasps and iron edges to its shut surface. I peered in, seeing rolls and rolls of cloth and a thin brown man wearing a white turban seated on a stool, stitching diligently into a dark puddle of cloth. A Japanese salesman gathered up samples into a bag and pushed past me back into the street. The tailor spotted me, saying, 'Please, please,' amid gestures of welcome for me to come in.

I stared around at the bales of cloth that had come from the looms of Tokyo. Once they would have been from the mills of Lancashire. The cloth colours were drab and dull, rain-cloud grey, some with fine metallic threads to brighten them up, but which only gave the cloth a touch of down-market tat. There was a strong smell of paraffin, and old cooking, and sewage. There were flies circling idly in the half light, and I felt that I was now one of them, and about to be trapped.

The tailor said, 'Come, come,' and he pointed to a suit hanging up on a nail. 'You want? Very cheap.'

I nodded. The tailor whipped out his tape-measure and spread my right arm and dug into my armpit. I was embarrassed because I was sweating, but then realised that he was probably used to worse. With a carpenter's pencil he wrote down the measurements on a brown paper bag, which seemed to have had several uses already. He pushed the tape round my chest. I rapidly breathed in and expanded as best I could. A resigned look crossed his face and he lowered the tape, shaking his head. I tried to stand naturally. Cuffs, neck, back width, and leg measurements quickly made a mass of cat's-cradle pencil marks on the paper bag.

Then he gestured towards the rolls of cloth stacked up behind him. Feeling a bit flustered, I chose a sort of woodland green cloth that had the look of a fine tweed, that I thought would fit in with country life in England. Back then, country gentlemen were still very much of their ilk. My father had made me aware of how one should behave and dress, although I had neither the money nor the inclination for such matters.

The tailor was used to making himself clear without knowing many words of the language of his client. He held up his fingers to indicate that the cost would be twelve dollars, about eight pounds, and that it would be ready the same time the next day. He knew the word 'tomorrow', and repeated that several times to make sure I, an ignorant foreigner, understood. The suit fitted perfectly the next afternoon. And I could hardly believe that I had got such a bargain. The only problem was that I had not realised how much weight I had lost due to the Kabul Trots. When I arrived back in England my wife said she could only feel bones. On weighing myself I had lost two stone. She soon made sure I got back to normal. Almost immediately the suit was too small! It hung in the wardrobe for several years, and eventually was sent to a local charity shop.

My next adventure was with the police. I had done nothing about the visa that I had been told was necessary for my forthcoming trip, and thought I had better get that organised. From a window on an upstairs landing in the hotel I had a front-line view of a prison compound, a bare dirt square with a high wall, just across the road at the back, where a group of men could be seen. These eight men wore white turbans and long brown coats, and looked like any group of middle-aged Afghan men, except that policemen, in blue denims and caps, brandishing truncheons and firearms, guarded them. The hotel manager told me they were convicted criminals and had all been sentenced to death. When I asked what for, he just shrugged. One day the compound was empty. It all seemed rather grim.

So that, when I arrived at the police headquarters to ask for a visa to leave the local province of Kabul for my journey into the Wakhan, I already had a subconscious dread of the place. The man in charge of the police house looked just like the bandit in a bad Western film. He wasn't impressed by my forthcoming adventure. I explained that I would be gone for two months, so needed an extended permit to cover this time.

'You can have permit for three weeks,' he told me. The room we were in was dark, and very hot and stuffy. The chair he had indicated I sit in across the table was thick with dried sweat and dirt from decades of palms clutching at straws. I found my fingernails picking gouges out of it.

'Yes, but I shall be away for much longer than three weeks, it is a long way . . .'

'So then you apply here for a new permit.'

'But I won't be able to, I shall be miles away in the Wakhan.'

51

'Without permit you cannot go further. You must be arrested. Apply here for a permit.'

'Why can't I have a permit for eight weeks?'

'You do not need! You can go now. Here is permit for three weeks.'

Another policeman was edging forward to witness my discomfort, like the customs officer at the airport. He was looking eager and almost excited. The two kept exchanging glances. What the hell was I going to do? I repeated my case. He repeated his.

The tension made the now well-known pain in my bowels start, of all the places for that to happen. I clenched my buttocks together, and tried not to think of the shame of that. But I couldn't leave now: it would mean the end of the expedition. I tried to reason. I knew I mustn't be rude. I had a vision of that empty prison compound. These people were terrifying, and so was the whole country; being rude could quite possibly carry the death sentence, for all I knew. I could see, now that the confederate had come into the light, that his lower lip had once been cut through and healed into a fork. It made him look very sinister.

Then I suddenly realised what was going on. The second policeman was rubbing the fingers of his hand across his other thumb and grinning suggestively. Of course, how stupid I was! I pulled out my wallet from my jacket zip pocket. They leaned forward in silence. I brought out a couple of dollars. There was still silence. I pulled out another two, and looked at them, and made as if to put my wallet back in my pocket. The sinister one now let out a sigh like the hiss of a snake.

'OK, you want permit, OK,' said the original bandit, and scribbled out something on some sort of form. The interview was over. The hot air outside felt almost spring-like. I fled back to the hotel, in urgent need to use its facilities.

4

My next encounter was with a woman in the bazaar. I had gone there to check for skins and horns of endangered mammals, in order to report back. I didn't have to look far. There were pairs of ibex horns on every tourist shop, looking almost like royal cyphers or shields, proud and emblematic. They were attached well above eye level, so that they stood out against the blue sky like crowns, and they gave each shop displaying them an almost dignified air, like the badge on a club blazer. That the Afghans were proud of their heritage was the message, even if it had had to be captured and killed for them to show it to the world. I also found the horns of the very rare Markhor goat, and presumed they were the very same ones that I had seen confiscated at the airport, now back and ready for resale. They were old and grimy, and had probably trundled back and forth to the airport many times. The shop-keeper here tried to get me to buy them, and spat in my direction as I moved away.

Then I found the claws of a snow leopard, crudely mounted and embossed with Middle East silver, which I knew from old had more lead than silver. Snow leopard skins followed, again crudely preserved, and becoming soiled with age. I held one in my hands. The marbled imprint of the camouflaged fur, which had once hidden the magnificent animal among the scree of stones and glacial pebbles, mountain plants and melting snow, still gave that frisson of mystery of this high-altitude feline that somehow managed to exist in the clouds and peaks of a secret land. As a child I had seen a picture of one of these creatures in a book. Its mystery had gripped me: it was so different from the African leopards that everyone knew about. I had always wanted to see one, never dreaming that this might ever happen. Now I was suddenly and unexpectedly close, and I could scarcely believe it. But the dead skins made me feel sad and angry at the same time. I thought of that missing zoo animal: one of these skins might have belonged to it. What a waste of a magnificent creature. Now I was so near, I longed to see the living animal. I hastily moved on to the next shop, while the owner of the skins sighed heavily and muttered something to himself.

The next shop was selling locally-made carpets. The patterns were good but they were not quite top quality, with only 50 stitches to the inch compared to up to 80 to the inch in those from Iran – Persia – that I had seen in my RAF days. There was also a pile of Afghan sheepskin coats, with their cured skins embroidered with patterns of flowers and leaves, and curled scrolls in red and gold and green and white. I knew these were all the rage back in London among the hippy generation. What they did not know, and I certainly didn't, was that Afghans had no thought for the London rain that could destroy the poorly cured skin coats overnight. Nor that there was a possibility that these coats might carry traces of anthrax, one of the deadliest of diseases. My thought then was that one of these would make a wonderful present for my wife, and I started to rummage through them to find one dyed in the most unusual colour, although I noticed that the smell coming off them was pretty strong.

Then all at once I was confronted by a majestic woman clutching a baby. She stood right in front of me and began a harangue in her native language. She was thin but hard as mahogany, her long skinny arms a mass of sinew and muscle, her hands like those hand-cultivators which drag steel claws through rough ground to break it up after the winter. She had the face of a golden eagle, with a hooked nose for a beak. Her big black eyes were sunk in hollows and they were focussed directly on me as she thrust her face forward. The rest of her body was swathed in coloured rags, her head bound loosely in a turban of many colours that gave her a kind of crown of authority. She shouted at me and put her fingers to her mouth and threw her hand away again. I felt totally cornered and unnerved. What on earth did she want? She went on shouting and pointing at me and then at the baby, which went on sleeping through this tirade. Surely she wasn't claiming me as the father of her child? Then the shopkeeper came to my rescue.

'She want baksheesh, to feed baby,' he explained in a bored voice. Of course – a wave of relief swept over me. I had just been very slow on the uptake. I handed over a coin. I had no idea how much it was, but it looked bright and silver, so it should have been all right. She stopped shouting anyway. The shop-keeper ushered her outside by waving continuously with both hands as if he were sweeping cobwebs. But I was unnerved, and forgetting all about the sheepskin coat hurriedly left. The encounter made me realise how little I knew of the harsh world of survival that these people endured.

The hotel manager had told me that one of the specialities of the market bazaar was lapis lazuli, mined mainly in Badakhshan, and which came traditionally from the market at Khotan in China, along the southern route of the Silk Road. This curious dark blue rock, ingrained with threads of gold colours, was manicured into trinkets for the tourist trade. I wanted a piece, but not the finished object. I just wanted a lump of the raw mineral. I now wandered along, determined to find some, and soon spotted a specialist shop down a side street. I stood and looked at his stock. One object for sale was an ashtray. It was about four inches square, and about an inch high at the shoulders, with the centre smoothed out. It was heavy, and to me seemed an enormous lump of what I knew was semi-precious stone. The colour was a deep aquamarine, the colour of deep oceans in high summer, or the Mediterranean around the Italian coast. Or was the colour indigo, that depth of dark blue almost at the end of the spectrum? Whichever, it was very beautiful. The man said it was four dollars. I tried to think how much it would cost to buy in England: certainly a lot more than that! I nearly agreed to buy it, but suddenly saw myself as just another idle westerner, picking up trinkets, whiling away the time. And I was waiting to travel into the extreme conditions of survival. I would have to lug this object all over the mountains, and it would become an absolute nuisance. I remembered how I had brought back Dead Sea stone ashtrays from Jordan twenty years previously. Anyway, I could never soil that beautiful colour by crushing out cigarettes on it. Besides I no longer smoked. That had stopped when I got married, mainly because there was no spare money for cigarettes. So I left the lovely relic of a moment of igneous alchemy in the planet's deep and hidden past where it was, and bowing slightly to the shop-keeper, went on my way. I could hear his coarse muttering in my head long after I could no longer hear him.

I retreated to the hotel, where I was protected from the harsh climate, the dust, the frenetic traffic, the unintelligible babble, the pestering for baksheesh (to them I was a rich foreigner), the constant sly looks of hostility (for the same reason), the futility of a country going nowhere, the certainty that life was short and sudden death lay just around the corner. It would have been nice to have had a companion, a friend who could share my interests and thoughts and values, and who could laugh at the problems. There was nobody in the hotel except a few Japanese businessmen, German car salesmen, and Russian tourists. But were the Russians tourists? They did not seem to be enjoying themselves. They sat endlessly discussing something among themselves, handing round what looked like files of paper in a peculiarly furtive manner.

Staying in the hotel was tedious. I wrote long letters home, including the weekly articles I wrote for my local newspaper, and continued to read Hardy's *Tess of the D'Urbervilles*. The excitement of the day was the meals. For every midday lunch and evening dinner I was welcomed by four or five waiters, superbly dressed in starched shirts and white ties, white gloves, black trousers, and highly polished shoes. Usually only six tables of the twenty in the dining room were filled. I was always first down, and the welcome was palpable. Their moment as exhibits of civilised dress and rules could begin. They perhaps went home to hovels and labouring parents, but here they were the elite among their tribe, and they revelled in their position. For over a century there had, after all, been a tradition of English people keeping the borders of the Empire in place. They had paid their bills and laid down a tradition of behaviour that was still adhered to, even if it was all now a pastiche.

These attempts at grandeur were not upheld by the choice of food, at least not for the main course. The first night I was there, the dish was lamb steak. The next it was lamb burgers. The third, we could choose the only contestant for our attention, which was lamb chops. The fourth night the menu showed just 'lamb grilled'. I pointed out, tongue in cheek, that in English it should be 'grilled lamb'. He just smiled, having no idea what I was talking about, said 'So sorry Sir,' and proceeded to remove my spotless set of knives, forks and spoons, and replaced them with an identical set. On the fifth night the menu began back at the beginning: lamb steak.

After this course, the pudding trolley appeared. Here were remnants of the culture of the 1930s, perhaps even the

Edwardian era. This trolley had silver-plated handles and two old mahogany decks, and the little rubber wheels were possibly first made by Mr Dunlop back in late Victorian days. Their axles had known no oil in a century, so they squeaked as they were pushed around the tables. To begin with this was amusing, but quickly became irritating. The contraption held enormous puddings of the Raj era: blancmanges made in ancient copper casts, chocolate castles beginning to collapse, sodden cakes soaked in sweet syrup, ice-cream slabs with glacé cherries. The only way to pass these interminable evenings was to try to eat slices of these monsters slowly and deliberately. There was of course no wine or alcohol of any kind with which to anaesthetise the senses, and ensure sleep in the endless nights.

The weather cooled a little, and I continued doggedly looking round the suburbs, or rather the outskirts, absorbing, or trying to absorb, the atmosphere of this city of Kabul. The small mountains near the city now looked like crumpled cardboard. The nearest hill had the noon-day gun perched a thousand feet above, and its boom was a comfort of regularity. It marked off another day, that time was passing, and I was a day nearer to when I could get out of this oven and away into the fresh snow and silence and vast emptiness far from the human mass, with only wild animals and eagles, and the flowers of the alpine meadows; a day nearer the time when I was due to report back to Mr Ali Sultam, vice-president of the Afghan Tourist Authority, who was arranging my trip to the mountains. Then I would meet up with the two American hunters and a guide for the journey. I was curious to see what they were like. My brother lived in Canada, and told me wild tales of hunting out there. These men would be pretty tough. I wondered if they would resent having an Englishman foisted upon them. But none of that would matter: at last, I would be able to explore the mountains.

*

I met the Americans in the lounge of the Tourist Authority building. They were of course staying at the Kabul Hilton, away from the centre of Kabul, and so I had not met them before. One was dressed in a fine green woollen shirt and green tweed jacket and trousers to match. It was the kind of uniform that English deer stalkers would wear. This was a guy by the name of Don Teters, in the business of making lifts for skyscrapers, as he announced on greeting. He was forty-five years old, but looked much older. The two men had been told about me, but he did not seem too interested in my existence. His companion looked me in the eye as we shook hands when I introduced myself. I could see he had an eye that noticed things. It was an eye looking for detail, with a smile that began at the corners of his mouth. He had a sharp nose and a big frame, and a hand-shake that showed hard palms. He was Pete Serafin, he said softly. I liked him immediately. We sat down in the big armchairs again, and waited for Ali Sultam. Pete went to sleep almost at once. Don sat silently. After twenty minutes, the regulation time to establish his importance as a very busy man, the vice president appeared.

'I am Director of Special Projects,' he told us importantly.

Tea was brought in by a young lad and poured out and handed round.

'OK,' said Don. 'I guess we want to see Marco Polos. So, what's the deal?'

'You will see these animals. Also ibex to shoot. But first! Please! We must get you there. There are many miles. First you have to fly north, over Hindu Kush mountains to Faizabad. Then is truck, car, to Wakhan. Then horses, then into mountains on yak to hunting place.'

'The sooner we get out of Kabul the better,' replied Teters. 'The place is not too healthy.'

As if on cue, flies had begun to land on the rim of his teacup where his lips had just left a damp semi-circle, but he did not seem to notice. That alerted me at once, and I kept waving my hand over my cup as if cooling its contents. Mr Sultam automatically tipped his cup so that boiling tea washed away any dirt before he drank again. Pete left his tea in the cup untouched. Later he told me that he had brought along the only tea he would take, which was some sort of herbal mix that his wife back in Oregon had made and ground up for him, and put into little linen bags. He had brought along some iron rations too; dried strips of meat he called jerky. I was to discover that he was one of life's most dedicated survivors, while Don was certainly not. Just now he was biding his time and surviving Kabul's foul dust, the long haul from America, and the expectation that the one bullet he was going to be allowed to fire here, and which had already cost him seven thousand dollars, might end in a clean miss, with nothing else to show for it.

'Klineburgers said there would be a doctor on board this outfit,' Don told Mr Sultam. 'I guess you know about that?' Klineburger was the hunting firm which had arranged this expedition. They organised big-game hunts world-wide for clients from all corners of the planet. Even I had heard of them, though I had not the slightest interest in shooting big animals. His slightly belligerent tones continued, 'I heard an American hunter did die last year up these mountains. The guy was my age and there was no doctor, no oxygen, no nothing.'

'Yes, is very unfortunate about that man.' Mr Sultam beamed briefly, and spread his hands, then pointed at the ceiling as his expression changed to determination. 'Now is much safer. We have employed a new doctor. He has trained in your country – yes, believe me, he has trained for safety with NASA on high altitude. He will make this safe, for you to go to high altitude, believe me.'

I wanted to know about the conservation of these high-altitude animals we were hoping to see, so I asked Mr Sultam directly, right there in front of the hunters who had paid fortunes to shoot them. Dr Nogge had already told me what he thought happened to the monies paid by hunters, and he had been an impartial observer of the politics, forming his opinion after talking to other leading specialists in animal conservation from around the world. He was very dubious that the money went to where it was supposed to go. But I was curious to see what the official reaction would be.

'Money from the World Wildlife Fund and some of the money which the hunters pay to the Afghan government and to the Afghan Tourist Authority is intended to pay for the conservation of endangered animals in the Wakhan and the Hindu Kush,' I said. 'How is this money spent, and is it helping to protect and keep a good breeding stock of species like the Markhor goat, snow leopard, Himalayan brown bear, and Marco Polo sheep?'

Mr Sultam smiled again, wider than before, his hands reaching out to embrace this question that he must have seen coming from a thousand miles away, ever since he had been briefed that a nuisance was coming all the way from 'the BBC' who would want to probe into this shady area, and replying with the most reassuring of answers.

'Believe me! We know what we do to animals in the mountains.'

I wondered what was coming next after this surprising volley.

'Yes!' he continued, certain of his ground if not his English. 'The animals are protected of course. You yourself have come to see them. English BBC will tell the world. Many more will come. Yes, all animals are protected. We have two Wakhi men there, protecting them. We pay them to be sure to stop mountain people killing the animals.'

I wondered what on earth they thought two men could do to protect such a big area, but decided to let that pass, and went on to my next query. I also wanted to know whether alpine meadow grazing by herds of domestic sheep was diminishing the food supply of Marco Polo ewes when these were lactating. This was something the WWF was most concerned about. They had had reports of increasing flocks belonging to nomadic pastoral tribes which were depleting the meadows, and I had been primed to check that out. Some of the money raised was supposed to be paid to the nomadic tribes so they would not have to increase their own grazing for income. Mr Sultam had done his homework.

'Of course, this can happen. Yes, we pay the people there in Wakhan to be careful. The Marco Polo has plenty food. Plenty. Believe me.'

The man was not going to admit any fault. Dr Nogge had said he had his doubts as to what happened to the money. I had not expected to be given any true answer, but at least I had made the point that it was under question. And I would soon be able to see for myself to some extent.

At last, it was time to go. We three went by car to what was then the only supermarket in Kabul, to buy for ourselves any special delicacy we fancied for the six weeks ahead in the mountains. I bought a few bars of chocolate, remembering the thrill that these gave us children in the war, when American soldiers in jeeps, stationed near our farm on the north Norfolk coast, cruised down the village street and threw them out for us to pick up. Americans and chocolate and chewing gum were synonymous. Those were golden summer days of innocent excitement. The war itself held no meaning for us children, other than the noise of bombers droning overhead, the thrill of finding bits of red target from the practice drones, and the sight of soldiers camped on one of our fields. The chocolate bars in Kabul that afternoon triggered a moment of resonance that had its root way back. Perhaps it was something to do with the same temperature, the same height of the sun above the horizon, but suddenly all my senses were sharpened. I felt supremely happy and confident. I was in good company, and, as in childhood, on the brink of a great adventure that would give complete fulfilment.

At Kabul airport, a dusty old red and white single-engined de Havilland Otter passenger plane awaited us. Immediately I noticed that one of its small tyres was almost flat. Its walls bulged. I knew about tyres, having to maintain the large number attached to my official tractor, trailer, cutter, Land Rover, and my own vintage car. My life depended on tyres, from motorways to the steep stony tracks on the nature reserves of the South Downs. My father had taught me to have an obsession with tyres. He had driven at peak speeds, clocking up huge mileages around England and abroad, and often showed me how to grip the steering wheel if a tyre blew at speed. He had watched many of the great racing drivers at the wheels of such cars as the pre-war Silver Arrows Mercedes and the BRMs after the war, in the hands of Froilan Gonzales and Graham Hill.

The pilot grinned at us as we prepared to embark. I pointed out the half-flat. Why did I bother?

'Sure, is OK, please to get on.'

The two Americans looked briefly, but seemed untroubled. When we settled into our seats, Pete told me about a Russian plane he had been on once when on a hunting trip, which had been unable to get airborne due to being over-loaded. All the passengers except himself had been terrified, he said, and most of them had been sick during eventual take-off, with the gangway awash with the contents of forty or so stomachs.

This aircraft held twelve passengers, with a lot of extra baggage dumped in the aisle at the last minute, much of it being sacks of what looked like melons.

We headed for the Hindu Kush mountains, which soon began to rear up ahead into a mighty barrier. At a distance, they were the same cardboard colour with jagged peaks topped with snow. I wondered how we were going to get over the peaks without pressurisation or any sign of oxygen. But then I could see that the plane was headed for a pass. Pete was talking to an Afghani government official, who said he was the Secretary of Agriculture of Afghanistan. I leaned over and asked if he knew how high the pass was. About sixteen thousand feet was his answer. Kabul had been five thousand feet, so I was acclimatised to a certain degree, but this was quite a rapid ascent. We were on the edge of that spine of mountains raised by the six-million-year-old tectonic plate collision that was still actively forming the Himalayas, giving planet Earth a wrinkled hump.

The agricultural minister was telling Pete about how local crops such as barley and melons were being grown when he suddenly stopped with his mouth open, and then began to slur his speech and roll his eyes. His head dropped on to his chest for a second or two. Other passengers were beginning to roll their heads and hold them in their hands. I realised the cause was lack of oxygen, and wondered if I was going to be all right. The pilot of course would have a mask for his own use, or perhaps he was acclimatised to the conditions. No mention had been made of this possible problem when we boarded.

As we came near the top of the pass strong wind currents caught the plane, and it veered to one side, then was caught in a gust that lifted a wing, and began to throw us about. The ground looked uncomfortably close. Then suddenly we were over the pass and diving down. I was OK, though my head ached a bit, and so was Pete, and we grinned at each other with mutual silent congratulations. Don was holding his head and muttering to himself. Out of the window I could see scrub and flocks of sheep and a land of pale limestone shot with streaks of red, all smoothed by winter snow, and with small flat alpine meadows in between. We looked down on fields of cotton and rice, grown on the alluvial outwash from the mountains, a soil that was fifty metres deep. It was all green enough to look like Dorset farmland, with its small green fields, tall hedges, copses, and single trees.

The plane landed in a trail of dust and small stones thrown up almost to the wings. The pilot announced this was Kunduz, and that we could get out and stretch our legs, but to stay close. Some passengers got out, but more got on, some children sitting on their mother's laps while yet more sacks of whatever it was were piled high in the aisle.

'Goddam plane won't lift all this,' Don Teters complained. I presumed it would. The pilot obviously knew his job, and this trip was just routine to him. We did get off of course, and Pete went to sleep very briefly, waking up just as suddenly to peer at the ground, saying it looked just like the wheat country of Oregon, which was where he lived. He now presented me with his business card. It declared, simply but effectively, the cornerstone of his whole life and how it had given him the riches to be able to afford hunting trips for big game all over the world. Not in actual words of course – but implicit in its message: 'INVESTMENT TODAY, SECURITY TO-MORROW', with his address on the other side. Real estate was his business, although it was many years later that I realised just how much of an interest that was.

We had taken nearly two hours getting to Kunduz, although it was only about 150 miles from Kabul, probably because of a head wind. Now we turned east for the hundred miles or so to the town of Faizabad. Below us we saw the river

Kokcha, which flowed from the mountains of Badakhshan to the south in the Hindu Kush, and then onwards west, to join eventually the Oxus at Khoja Ghar, on the Russian border. We landed among another welter of small boulders and rocks like shrapnel on the dirt strip of Faizabad.

The pilot grinned at us as we got off; he exuded what seemed to me to be an immense sense of relief at having got there. But perhaps it was my own sense of relief that the dud port tyre had not hit a rock on landing and got ripped off its rim, when we would have careered in a semi-circle into the sides of the mountains that now towered above. An Afghani man was waiting for us when we got off the plane. He greeted us and told us his name was Pia.

'Your guide.' We shook his hand and introduced ourselves.

5

On the right-hand side of the road were the bright blue waters of the river Kokcha, flowing quite swiftly, for we had come back into mountainous country, the heights that ran north into an area called Tadhjik, which was in Russia. On the left, the biscuit-coloured rocks rose as a precipice perhaps a thousand feet or more above us. As we drove down this road to the town, there was a sudden hissing sound and a huge boulder hit the road fifty metres in front of us, and smashed into pieces, bursting up like an exploding bomb. Bits of smaller rock showered around us and one hit the roof of the Toyota. We stopped dead with a long skid. The Afghani driver leaned out and shouted to the vehicle behind, and both Toyotas reversed back hurriedly about a hundred metres, and we all got out to see what sort of danger we were in.

'Jesus! What the hell! That rock was five tonnes at least!' shouted Don, wiping his face with a red handkerchief.

We all looked up at the precipice to see if anything else was falling. The Afghani guide and the driver of our vehicle started talking and pointed up into the sky, but didn't seem unduly alarmed. Looking to where they were pointing, I could just make out a movement on the edge of the precipice, towards the top. I got out my binoculars, and then could see five men up there. They had crowbars and were levering away at the sheer face. God knows what they thought they were up to, or how they did not themselves fall. I told Pete and Don.

'Those goddam guys are trying to kill us,' was Don's response. Just then another boulder was levered off the cliff face. I could see the sun glint on the crowbar. This one was part of an overhang and it went wide of our road. With a hissing roar, now much louder because we were standing out of the vehicles and the engines had been turned off, it disappeared with a mighty splash into the river. Another smaller boulder, the size of a car wheel, followed. Then two men appeared on the road ahead and began hauling the pieces of the first rock to one side. Even Pete was now getting annoyed, as the rocks continued, some quite close.

'What the hell are those guys trying to kill us for?' he demanded of Pia.

'No, is OK,' Pia said. 'These men work for the town on the roads. In the winter frost loosen the rocks and so they fall and hurt people, so they get rid of the rocks now.'

Don turned away, muttering 'Goddam crazy country' to himself. I hoped the Afghanis had not heard him. We were totally dependent upon their good will. I suddenly saw the funny side of it all and said, 'It's the rolling rock show,' and Pete laughed with me. Don just hunched his shoulders. For the Afghanis it was all quite normal: this was how their country was.

'God willing we will not get hurt.' Pia remarked to himself. And to us, 'We go on, OK?' We decided to take the risk. The driver shouted to the men clearing the road, started his engine and drove slowly forward bumping over the shattered debris. After we were through, I looked back and saw the road-workers were putting out two battered red and white cones to stop the traffic. Very helpful, I thought. Stable doors crossed my mind, but I decided to keep quiet.

Now we came upon another hazard for which there were no signs either. As we stormed round a bend, so a herd of about three hundred goats and sheep filled the road. Big sly dogs looking like wolves, with slit eyes and with all their ribs showing, were guarding the animals, and they snarled and snapped as we passed between them, the herd opening as we travelled without slowing, missing them by millimetres. Our driver shouted at the shepherds out of the window. I presumed he had sworn at them. I asked Pia about them. It was all interesting, and part of my remit. He said the men were from the Muchinsa tribes, explaining that Muchinsa meant nomadic. 'Winter is coming. Much snow. No grazing so they move down. The goat animals are Karakuz. The dogs Kuta.' I wrote in all down in my notebook.

Faizabad had a long muddy street with shops and houses along both sides. The weather was dry and fine, with a blue sky and a cooling, brisk wind from the mountains to the east. Yet the street was extremely muddy, with large puddles that locals had to avoid. It seemed very odd. Then, as we sat on a bench outside a street vendor, eating naan bread and goat cheese before the journey ahead, we discovered the reason. A large green and grey tanker came rumbling towards us along the street, spraying water from gravity-fed pipes at the back. The café owner told us with some pride, with Pia translating, that the tanker had been a present from Czechoslovakia, Russia, to lay the dust. It laid the dust all the time, every day, and never stopped this work, and it was very good, very good. It certainly was refreshing after hot and dusty Kabul. The man went back inside, chortling. Pia said, 'He is telling everyone that the feranji – er, foreigner – said Faizabad is better than Kabul. He will tell everyone that for several weeks!'

We had an hour before starting off again, so I wandered along through the mud to see what appeared to be a medieval community. One of two wealthy owners had built ranch-style wooden houses, but generally the homes and shops were hovels. A mullah, recognisable by his long grey beard, came striding along the street, avoiding the puddles, so his passage was rather erratic, his long grey garment wrapped around his body, and held up out of the mud, his white turban rolled into a tight neat shape round his head. He looked like a grey heron, thin and with a pointed beaky nose, and eyes that pierced the way ahead. He saw me at once, stopped briefly, and then turned his head away and stalked past, ignoring and disapproving of this westerner, an infidel in his mind, in his town. It was a slightly chilling encounter. I had heard mullahs had extreme power out in these hills. They could order death by stoning for what we might consider minor crimes, especially women for adultery.

I stopped by a butcher's stall. Skinned goats hung in the blazing sun, their dark red meat being gnawed by scores of hungry wasps and hornets. The meat, what was left of it, was 13 afghanis a kilo, about six pence. One carcass was almost bright yellow all over with the wasps. Two very young girls were selling bunches of fresh mint they had picked somewhere along the nearby river. They were dressed in flowery pinafores and shawls, which I thought were probably imported from Pakistan.

Next, I stopped to watch a boy of about seven or eight helping someone whom I presumed was his father to make horseshoes. The old man – he was probably only in his late thirties, but I had already realised that the men aged very quickly in this country – was heaving on the cow-horn handle of his home-made bellows. The air forced into the bed of cinders made them glow white, and the roaring air scattered sparks into the young boy's face. His father shouted at him to move the shoe around to the hottest places with the tongs he held in his small hands. The boy had sweat running down his face and bare neck. His only clothing was a grey shirt, which might once have been white, reaching down to his knees. His rather pinched face had a serious, almost frightened look as he concentrated on the job he had to do to survive life in this mountain village.

I had watched similar scenes in my own village when I was

a boy on our family farm, but they had been fairly jolly occasions. This was deadly serious. His father pumped the worn bellows, which were patched with shreds of goatskin. I knew the horseshoe would soon be ready for the man to beat flat, and then punch holes through for the nails. Then the boy can have a breather, I thought. A battered anvil stood near them. The bellows stopped pumping, and the man shouted to the child, who placed the white-hot metal on the pointed end of the anvil, picked up the mighty hammer, and began beating it into a tighter circle. More shouting then. I guessed the metal had started to cool and harden up, and the holes still had not been made. Our horseshoes always had six holes. The lad held the semi-circle on the flat top, over a large hole. The father placed the piecing pin on the shoe and beat holes through with two mighty strokes. Somehow the small boy held it steady beneath these crushing blows. The shoe was now dull red. The man peered at it, holding it up against the sky with the tongs, then dropped it with a clatter on to a pile of others, all still a dull blue from recent heat.

This is how it would have been in the iron age in England more than two thousand years ago, I thought. Living on the edge of existence, like all birds and mammals, and it didn't matter, because that was all you knew and life was lived from day to day.

Next door a man was making shoes. Not normal shoes of leather, but of worn-out motor tyres. He was holding the tyre in a grip between his knees as he sat on a wooden bench, sawing away at the rubber, steel and canvas with a hacksaw. He got the foot shape sorted, then he cut two more pieces, one to curve over the toes and the other to hold the ankle. Most of the people there were wearing these motor-tyre shoes. But not the mullah, I recalled. His shoes showed his dominant status. They had been leather of the best quality.

There were tin trays for sale, piles of green melons, raisins, and one could buy a kilo of saffron for 25 afghanis. This I could hardly believe, remembering how expensive – and precious – saffron was in England. For a moment I thought I must get some to take back home for my wife and how pleased she would be. But again, the thought of the days ahead became dominant. I only needed the bare essentials for myself. I was living in a minimalist world. Wanting a bulk purchase of the yellow stamens of flowers was almost as bad as wanting collections of butterflies or birds' eggs. Let the crocuses alone. Let them live. All these years later I still have the memory of that moment.

I also carry a sound memory from Faizabad which I shall never forget. It was the sweet sound of the lonely places I first heard as a child in Suffolk. It was the song of windy heaths, still crisp with winter cold, but coming forward to spring. It was the song of a goldfinch, whispering, almost; but insistent, not giving up, hoping for better times to come. I followed the merest ripple of this song down the street, past the stalls and the clangs of the blacksmith and the shouts of the people passing by. It was a kind of thread that was reeling me in over the mud and the slop pails, until I found the bird, not as in my youth, in a Suffolk whin bush where it had its nest, but in a cage hanging in a shop next to yet more carcasses. It turned this way and that on its perch, its gold wings dull and grimy in the sun, the purple-red mask of its face like a visor, drawn down, waiting for the next lance-like blow of life with the courage of a medieval knight in battle. It was blind. Its eyes had been pricked out with a hot wire, to make it sing for ever. It was a custom that I knew had been used in Britain not so very many years before. There was the shadowy shape of a woman just inside the shop, her face too with visor down, covered from head to toe by her chaderi: she too was having to hide from the world.

We found Pia had bought a pile of rough blankets, a couple of sheep skins and amazingly a camel skin.

'We are sleeping bag short. I use these. You, Reeshard, have good American sleeping bag.'

For the first time I realised that I was actually 'extra' for the planned trip. The Americans explained that their American travel firm provided special sleeping equipment for its clients and regular staff. I offered to have the blankets. Pia shook his head.

'No, you are client. English BBC. Is OK. I live here. I know cold.'

Pia had also bought some saddle-bags. They were a rough weave of red, black, and white, with strong handles so they would carry heavy loads when slung on horse pommels. He explained that first we would continue to travel in the Toyotas for about 120 miles, then we would need to change to horses for about 60 miles, and then on to yaks for the final leg.

'Sounds a cinch,' said Don.

It wasn't. I was in the leading Toyota on my own with just the driver, who had no English at all. His name was Ahmed. The others followed behind in the second vehicle. Wanting to record every impression I decided to write as we went along. My notebook, in shaky writing, reads:

The Afghan drivers of the Toyotas are crazy. I am hanging on for dear life while writing this between the bumps. We roar in clouds of dust between the bends with the ice-blue torrents of the Kokcha below us. It is very hot. The windows are tight shut. My head just cracked the roof and I am running sweat everywhere. The mountains outside the windows are like a denuded Scotland, with dry stone walls of glacier pebbles. But the scenery is more savage than anything in Scotland. Sometimes there is little more than an inch of road between our tyres and the sheer drop down a hundred feet into hurtling water.

At that point I gave up trying to write. I needed both hands to brace myself tight to the seat. Several times we came round a corner to meet a herd of goats and sheep, with small boys and their father in charge. There was no room for the two parties on those tracks. The animals and the shepherds were made of bone and blood and were softer than the iron girders of the Toyotas, and the drivers knew it. They just drove straight into the sheep and children without noticeably slowing. Here, drivers of vehicles had the chance to show dominance and, boy, did they enjoy the experience. This was unbelievable to me. In England I would have shouted at the driver and lost my temper, and told him to slow down; but I was in a strange country and was more worried about upsetting the driver.

The young boys were nimble, and jumped and scrambled out of the way. Animals scattered in all directions. The shepherds pressed against the rock-face, glared at us in fear and hatred, and shouted what were clearly obscenities at us. The driver shouted back in return. I felt that if we had to stop we might get lynched, and perhaps the driver felt the same way.

I had brought with me my old camera, a Finetta 88 of German make, bought in Iraq twenty years before. In those pre-digital days cameras used film which took negatives. Anne had bought me a few precious rolls of film in that hectic rush before leaving England, thinking that I would be able to get more on arrival. But such a commodity had not been available, and so I had decided I would have to be careful about the photographs I took. I did manage to get one picture of this mad drive into herds of sheep and goats. I was lucky that my old camera kept working. The cameras of the two Americans did not, jamming with the mountain cold or dust, or both.

Another hazard was donkeys carrying huge bundles of sticks, thrashed by their drivers on their rumps to make them move smartly out of harm's way. When we stopped to relieve ourselves, I asked Pia where these sticks had come from, in this seemingly barren country. He said that trees had been planted farther along the road by the Czech government for the use of the local people, to provide building beams for their houses; but that they got used for firewood.

'We will come to them soon.'

We came down the side of the mountain to a plain where the river had gorged itself on the rock boulders, rolling them into huge egg shapes that it was gradually digesting, levelling the land flat as it flooded during the monsoon. Now we could see the trees – or what was left of them. They were some species of willow. A few of the trees had managed to grow taller and were about forty-five feet high, but most had been hacked down by villagers for the bundles of firewood we had seen being carted down the road. Goats had nibbled the bark away as well. I saw a couple of older animals reaching up high to nibble the few leaves still in reach. To my English mind and eyes, it was all a forlorn sight. But of course, I was thinking like some western tourist. Here was a different and very hard way of life. They had to do the best they could in a primitive world.

I soon lost interest in the trees, because suddenly I noticed there were various birds flitting about in front. Among the material handed over to me by The Voice back in England had been a book on the birds of Afghanistan by the Director of the World Wildlife Fund. I had looked at it carefully during the period of waiting in Kabul. The first birds I recognised were wagtails. There had been others, but I had been so concerned with my own safety that I had not really registered them. Now the road was less hazardous the driver seemed to be calmer, and I was able to relax a bit; or perhaps I was becoming used to the wild rush of dust and rocks and nearly killing people. To the Afghanis it was all part of normal life. The taxi drivers in Kabul had driven like drunks would in England, but that was usual and unremarkable. I began to realise that I had perhaps lived a sheltered life, despite all the mayhem in Cyprus with EOKA terrorists back in the Fifties. I decided I needed to forget my western prejudices and inhibitions and take this all more calmly. Pete was calm most of the time, having travelled every year to out-backs across the globe. I needed to learn to take it all in my stride.

I looked more carefully at the wagtails, so I could see what subspecies they were. Its head was black and white, like the pied wagtails I was used to in England and had known since childhood, catching flies on our local church roof; and also, I suddenly remembered vividly, on the open market stalls of Norwich. A wave of nostalgia flowed over me, a sudden longing for the safety and delights of childhood, but I resolutely shut it off. I knew thoughts like that would lead to depression. I was here to do a job, and it was a marvellous chance in a lifetime. I knew my problem was that I was alone here and had no one to share my thoughts, no one even to talk to. But I must concentrate on these details, which were part of this adventure. The sort of adventure, I reminded myself, that my mother's cousin Sir Francis Chichester had undertaken in his odysseys across the Australian outback in a Gypsy Moth biplane, and then again across the oceans in his boat as he circumnavigated the globe – the first human ever to do so singlehanded.

Focussing my binoculars back on one of the wagtails I could see its back feathers were dove-grey. That made it a white wagtail not a pied. I had only ever seen a single such bird before, when I was still a child on the Norfolk farm and had been out birding on the sea-marsh at nearby Cley with the very knowledgeable and well-known birder, Richard Richardson, also a talented artist who had been the first man to illustrate *Collins Pocket Guide to British Birds*. He had pointed it out to me and told me how to identify it – and many other birds. How lucky I had been in those far-off golden days.

I thought about the life of these tiny wagtails here in this remote valley. Some good days like today, flitting about catching flies and other insects, but some terrible; with fierce cold, no food, head winds, the claws of a falcon hissing past, narrowly missing its tiny frame of needle-thin bones and palpitating flesh in its envelope of feathers.

I pointed them out when we stopped again: the two Americans looked at them briefly. 'Funny little critters,' Don said. Pete nodded his head. They were not interested in such minutiae: their minds were on the big prey that lay ahead.

More birds appeared by the wayside. I spotted a hoopoe picking about among the rocky soil looking for ants or perhaps finding a big black harvestman, a member of the spider family, with a tiny brown ball for a body the size of a grape pip and legs as fine as fuse wire. The bird was sandy pink, the size of a crow, and its curved beak was as long as the curved feathers of its crest, the two balancing each other – one down, the other up, in perfect balanced symmetry. It flashed a sudden signal of black-and-white fear with its wings, like a mass of semaphore signals, as it fled the roaring noise of the Toyota truck bumping through its territory.

We stopped at a small hamlet called Bahrak. A lunch of stewed goat and rice, complete with flies, was served. Willow and pomegranate trees gave a soft, dusty shade. Men dressed in the same quiet shades of earth brown watched us silently. Sparrows chirped in the roof of the shed which was the café. I mentioned them to Pia. He told me they made their nests in the roof and the locals took the chicks just before they could fly, as a delicacy, so the birds just kept on breeding. 'Just like chickens and their eggs,' he ended laconically. They were not quite the same markings as our familiar sparrows, and I thought probably of the Italian subspecies, but I wasn't too sure. Pete and Don were cheerful in this ambient place. They talked of former hunts, exchanging tales of survival in far worse mountains and deserts than here. I smiled to myself, wondering if this was bravado: we all knew we were only at the start, and still in the foothills of this greatest of mountain ranges in the world. Perhaps they were already feeling the pressure, or rather the lack of it – we were all getting a little breathless with the altitude, as the air pressure dropped.

Pete said, 'Mongolia was one of the worst places I ever been, dry and dusty, no shade whatsoever. The driver was crazy too; crazier.' He glanced at our two drivers, grinning. 'The guy just kept going through the desert at sixty miles an hour. One day we took off when he didn't see a shelf. That shelf was a twenty-foot drop to the sand below. We landed like a plane landing just on its front wheel and the rear wheels caught up when it bounced. One hell of a bump. Yeh – I hurt my back pretty bad. Still feel it sometimes. No matter, we always come out OK.'

'Sure,' said Don, capping the other's story. 'I had bronchitis once up in the Andes. I just got cold. The mountain air cleared that all right. Yes sir! Nothing like mountain air to clear the lungs.'

Nearby an old man was weighing up sacks of walnuts. Pia said they had been gathered from wayside trees and would eventually be exported to Europe. The man would have looked at home in the Neolithic culture of six thousand years ago. I asked Pia to come and talk to him for me. His black hair and beard were shaggy and unkempt, and filled with straw and dust. His lips were sore and cracked, and his tough yellow teeth grinned at us as he shouted something in his own language. His clothing was a sort of soft brown sack from which his bare feet, with their splayed toes and black nails, moved like the branches of a tree. He had a weighing machine of wooden uprights slung together, holding two dusty platforms of timber that had almost shredded away over what could have been centuries. It looked that old, and so did he. But Pia said he was probably well under thirty years of age.

He lifted an enormous stone on to one platform and, placing a sack of walnuts on the other, threw in more nuts until the two balanced. It gave a new meaning to our sadly no longer used English 'stone' weight. I asked Pia the Afghani word for the nuts. 'Charmus,' he replied. The man looked up.

'Can I take his photograph?'

Pia asked him, and the old man grinned. So I took the walnut man's picture, as good a snap shot into the distant millennia of the Bronze age as I was ever to see. Ancient times and people also fascinated me on the Sussex South Downs where I worked, looking at the earth works and lynchets and winnowing circles and burial mounds of past ages. Here they were still living the same kind of life that had passed into history in our own country.

'Ask him about his life,' I urged Pia. The man was pleased at the interest, grinning broadly, and Pia translated. His mother had died when he was a boy, falling down the side of the mountain. His father was dead a long time ago too. It was the will of Allah that his father had to drown in the river, falling through a hole in the ice and never to be found.

I handed over a few afghani coins, and he immediately picked up a handful of the nuts and pushed them into my pocket. The gesture said we were equals. He was proud and did not need charity from a feranji. As the days went on, I ate one or two each evening, laughing at myself as I remembered the letter that Lawrence of Arabia had written to my father, who had sent him a small bag of pecan nuts from the United

States in the early Thirties, saying that he kept them at Cloud's Hill and ate one a week when he visited the cottage from camp at weekends.

We wandered along to the small bazaar. One stall was selling those same sandals from Faizabad made from rubber car tyres, and there were also water melons cut open and looking like the setting sun, with flies drinking the juice. Pia bought us a slice each.

'I guess those flies have just come out of the shit-hole,' Pete remarked.

'I'll get out of this place alive if it kills me,' Don replied.

At the time we did not know just how portentous his remark was, as things would turn out. I had a folding knife in my pocket, and with the blade carefully scraped off the surface juice of my slice.

A rock partridge picked about in the dust round our feet, finding the melon seeds we spat out. Maybe it was a pet, but more likely someone was nursing it for the spit-roast. The name for these birds is chukor, which imitates the sound they make as they call to one another. I knew the bird well, as many years before, when as a young and rather wild young lad of eighteen and stationed with the RAF in the Jordanian desert, I had gone off with a friend on a shooting expedition for rock partridge in the old Roman city of Um-el-Jimal on the Syrian border. They had been very plump birds and very good eating. I remember thinking then how extraordinary it was for such large numbers to exist in the almost bare Syrian desert. This country apparently had enormous numbers at one time, as reported by Victorian military explorers who were defining the boundaries of the British Empire, and keeping India safe from Russian expansionism. I thought of the Raj officers having partridge drives along these valleys. What a strange and troubled history this area had had – and was so soon to have again, not that we knew it.

We set off once more, Pia coming into the leading vehicle with me. Soon we came to a fork in the Charkaron valley, leaving the right turn to Jurm and the Kokcha River, and pressed on east to follow a tributary river that was draining the mountains of the Hindu Kush in Western Chitral. Now we saw where the walnuts had come from, for the trees were well spaced along the valley, together with orchards of mulberry trees. Fine stone houses had been built.

'Very like traditional yurts – same size,' Pia said, adding, 'Yurts are the collapsible skin and pole tents that the nomad tribes live in.'

I nodded. It was quite difficult to hold a conversation in the noisy vehicle. There were stone cairns, too, next to open spaces.

'Cleared by the local farmers to make area to grow barley.'

These pebbles and boulders were a complex weft and warp of colours which I presumed were both volcanic granite and ancient sea-bed marble. Pia said that some of the rock pyramids we passed were in fact tombs of people who had been condemned to death for misdemeanours including stealing or adultery. These people had faced village tribunals headed by the local mullah. They had been pinned to the ground and heavy stones placed on to their bodies, crushing them to death, until they had been entombed completely and for ever. I shuddered: it was barbaric – but a very good deterrent against wrong-doing. Pia said the Afghan Tourist Authority would deny this practice and make it clear that it was an unwelcome subject.

About fifty miles ahead were white snow peaks from which the ice-blue water was tumbling. This was the Tirich Mir, with a peak of 25,230 feet, the thirty-mile-long range which also fed the Chitral River, that in turn fed the Indus in India's distant plains.

'North is Russian; south is India.' explained Pia.

We were coming towards one of the mighty water-sheds of the Hindu Kush and Pamir Mountains, and the barrier between mind-sets of cultures and countries. It was as though we were being squeezed between the two. The two vehicles stopped so that we could relieve ourselves. I had a strange sensation, though it was more in my mind than real. The mountains were being pushed upwards and northwards by the forces of nature, and I suddenly sensed the hundred-year-old British dilemma of holding it all apart like Samson pushing the pillars of the temple. I found my muscles had tensed. It was a strange and unsettling feeling.

Looking up, I could see specks in the sky ahead. I knew they were birds, although they were so high I couldn't tell what species. But that wasn't important just then. All I knew at that moment was that I was entering a new world. It was the beginning of a vast expansion of the mind.

Pete and Don seemed to feel the moment too. They were staring at the peaks of snow above us with mouths slightly open, also lost in a moment of reverie. For them this was the opening scene of a life-long ambition: the hunt for the impossible. A good Marco Polo head was the top of the list of all hunting trips. They would go home as the great adventurers they wanted to be seen as: Don for the trophy head; Pete, I thought, for his own satisfaction. In that I was wrong: Pete's need for *the* trophy head turned out to be paramount.

For me, I knew all at once that this was the realisation of all my years of picture-book wanderings, of longings for the far-away distant places seen on maps of the world, of those places where only the fiercest, the tautest and finest of form could live. These longings had haunted me all my life. Sometimes music had shown me these dimensions, had taken me into a world beyond and outside myself: Beethoven, Mahler, Ricard Strauss, they all had this power. I felt the same when reading my father's great winter scene in his book *Tarka the Otter*, and in looking at Peter Scott's painting of lesser white-fronted geese over the Iranian mountains. For a moment there was the connection of the mind to distance, almost a fourth dimension. Here, for the first time in my life, I knew I was actually in that place. It was thrilling.

The specks above began to take shape. They were wheeling in circles: eagles, vultures, falcons, hawks. There were ravens and crows too. Possibly there was a dead creature below that they could feed on. The snow high above was all the while changing, from a distant scene as one might see in a photograph of mountains to multitudes of shadowed whites and greys, of blue shadows, and gold and silver sunlit slopes, of sudden crystal gleams. We could see exposed rocks without snow on them, perhaps too steep for snow to cling. They were grey-brown, the colour of snow leopards. I stared intently and longingly at these fragments, and imagined there to be one sitting on one of the ledges, just staring down, watching the trail of dust we had been making, adjusting its movements to allow for this intruder into its territory.

'One of them snow ledges could hold a big sheep just watching us go by!' Pete said, thinking aloud. We exchanged glances. I nodded. Our thinking had been similar, but for very different reasons.

'Huh!' Don replied, also craning his neck to look up. 'I want one a bit easier than that.'

He was to find, much later, that it would be much harder than that.

6

We stopped for the night at a cluster of mud huts alongside the track, called Barshenn. Our sleeping quarters was a dark cowshed filled with about twenty-five animals, small black bullocks and heifers, and some milking cows. A couple of candles showed us where we would be sleeping, this being a platform of hard earth just half a metre higher than the cattle. I hoped the beasts would not jump in among us in the middle of the night. At present they were beginning to settle down, chewing their cuds, belching, letting forth streams of green shit on to each other's backs, and just keeping each other warm for the cold autumn night ahead, safe from wolves and bears. There was a flock of sheep in a fenced area next to the hovel, pushing close together, couching and belching, and doing their own streams of hard pellets over each other. It was quite medieval, and had a biblical ring about it, especially as Don muttered 'Christ' every few minutes. The proprietor of the inn brought us tea and hard-boiled eggs and naan bread, which we ate sitting on a bench outside. He was a big silent man with a boxer's jaw, black stubble and straw in his black hair. He had two small daughters, one of whom was greatly excited by the sight of feranji, and whose name we learned was Ahmana, as he called her sharply away. I could recognise the word 'feranji' in her chatter as I had heard men muttering the word everywhere we had stopped, and Pia had told me it meant 'foreigner'. The man's wife was nowhere to be seen. Pia explained that it was not allowed for a feranji to see the women. Her work was in the kitchen out of sight.

After we had eaten I went for a walk in the dusk, feeling the breathlessness of the altitude already, although it was only 9,000 feet. However, I thought it was a good chance to get acclimatised before moving on again, and I needed to stretch my legs after sitting all day in the stuffy Toyota. Pete and Don decided to join me, and we walked a little way along the dirt road. Pete had his cowboy hat on with its wide brim, and Don was wearing a wide-brimmed hat as well, together with his green shirt and green cloak, of the kind that English deerstalkers had once made fashionable. He had green tweed breeches, with little webbing garters in yellow, like those that boy scouts used to have to keep their socks up. He would not have been out of place in a Sherlock Holmes film, except the hat was wrong.

The hills were covered with luxuriant herbs growing almost as dense as heather. In fact, it was a bit like Scotland, except for the turbans and donkeys. I said so, but the only response was a grunted 'Yeh.' However, my remark seemed to trigger something in them both, and they became expansive in the rapidly cooling air.

'I made lifts,' Don announced in a slightly aggressive manner. 'My lifts are in all the sky-scrapers. I've done well. My business helps run America.'

He didn't actually say, 'And now I'm here, in the most prestigious, most expensive hunt the world can offer, and just because I have been successful. This puts the feather in the cap of my life and so I'm happy.' He didn't say that – but the tone of his voice implied it. I wondered about him, suspecting that he was a bit out of his depth, finding that all his worldly sophistication, recognised in the smart business world of New York, counted for nothing here. Also, he must have known that he was not as tough as Pete. That was evident to me already. He coughed quite a bit. I wondered how he would stand up to the rigours as we went on. But for now, he was determined to let us know that he was somebody, and we weren't to forget it.

Pete joined in: 'I've hunted every corner of the world. Done one hell of a lot of things. Been on the Fortress Bomber (Boeing's Second World War B17 Flying Fortress) assembly line in the war. I've dynamited rocks for a living, and picked a million prunes to earn my keep. I've hunted the Arctic, the deserts, the mountains, the forests. I've taught myself to sleep for exactly four minutes only, and to sleep in the crotch branch of a tree. I've had a hell of a life – but I guess this beats everything.'

Neither was really talking to me, or even to each other; just to themselves. However, I felt I needed to add my own pennyworth, even although I was by far the 'junior' and was from England, to them a little country they could dismiss in their minds. I found myself talking about my own peaks: not of business, or physical adventure, not even of my life in the deserts of Arabia with the RAF. In keeping with the brevity of those two summing up their existence so far, I heard myself talking of the great mountain peaks I had been on – when listening to the symphonies, the sonatas and sublime quartets of Beethoven. There was a short silence. A big bat flew over our heads as the light finally faded.

'Guess I'll hit the hay,' Pete said. Don just grunted.

We settled ourselves as best we could, in our clothes, in the dirt. We westerners were up one end while the Afghanis arranged themselves at the other. I found myself wanting to laugh as I looked at Don, lying on his side next to me, his head on his saddle bag, his best American green tweeds changing to a smeared pale ochre as he turned over several times in a hopeless attempt to get comfortable. 'Hitting the hay' had taken on a new meaning – if only there had been some hay to hit! He was so far out of his known world of business I found it hard to believe he was here at all. Yet he must have been on hunting trips in the past, but I suspected with everything laid on and within his known environment. Pete, however, was a very different type. He really was a person who had roughed it to extremes. Like Lawrence of Arabia, and Wilfred Thesiger, and Eric Newby, and all the other great explorers, he revelled in discomfort, or hardly noticed it. He knew his body was tough and wouldn't get hurt by cold or dirt or the discomfort of hard rocks in his back. He had trained himself for every eventuality. How did one train oneself to sleep for four minutes only, I wondered, or even at a moment's notice. His half-open mouth showed me that he had been telling the truth.

I curled my legs up into the foetal position for warmth and hoped for the best. Then I noticed a huge flea crawling rapidly and anxiously over Don's tweeds. The candles were still alight and gleamed minutely on the chitin body and long legs with their big brown claws. Suddenly it leapt, and I hoped not on to me. I tucked my bare hands between my legs. My new nylon sailing coat would not give the flea much of a hold, I thought. My mind brought up an image of the Black Death that had devastated England, when infected fleas had burrowed into rolls of wool cloth and been transported by merchants from the cities into even the remotest villages, living for months without food before feeding voraciously on the fresh source it found at the end of its journey.

I thought I was not going to get to sleep at all, but the rough road and the hours of bumping and clinging on to the seat of the truck must have exhausted me, for it seemed, after a few minutes, that the discomfort of the ground melted under me, and the noises of the beasts' contented snuffling and farting became like the comforting noise of the waves on the seashore of my youth, or the wind soughing in the trees of the woods where I now lived, and I slept.

The next minute, it seemed, I was suddenly awake again; yet the candles were well down their stems and their flames were being blown sideways. The time by my watch was 3 a.m. The door to our cowshed shelter was wide open. And outside an engine was revving up, and there was a lot of shouting and banging about. Pete sat up at once and held his rifle pointed at the doorway to face the mob that was possibly going to rob or even kill us.

'What the hell's going on?' he asked Pia. Pia sat up and shouted at the men. After a bit of talk he lay back down again, and said dully, 'Is OK, men are road builders. They make the roads. They come to sleep for the night. There is no problem.' With that he turned over and lay back, and closed his eyes. Don was muttering and swearing to himself. Pete leaned over to me, 'Keep your belongings well hidden.' I nodded. After interminable discussions and arguments, the navvies lay down on the platform amongst us, head to toes like sardines. There were about twenty of them. I had a pair of large sandals made from lorry tyres thrust up against my face. The only advantage was that the extra number of bodies made it a bit warmer, but the noises and smells they made rivalled those of the animals.

An hour later I had had enough, and struggling off the platform I stumbled out of the cowshed into the first streaks of daylight shooting over the mountains above. It was pretty cold, but it was going to be a fine crisp day, and the sense of relief of being out of that hovel and into the natural surroundings of clean air and mountain purity was palpable. A small hawk, I wasn't sure whether it was a kestrel or a lesser kestrel, suddenly shot out of the willow trees and caught a bat, which screamed with a very high thin cry before going limp in the bird's talons. I was very happy to have seen this little scene of natural life. It was worth being huddled into that hovel and suffering the fleas of the night. For that flea that had jumped ship from Don, or one of its many comrades, had found itself a safe harbour under my armpit, where it had gorged itself. It had bitten like a carthorse, and now it itched like fury, and I bore the mark of it for six weeks. Evidently Don had taken the proper safeguards of using chemical warfare against such intruders.

In the distance I could see ravens rolling as they dived among the crags. They could feel the clean air of autumn, and were enjoying its bounty. I thought of the woods at home: the balm of St Martin's Little Summer, that sudden warm spell in late autumn that would entice birds to sing and even small woodland flowers to bloom. I had seen precocious violets and primroses suddenly encrusted with ice when the reality of winter ended their dream. The ravens knew that winter was coming. Rolling over as they dived, cork-screwing through the sky in sheer exhilaration: it showed they always lived in hope. Hope of a spring to come? Probably not, but they knew that winter lay ahead. There would be five months of piercing cold that could paralyse them in the ebony black of midnight, or days of starvation as they waited for something to die before they did.

I felt a moment of sheer fright. What on earth was I doing here, at the end of autumn and with another two months ahead? I had got here because a couple of over-eager American big-game hunters at the end of a long queue had been persuaded that there would just about be time for their expedition before winter set in. I thought of all those flocks of sheep and goats we had seen on the Faizabad road, teeming down from the mountain summer pastures. If the nomads were on their way out, what were we doing going in the opposite direction? I could see that we could easily get stuck up here, miles from any help. It felt like some kind of nightmare, but it was too late now to do anything about it.

There was movement behind me. Pete emerged, and

greeted me and the bright cold sky cheerfully.

'Morning, Rich.'

'Hell of a night,' I said.

'I've known worse. The day is going to be good though.'

However, that turned out not to be the case. Yes, so far the day was good, with bright blue skies and heat bouncing into the Toyota cabin from that crisp metal-cooking sun. We were sweating again. The windows had to be kept closed, because we were now the second truck, and dust was clouding up from the one ahead. We came upon another small group of hovels, and three kids ran out in their blood-red and tangerine rags and wild shaggy hair, and stared excitedly, and pointed at the wheels going round in circles, which seemed to amaze them. There was a donkey there, with a small sled that it had to pull, wood runners worn down as thin as blades. It was loaded up with sage bushes which Pia, again travelling with me, said the kids would have collected. It made me think of the gorse-bush harvesters in the Thomas Hardy novel, who had had to gather gorse from the Dorset Downs for winter fuel and cattle food. There were small clearings on the tumble-down slopes of scree where boulders had been hauled to one side, and made enough room perhaps for a crop of barley that would just about hold this family in food for the duration of the coming winter snow.

It looked very bleak and I wanted to stop and photograph the scene. But Pia said, 'No, you might see the woman, the mother. She is hiding in the shed so that you cannot see her. It is not allowed. Also, they think here that if you take photograph, you will have power over that person. It is a bad thing.'

It was then, of course, well before the time of mobile phones and media sharing. Looking back now, I am glad that I saw it all in the last stages of that early civilisation. At that time, in the early 1970s, the incursions of the Raj a century before had not altered the way of life of the Wakhi tribes who lived there. Farther along the Wakhan, in the Siankiang borders, was the province of the Kirghiz tribes, who had preserved their integrity to an even higher level.

We rumbled on, and climbing up over sandy alluvial outwash hills, came to another low rocky hill, where the same shrubs as we had seen the night before were again growing in profusion. They had become withered and dried and skeletal. We stopped here briefly, and although I went over and looked at them I had no idea what species they were. We now decided to all sit in the same Toyota and lead the way, to avoid the problem of dust clouds for those in the one behind.

A bit further on we came to a field of poppies. Pale violet petals lounged languorously in the hot sun, spread wide with a kind of waxen welcome, their centres blushing black and holding up umbrella handles of fat stamens. Many were slumbering into the tight sleep of seed, their round globes scratched and oozing white sap. Pete was staring at this scene and shaking his head.

'Why on earth are these people growing flowers!' he exclaimed. 'They're almost on the verge of starvation – they want barley not goddam flowers! They can't eat flowers and they can't sell them up here.'

Pia and I looked at each other. I could see Pia was thinking the same as me. Surely this highly experienced American could not be so naive. I shrugged and left Pia to answer him.

'Opium trade. Very valuable crop,' he said briefly.

The road petered out. We came to a wide flood plain, and there were boulders as big as footballs everywhere, impossible to avoid. The drivers just ploughed into them, and I thought the Toyotas' suspension would never be able to stand up to such punishment. The wheels were just bouncing up and down continually and the noise was deafening. We were hurled about the cab and had to cling to the seats and keep our heads bowed forward for fear of a crushing blow to the skull. We kept up a steady forty-five miles an hour. Driver Ahmed, of course, had the steering wheel to hold on to. He seemed to be in his late twenties, skinny and muscular and cheerful, full of bravado: very male. He probably thought he was on a horse playing the wild national game of buzkashi.

'This guy's just playing with us,' Don muttered. 'Goddam driver; he'll finish us.' He looked grey and worried, and almost on the verge of breakdown.

Pia said, 'Is only way. He knows his job. It has to be fast to get through. Slow is no good, we get stuck.'

I nodded. I understood that. Much of my work with Land Rover and tractor on nature reserves was over rough terrain, though not as bad as this, and had to be dealt with in the same way. Pete was silent, just staring ahead stoically at the miles of smooth round boulders which we still had to cross. I felt he had almost put himself into a trance to avoid the discomfort. A man who could go to sleep at will could surely do that. I knew that shamans or holy men could do this, and men who could walk over hot coals in a circus act or lie down on a bed of nails without feeling any hurt.

Our road, such as it was, followed a river. It was a blue strip reflecting the sky above, but with white crests running all along its length showing tumbling little rapids. I asked Pia what it was. He said this was a tributary of the Kokcha, and it had drained down the Khattinza Pass from Sanlich, under the shadow of a 24,000-foot peak about fifty miles away in Chitral. I made rough notes as best I could. I could check things properly later.

'You take much interest,' he said. 'It is good. I like to tell you these things.'

After a while the road came to a bridge over this river at an area that Pia said was called Sovian. There was a gorge cut by the river, and there was a reach over it of about twenty metres. Sometime in the distant past this bridge had been constructed for a donkey and a man. It looked impossible for a vehicle to cross. Boulders had somehow been lodged on the cliffs either side of the gorge, and then long poplar trunks had been placed flat on top of them and weighted down at their ends, forming a cantilever structure. Where they met in the middle they were tied together with ropes. Small branches had been laid across these trunks and tied on to them forming a track. The Toyotas went over singly, although without much further care, and the bridge swayed up and down. On the far side we got out with much relief.

'Don't forget we have to cross again on the way out,' remarked Pete drily. Don was silent, then muttered 'Goddam crazy' under his breath.

'Well, I suppose they're used to it,' I answered. 'We're not the first party to come up here this season. They must know what they're doing.' Their next action made me wonder if they did indeed know what they were doing.

To my utter amazement, the two drivers now scrambled down the steepish bank to the river and filled a pail of water. Scrambling back up they lifted the Toyota bonnets, and threw the pail of water first over one engine, then the other.

'What on earth are they doing that for?' I asked Pia.

'The engine hot,' he explained. 'They need to make cold, to give drink, like horses.'

'What? But there's no problem. There's a thermometer on the dashboard. I was looking at it to see how the vehicles were behaving. It was perfectly normal. There's nothing wrong with the engine. Well – there wasn't. They won't start now, the electrics have got all wet.'

Pia shrugged and spread his hands wide. Sure enough, the engines didn't start. I was worried they might run the batteries down, for then we would be in real trouble. When I said,

'See?', Pia assured me that it was just that the engines were tired, 'horsepower' needed a rest, then would be OK. I turned away. I was angry, but also wanted to laugh. It was so ridiculous. I thought Pia would have known better, and surely the drivers had to know how engines worked.

So we lounged on the grassy bank, among the sea buckthorn bushes, and stretched out to rest our bruises. It wasn't a bad idea to have a rest. We ate a bit of naan bread and a lump of local cheese, and scooped up a handful of the cold river water to wash it down. The two drivers sat slightly apart, smoking rough-looking handmade cigarettes. Pete went to sleep, knowing there was nothing he could do, and accepting that this was how it was in this strange country, and it was no use wasting energy on it. Don just sat there in his green tweeds, and spent the time clicking his rifle open and shut, smoothing the stock, and wiping all the gun-metal surfaces with a large red handkerchief; and looking annoyed.

I spotted a hoopoe, and watched it stalking about on the brown crag and green grass slopes of the river bank searching for ants. It had a long thin, curved black beak, which it poked among the stones, and every now and then nibbled a black wriggling ant that died a useful death in keeping this exotic bird alive. I hoped there were no local people around who would shoot it. It was such a masterpiece of design, finer than any Chinese fan of coloured silk. The complexities of pattern as the black, white, and pink feathers of its crest were flashed open when it flew forward a few yards, or became excited as a morsel presented itself, enthralled me for nearly an hour. No one else seemed to notice it. I was amazed that such a display meant nothing to them, despite the boredom of the interlude. I pointed the bird out, and asked: 'Name? This bird, name?'

Pia shook his head. 'Ask the drivers, they might know.'

They started a conversation, and finally Ahmed looked at the bird, and said a name. It sounded like 'hooduduck'. I wrote

94

it down, spelling it as it sounded. Pia said, 'It is Persian name.'

Up in the sky I saw a raven, tumbling and croaking in its unmistakeable deep voice. I asked what the name for that bird was in their language.

'Zarr,' they replied.

Then I heard the cackling of jackdaws, very much at home, and not bothering about the strangers below them.

'So what is the name of that bird,' I asked, pointing at the flypast of half a dozen of these much smaller birds of the corvid family. The two men were alert now. They were now used to my question and eagerly shouted, 'Zarr!'

That was rather puzzling. Surely they could see the birds were different. All right, then that was their name for both birds, so I wrote that down in my notebook. Then I heard most extraordinary calls from birds above, which were whistling as they dived in fast and feisty flight high up among the mountain walls. I recognised the birds to be choughs, the first I had ever seen. I knew they were a close cousin of the choughs of Wales and Cornwall, which I had longed to see on holidays in Devon with my father, as a boy.

'What do you call those birds?'

'Zarr.'

The excitement over, they turned away again. I asked Pia what the word meant in their Pashto language.

'Black,' was all he said.

Some months later, going over my notes and talking about this to my wife at home, she exclaimed. 'Ah – that's interesting, because the word "tsar" has some symbolical meaning to do with black. I remember reading about it somewhere. It must have had the same root. Perhaps it was the same word even.'

After about an hour, the heat and dry atmosphere eventually dried out the electrics and the engines were started up again. The drivers grinned and said something to Pia. He looked at me and imitated my 'See?' It was my turn to shrug and say, 'OK.'

We carried on. Suddenly, around a bend under the great bare, brown mountain walls, the whole sky opened up, with snow peaks much higher above. We had glimpsed these from further away, but now they were towering vertically above us. I had never seen anything like it before. They were like solid clouds. Even the Alps were nothing to this vast height.

'That is Tirich Mir,' Pia said before I could ask. '25,230 feet. Highest mountain in Afghanistan.' (Later, when I looked at my map, I thought it was actually over the border, in Russia.) It was part of the Hindu Kush. I worked out that it was about three miles above us, and almost straight up.

The driver saw me looking.

'Howguch Kronmanjon!' he shouted, relishing his role of informing the feranji.

'Kronmanjon means mountain,' Pia explained. 'There are many different local names. I have also heard "Nowshok Kronmanjon". It depends on the tribe or even the area.'

I was to discover for myself that each village or mountain or valley had different names to those listed on the official maps, and often I had to write down different names given by different people, and work out afterwards to where they actually related.

At that point we came to something critical. Our little convoy of vehicles came to a halt. It was another cantilever bridge.

'Sangreach,' said Pia and Driver Ahmed in unison, before I could speak. I dutifully wrote down this place name: but discovered later that the word just meant 'bridge'. This time it was over a real, and deep, gorge.

'You must get out of the truck,' said Pia.

Far below was a torrent of black, shadowed, icy water. Pia said, 'From glacier on the mountain.' Even with the rock

96

constructions, which Pia said were called 'berms', to reduce the open span, it was about fifty feet of bridge hanging in open space. One of the rocks had fallen out of the basic construction, leaving a gap a metre wide in the supporting structure. It all looked very primitive and very unsafe, far worse than the first bridge. The drivers began unloading anything that was movable, which included the spare gallons of petrol, all our baggage, even the spare wheels, tools and seat cushions.

'I can't believe even a wild goat is going to cross that thing,' Pete commented. I looked at him. He had hardly flinched so far. If he was worried then I certainly needed to be.

Pia said, 'Is no problem. We do this all the time.'

Pete looked at him. 'It's nothing but a bunch of sticks. They're cottonwood and aspen and look pretty rotten. There must be a better way. Let's have a look round.'

Pete and Don walked down along the edge of the gorge while I went upstream, but couldn't get very far. I thought of those Victorian explorers who had been this way, and back even further, to Marco Polo and all those Silk Road travellers. Perhaps many had crashed to their deaths in that chaos of black water. Perhaps the bridge had been stronger then. I went back to the bridge. Pia said, 'It is repaired at the beginning of each year. It is strong enough.'

Maybe, I thought, but this is the end of the year and it has taken quite a lot of traffic, and this might just be the last straw. I went to meet the other two. Pete called out: 'Nothing that way. You?' I shook my head.

'I feel like bunching the whole trip. Even if we get across this miserable load of junk now, it may give way before we come back in a month's time, or while we're on it. Then we've had it.'

'It's seventy feet down,' Don added morosely staring at the water. 'If that thing gives, there's no hope. We're corpses all

97

the way to the Aral Sea.'

It was now or never to decide whether we continued. But then the Toyotas started up.

'Jesus!' muttered Don. The first one drove straight on to the bridge and crept across. We three just stood in silence and watched it go. Bits of branch cracked and fell into the chasm. We just could not believe that three tons of vehicle got safely over. Then the next one crawled its way across. And then the two trucks and all the Afghanis were on the other side, and we three were left looking like the soft westerners we were.

'Well, that's put us in our place!' I laughed nervously. I thought to myself that they must be the most resilient people left on the planet today: on the far side of the divide in every sense possible.

They came back over at once and began to carry all the stuff that had been unloaded, and we mucked in to help; though they rather pointedly gave us only the lighter pieces to carry. Even so, we kept ourselves well spaced out to spread the weight; but, I thought wryly to myself, really so that if one should fall then the others would live to tell the tale. We had to step very carefully, because there were holes in the surface, and looking down you could see that black noisy water far below. I could see that it was probably stronger than it looked, but even so it was precarious going.

Over the far side the Afghans were chatting away noisily, giving us sly looks. Our driver suddenly started to shout and almost to crow, rather like a song. While they were stowing stuff back into the vehicles, I wrote down as best I could as many words as I could catch. Several were repeated several times, so I got quite a few of them.

We found that all the gear had been put into the front truck, so we let them get well ahead so as not to suffer from their dust. It was a move we were shortly to regret deeply. Then Don had to find a rock to go behind, which held us up further. When we were all settled again and on the move, I asked Pia what Ahmed had been saying.

'I do not know these words,' was all that he would say. At the very end of the trip I asked him again, and handed over coins as a tip or a bribe, and he laughed, and said he did not think I would want to know what the driver had been saying.

Ahmed was still on a high, smirking and shout-singing, and waving his hands about with a flourish of triumph. But he did not hold the moral high ground for much longer, because he came round a corner on that rocky road too fast, and crashed. We ended up in the drainage ditch nearly upside down, but fortunately the truck teetered and hovered, and fell back on its side. With some difficulty we struggled out of the doors that could still be opened, and stood there in some bewilderment, feeling our bruises, and checking that no one was bleeding or really hurt. Pia was a bit pale, and spoke very sharply to the driver, who now looked like a pricked balloon and moved a few yards away. Don sat down on the side of the road, muttering under his breath.

'It's OK,' I said, 'No one is really hurt, which is the main thing. But we need to get this sorted out quickly. A pity the other truck has gone ahead. We could really use it now.'

I knew what to do. I had dealt with similar situations more than once in my job. And now it was a chance to take charge, and show that the westerners were not so useless.

'We need to get rocks and all push from one side, and try to get rocks under the wheels in the ditch.'

We all wandered up and down, picking up what we could find, but as chance would have it there were no stones big enough for the purpose; and if there had been we couldn't have moved them. When we had a small pile, we tried to rock the vehicle to get them under the tyres. But it was hopeless.

'Pia, ask Ahmed for the jack so we can lever the truck up.'

But that didn't work either. There wasn't enough room to

work properly, and the truck was too heavy.

'Well, we'll just have to wait until the other truck driver notices we are not behind, and hope he comes back to see what the problem is.'

I got out my camera to get a record of our plight. Hitherto Driver Ahmed had always leapt forward when he saw I was about to take a picture, and posed manfully in the foreground, his chin in the air as he stared into the far horizon. Not this time.

We stood around kicking our heels and wondering what to do. I interested myself in watching a small white butterfly, which must have been the last of the year, zig-zagging here and there, looking for a flower and then a piece of warm rock to rest on. Along the Himalayan chain there are at least 700 species of butterflies known to science today, with some yet to be identified. Most were on the southern side, in the scrub and forest zones within the monsoon rain shadow.

My reverie was broken by the sound of another vehicle approaching. To our surprise this was a lorry carrying the twenty road navvies who had shared the night with us in the cattle hovel. There was much shouting and laughter as they leapt out of the open back and between them lifted our Toyota back on to the track. That they had crossed that bridge over the deep gorge was almost unbelievable. And, I thought, it also meant they would cross it again, which made our own return even more questionable. But there was no use in worrying, we would cross that bridge when we came to it. I found myself laughing at such a silly thought, but really it was in relief at having the present problem sorted.

7

Afrer a few miles we came across the other Toyota, with the driver waiting patiently by the road. The lorry of navvies had passed him and told him what had happened. We decided that all of us being in one vehicle was not very sensible, in case of any further incidents, and so we set off again, with just me and Driver Ahmed in the leading vehicle.

While we had been stopped Pia had explained that we were now coming into the Wakhan Corridor, which runs for about 234 miles east to the border with China. The first part is the Lower Wakhan, and further on it becomes the Upper Wakhan. It varies from about 9 to 50 miles wide. The eastern end, where we were going, holds the Little Pamir Mountains, while the western end, which we were now entering, is under the shadow of Chitral, in the Hindu Kush, and locally called the Howguch. Pia also said that the mountains that would be on our left and to the north were known as the Goshaan Mountains. The Little Pamir runs on over the Chinese border into Taghdumbash Pamir and Mariom Pamir, that overlook the Shiankiang Province with the far town of Yarkang in China, and to the south, Gilgit in Kashmir, with its Karakorum Range.

Pia said that is where we would have our first view of Russia. He instructed Ahmed to point out to me places and any names that seemed important. Ahmed grinned. He seemed to relish this new role of teaching a feranji. It gave him important status.

We set off, and Ahmed duly shouted out all sorts of words.

I began to wonder if every stone was being recorded! We were in another smooth alluvial outwash geologically, and the round mounds of sand which had been pulverised over millennia from solid rock into soil were covered with smooth meadows of grass. It was nice and easy going for a while.

Then we came to another bridge. Pia had given me his map so I could follow our route, so I could see we were by the village of Zebak, where two rivers joined up, one from the north-east and one from the south-west, each being about 30 miles long and tributaries of the Kokcha.

We stopped and the drivers and Pia had a brief conference.

Pia said, 'OK, we go on. No unloading, it takes too much time. We need get on.'

This bridge looked just as bad as the last one, but I had decided that there was no use in worrying about it and trusted that the Afghanis knew what they were doing. I erased the thought from my mind that they might be fallible. That of course is a dangerous thing to do. It is the mentality of sheep. I must have been getting tired, with the altitude and the continual bumping and dust and noise and general mayhem after a poor night dulling my senses. We had been all right so far, so why not again? My warning light had stopped working. It must have been like that on bombing raids in the war. All is well, until suddenly it is not, and it is too late.

So it was now. As we had not unloaded the gear to reduce the weight, we were heavy, though that probably made little difference. Halfway across the bridge, the leading vehicle – that was myself and Driver Ahmed – stalled. A back wheel had dropped through a hole. The bridge gently bounced up and down. Ahmed half opened his door and peered down into the river. I decided to get out and try to walk along the bridge, but just as I was doing this Ahmed restarted the engine and put the gearbox into slow four-wheel drive. I had done this many times with my Land Rover at home when pulling trailers up steep inclines, or even when a wheel had got stuck in a hole as now; but then I had had solid earth beneath the vehicle, not this terrifying drop into fast-flowing icy water far below.

Now that one rear wheel was embedded into its slot, the front ones just revolved, grindingly and agonisingly. We were going to plunge into that chasm and there was nothing I could do to stop it. I could not move, and felt fear for the first time, real fear. Then suddenly the rear wheel bit on to the piece of cross-pole, and the truck heaved itself forward and rumbled slowly onwards as if nothing had happened. I was sweating profusely and so was Ahmed. He folded his hands together and turned his eyes to the sky, but his words were unintelligible. I presumed he was thanking Allah for his deliverance from danger.

We stopped on the far side. I found I was shaking. Pete and Don were out of their vehicle and had been watching us. They walked carefully over the bridge, stopping to examine the hole, now bigger due to our wheel's movements. Pete asked if I was OK, then demanded that wood be found and placed to cover the hole. Ahmed was obviously bragging about his prowess as a driver. Pia shrugged resignedly and looked around for wood. I found some sea buckthorn bushes growing nearby, and Pete unstrapped his hunting knife and hacked off several branches. These were tied down by the drivers, Pete supervising to make sure it was all secure. Don had gone back to their vehicle and was back in his seat. When Pete was satisfied, they made their way slowly over without mishap, and we went on our way.

Again, I was aware that the Afghanis seemed con-temptuous of this caution, and of our attitude. I was full of admiration for their ability in this hostile terrain. Even Pete was not as tough as these people. Their life was hard, and they faced far worse problems than we westerners now do;

although I thought to myself that we had had to go through much the same stage in earlier centuries. I considered myself pretty tough and able to cope – by English standards. Here I was exposed as a weak westerner. But the wild animals found here were way beyond the humans in terms of survival ability. It had taken them millions of years to evolve and successfully endure the extremes of habitat to be found up here. I caught my breath at the thought that I would soon be seeing these beautiful wild animals, the apogee of perfection, in this wild and hostile terrain.

We drove on for seventeen miles to Ish Khashem, near the border with Russia, and the last township. It was here that we met up with the returning hunting party. Their truck was decorated with two animal heads strapped on the roof-rack. One of the hunters was another American, a young airline pilot with red hair and a lot of complaints, which he off-loaded as he went into a huddle with Pete and Don. He was not a happy man, grumbling about the food, the cold, the lack of attention he had received, the hopeless guiding across the hunting ground, which had resulted in his having no success in gaining a big enough trophy. He had only got a forty-something-inch Marco Polo head, he complained. From the little I could overhear he seemed to think this whole experience had been a waste of money. I did not take to him. Yes, it was a lot of money, but surely the chance to see this rare area, that few other westerners had ever had the opportunity to enter, made up for the lack of one big dead head. I thought to myself that he had a big enough dead head long before he ever set foot in the Wakhan. The other hunter was a fifty-something-year-old French doctor. He was charming and friendly, and he and I got on well with our few exchanges. He had shot an ibex only, but was brimming with the experience, and full of fun and relief that he had got out alive. The brief meeting over, we went our different ways. Pia had been in earnest consultation with his compatriots, and re-joined us with the news, to the Americans' obvious relief, that they had left the camp doctor waiting for us at Sargass, still some way up the line. What I had gathered from this short encounter was that conditions ahead were a little grim. I did know that, but to have it said by someone who had just experienced it brought it home. The Frenchman's relief was more ominous than the American's complaints.

We still had 220 miles to go. We were in a vast, bare corridor of black and brown colour. The whole of this valley, forty miles wide at this point, would have been growing grass and sedges and herbs, if humans had not lived there. But it was bare and forbidding, seemingly to the distant mountain range. Only the nearby soft alluvial soil was green with growth. Pia thought that about 4,000 Wakhis lived within the Wakhan; they existed by farming, chiefly by raising herds of goats and sheep and selling these in the town markets. The animals had denuded the landscape.

Our lunch was hard-boiled eggs, naan bread, and water melon. On peeling my eggs I found a thick green layer between yolk and white – something I had last seen as a child when we had found some old eggs abandoned by a hen in the cow-shed, and which Mother had told us were not fresh enough to eat. We had eaten them though, secretly cooked on a camp fire out of sight of parental authority, and had been none the worse. So I just swallowed hard and hoped for the best.

It was now 5 October. I got out my little Swedish thermometer. The temperature was about 70°F, I announced. It was suddenly very pleasant as we relaxed in the shade of willow trees on wooden benches by the basic shack café. The Americans forgot the earlier altercation and became expansive again. I decided it was a good chance to concentrate on the birds that were passing through on their way south on migration, and pointed these out to everyone, whether they were interested or not: I felt they ought to know about these little creatures that were all about us.

Later I was to hear from a young guide and warden for the Afghan Tourist Authority, a young Afghan named Khasem, whom I met further up in the high mountains, that the Afghans at first considered me an object of derision, as I 'kept looking at birds and wanted to know the names of them'. 'Why?' they had asked themselves time and time again. 'What does he think he is up to? Obviously a bit soft in the head.' Then they apparently decided that my birdwatching was a camouflage for something else, something far more sinister, and that perhaps I was a Soviet spy. I was using my binoculars to look at 'things', and writing down a report for my masters. They had decided to go along with this apparent interest in birds in order to learn more about the subterfuge behind it. I was totally unaware of this attitude, but had realised that they never looked one in the eye, and always kept themselves apart, having long, furtive conversations among themselves. I thought perhaps they felt a superior resentment against any feranji, and tried very hard to be friendly (unlike the two Americans, who treated them as servants). Of course, in the light of what was to happen to the country in the very near future, when the Russians over-ran it, they were perhaps right to be suspicious. No doubt there were many Soviet spies around. Pia never said anything about any of this. He had to be diplomatic: he had two very different cultures to keep happy.

However, at this point I was ignorant of this feeling of suspicion, and concentrated on my bird-watching. I was over-joyed at suddenly seeing a wheatear, and after a minute or two, asking via Pia, found that the locals called it a worrk; the 'o' as in 'orange'. These birds were still reasonably common in

England during the migration period in September, as they journeyed to Africa from the southern uplands and Scotland. Their name derived from 'white-arse', I told the Americans, and that in the days of Queen Victoria they had been trapped in their thousands in small horse-hair snares by shepherds on the South Downs of England, and were a luxury known as ortolan buntings on the tables of the wealthy, as an hors d'oeuvre. Pete nodded.

Then I spotted a redstart, a cock bird with its slate-blue back, black bib, and orange breast and rump. As a boy I had found the nest of one in a hole in a cherry tree of the orchard near where I was at school in Worcestershire. I remembered a girl I had met then, fifteen years old, who had been shooting bullfinches as they stripped the blossom from this, her father's precious orchard. She was thin and muscular, with bare brown arms that showed the complexity of tendons like whipcord, a mane of auburn hair, deep dark, serious eyes, and fine teeth that grimaced at me, a boy from the posh school on the hill. With her .410 shotgun she had knocked over the rose-chested finches as they sped away in twisting flight, and laughed at me when I complained. Looking around at the scene in front of me now, I felt the connection between the two. In 1947, England had been almost as deprived and as beleaguered as these people were now.

All at once, as we lounged in the shade, Don launched forth upon the joys of hunting in these outlandish places of the world, in that same rather curious formal manner he had used before, as if he was giving a public speech. He handed me his card, which had the phantom of an *Ovis amon* sheep printed on it.

'I took that from a book called *The Great Ark of the Wild Sheep*, published by the University of Oklahoma.' He continued, 'The pleasure of international hunting is the exploration of wild places. I've seen people of all kinds. They can be kind, sincere, and do not want to do business with you. You pick up some of their habits, some of their customs. It makes it kinda interesting. I guess I could just be collecting other ways of life instead of trophies. Sure it's hard sometimes, but I guess life is kinda hard anyway.'

I wondered if he knew what a hard life really meant. Pete joined in, over-riding his compatriot.

'You bet. I was in the Gobi Desert once, a place called Ulaanbaatar. We drove 600 miles across this plateau. It's not always hot, as most deserts, it can be deathly cold. And there's no water. There's no ocean water to precipitate rain. That makes the dirt track hard, so you can travel OK. We came to a commune with about two hundred people. These people were sittin' on a coal vein right out there in the desert. They were grazing animals out there for food, but there was no fuel to be had except animal dung, so this coal made life easier. While I was there in that camp, I had a call of nature and made for the latrine. It was a trench dug in the ground with a sort of tarpaulin shelter put up along the trench to make a bit of privacy. As I squatted there a woman came and squatted right next to me and carried on with her call of nature too. I wondered why there was a screen there at all. They were very friendly people.'

'That's what I mean,' responded Don. 'That's not an experience you'd have in New York – or anywhere in America.'

'I'll say amen to that,' was Pete's enigmatic response.

I wondered if either of them was as experienced as they liked to think they were. It was pretty primitive out here too, and such a remark might be considered insulting. Luckily Pia, the only one who would have understood, had gone off to sort out food for later. I thought of Anne at home in our little cottage in the woods, with two small children, no electricity, no mains water, and no actual loo, but decided to keep quiet.

*

We drove on again. I noticed that somebody at some time in this bare and lonely area had placed every so often some of the huge, oval, smooth, black and white glacier boulders on top of each other. They looked like large penguins, some as tall and white as humanoid snowmen. I thought they must have been way-markers, maybe for travellers of very long ago when this was the Silk Road, before the Chinese closed their border at the east end of the Wakhan and traders had to go north via Samarkand. Ah! Samarkand! – James Elroy Flecker's play-poem *The Golden Road to Samarkand* sprang to mind, the most hauntingly romantic tale of anything our English master at school had ever read to us. Samarkand today, however, was explored, revealed, written about, and been dragged into the present time. The Wakhan had not yet entered this century, and was still a hidden, forbidden place of mystery, and I was entering it. The thought struck me suddenly and forcefully with a resounding effect. Here I was only at the cliff edge of romance, in the black pit of uncertainty, still to climb up into the mellow light of bygone time, which was the sunlit uplands of romance as seen in retrospect. This was an adventure certainly as great as theirs. *For lust of knowing what should not be known, we take the Golden Road to Samarkand.* What a tale to tell the children, unless it all ended in disaster like Captain Scott's ill-fated trek to the South Pole, which has only become romantic in retrospect: at the time it was hell, and ended in death. Not a happy thought!

We followed the course of the old Oxus River, now called Dary-a-panj. We came to a small stream flowing into it, and Ahmed and the other driver stopped yet again to baptise the Toyota engines. Across the river, one hundred metres to our north, was a new tarmac road just over on the Russian side of the border. There were three or four small concrete block houses too, looking like lumps of icing sugar. One or two

Russian lorries were passing along this road, and a motorcycle. When Pia saw me looking at this through my binoculars, he told me to stop.

'It is dangerous to look. They watch us.' he said.

I asked him what it was all about. He shrugged. 'We do not want to know,' was his only reply. Later I realised that my interest in the Russian road had added to the 'spy' theory.

Eventually, after sixty miles of rough driving, we got to the end of the motor road, at a place which Pia told us was called Quala Panja. This was the boundary of another province, over which local chiefs had been the rulers way back in time. From here on, the present government did not collect any taxes and nor give the inhabitants any sort of medical or social service of any kind; and never had. Ahead there were the wild tribes of Wakhis, who were a law to themselves. It was here that we would change to horseback.

In front of us was a mud wall about twelve foot high, running for about forty yards and making a square, rather like a fort. In the middle was a wide-open gateway with a couple of ibex horns pinned on to its wooden lintel.

Pete said he thought ibex horns were there to bring good luck. He had seen ibex horns in Mongolia too. Don was looking glum. He wondered if they had anything to do with keeping a strong stomach.

'Dysentery could kill you up here along with all the other illnesses you can get in dirty places and high altitudes. I'm going to take a pill.'

Pia said the horns were there to ward off the 'Evil Eye'.

The sun began to lose heat now and shadows swept up the valley floor like a black flood; there was suddenly an icy wind like liquid glass coming off the mountain walls. High overhead, vultures were circling in a last search for anything at all to eat. We were now close on ten thousand feet up, and still had a long way to climb tomorrow and for the next weeks.

Strangely the distance to the snow-line seemed close enough to walk to before supper, but Pia said sharply that it was two or three kilometres away, and anyone breaking a leg slipping on the boulders would cause everyone else a lot of trouble. I said I would wander about nearby for a bit to stretch my legs.

'OK, but don't go out of sight.'

I was totally engrossed for some time, just wandering about and staring up into the ice and snow rising vertically for about two and a half miles, and watching the vultures which were going to roost on their icy pinnacles. I was glad that I was going to be far more comfortable than they would be. I could smell the cooking, which Pia had said was to be pilau rice and kebab, and which was wafting over the fortress wall. So, feeling cold and hungry, I followed the others inside the fort. But I was in for a surprise. When I went through the gateway I found there was nothing inside the fort. There were no rooms, just the surrounding bare walls and a large quad-rangle of earth open to the sky. Pia was cooking on a primus stove on the bare ground near the gate, where another short wall jutted out at right-angles. Our bedrolls were thrown out on the earth nearby. I thought to myself that Pia had kept very quiet about the 'hotel' arrangements here! Don as usual was muttering to himself.

When Pia saw I had come inside he sent the two drivers to close the big wooden gates and place a huge bar across to lock them together. I wondered about the place and what it had been used for in the past, but Pia seemed particularly distant and so I kept quiet.

We huddled around the stove. The blue ring of roaring flames spread out into wavy flames of yellow up the edges of the aluminium pot. There was no sign of pilau and kebab: the large pot contained lumps of goat meat cooking in water. Pia had obviously been joking. Of course, he had bought goat meat in the village where we had stopped for lunch. Pete reminded me that at that altitude water boiled at a much lower temperature than at sea level.

We wrapped the warm meat in rolls of naan, poured some of the liquid into our tin mugs, and chewed and slurped our way through our supper. We were hungry and it wasn't too bad. I remembered a meal once cooked by my mother in which the meat hadn't been anywhere near cooked.

'It's all right, dear,' she had said. 'It's meat from a sheep. They are clean eaters. It's not dangerous.'

Well, goats were like sheep in their eating habits, I told myself. You couldn't do that with pork. Pigs would eat anything and everything, and often it was filth. That was why the Arabs would not eat pig meat. It was unclean, unholy, and in a hot country worse than in one like our own.

There was no twig fire to stretch out around, so we sat huddled close as the cold began to bite into our bodies. I made some remark about how well the trucks had stood up to the punishment of rough riding the miles and miles of boulders, and suggested that not even a Rolls Royce would be able to stand up to that kind of treatment. Don looked up, suddenly animated.

'You should be made to stand to attention in the corner and wave the Union Jack over your head, and drink a bottle of Schweppes for such heresy! Don'tcha know your Queen has a Rolls Royce?'

'Well, maybe she has, but she's also got a Land Rover or two!'

We all laughed: a little light relief in this dismal place. Pete then launched into another story of how he had once hunted wild goat in Alaska, and got caught by night falling, and had had to hunker down among the boulders without any provisions or sleeping bag, other than some 'jerky', which he always had in his pocket – 'Never go nowhere without it.' Then the frost had begun to dislodge rocks higher up and these tumbled down, and he had to hide behind a massive boulder so 'they could not have their fun with me'. He had passed a cold and restless night, but knowing he was in the right place to bag a prize billy, he continued up the mountain at day-break. He had crept around the icy rocks for the rest of the day, finally shooting a trophy head, as night began to fall again.

'By then I was pretty cold and hungry. So I hacked off that goat's head to keep, and skinned the critter. I wrapped its raw fleece round my shoulders and chewed on some chunks of tallow fat from around its ribs. That was as sweet as candy right then.' In this way he spent his second night on the bare mountain.

We prepared to turn in. The night was black as the Shuck Hound of folklore, with no stars, for a dull sense of coming weather hung about the sky. This seemed to be worrying the Afghans, for they had moved apart and were looking up into the night sky, and talking agitatedly. Pia seemed to be giving orders, although of course I couldn't understand a word. But whatever it was, it seemed that it was not good news. Then Pia came over to us and told the Americans to have their rifles ready and loaded by their sides, in case we were raided in the night. The mud walls could easily be scaled by thieves, even though the gate was now locked.

'These people will have no care for the law or for anything. They are very bad men. Back in the last village a man told us there might be trouble. If people come into the camp, be ready to shoot them,' he told the hunters.

I felt more concerned about the weather. I didn't like the look of that sky at all. What would happen if blizzards struck now? There would be no way out. The snow could be a metre deep in an hour in wind drifts, even in England. I had seen it happen in the winter of 1947 and again in 1963. Transport was crippled very quickly. I had once been in a cottage on

113

Dartmoor with a mild west sky at sunset, then at dawn, on opening the door, found a wall of frozen snow covering the entrance six feet in height. Helicopters were not an option here, we had been told before we set out from Kabul. Neither did we have those Bactrian camels which nomads used in such places when winter came. I mentioned my concern to Pia.

'No problem with weather tonight. Is OK. It is not the weather that worries me.'

I wondered what he had heard. Of course, our presence – rich Americans – would have been spread around the locals. They could have been watching us all the way. There was nothing I could do about it, but I looked around and found a stout stick to have by me in case of trouble. Taking off our boots, but keeping our clothes on except for coats, we quickly got into our sleeping bags, for it was too cold for sleeping on the dirt floor as we had the night before. I felt a moment's guilt about Pia only having rugs, but knew he had also bought some skins in one of the villages, and one underneath to keep the damp away with another on top would keep him quite snug, I was sure.

I had learned many years before, on camping holidays at Father's field in Devon, how to warm up a sleeping bag. He had learned the trick in the trenches in the First World War. Cover the head completely and breathe precious heat from the lungs down to the feet. Hold that heat in all the time, breathe in through the nose and out by the mouth and occasionally take a breath of fresh air so you don't suffocate yourself. I thought of all those vultures up on their pinnacles, with their scrawny heads tucked under their huge wings, breathing in warm air and breathing that out again into the feathers around their main organs keeping heart and lungs happy. What about their scaly legs and feet? I knew birds at roost alternately lifted one leg then the other to warm in their breast feathers. Vultures no doubt would do the same, or perhaps they squatted down in a sitting position.

The thickening clouds kept me worrying for a while. I wasn't sure that Pia really understood weather signs. Then there was a far-away rumbling sound. Was it another truck arriving? Abruptly it ceased with a crash some way off. Both the Americans and I sat up with a jerk.

'Is OK,' came Pia's voice. 'Frost moving boulders off the mountain. Too far away to have fun with us this time.' Pete grunted to show appreciation of the joke.

8

We all slept well and heavily, despite the occasional sound of boulders rumbling off the mountain. To me they sounded like waves rolling on the seashore, or the roaring of trees at home, when the gale came through the wood and made the house creak, and I found that quite soothing. But we awoke soon after dawn, stretching and exchanging grunted greetings. As soon as we got out of the sleeping bags we could feel the cold air of the night entering our bodies. While water was being boiled for tea, I went for a brisk walk round the inner wall of this compound to get my blood moving. I looked up into what had become a white, almost milky sky, which had about it that pale loitering look of possible snow not far away. The mountains rose a mile overhead and out of the crags came one vulture after another, swinging out as the tiniest specks from their roosts. I felt apprehensive: a feeling that the danger level of this place had been notched up another tooth. Winter was closing in on us. I hoped that wasn't going to be a problem.

We were finishing our breakfast of a local hard goat's cheese and naan bread washed down with tea, when suddenly there was a lot of shouting outside the wall. The Americans reached for their rifles, but Pia assured us this was expected. 'It is our transport.'

He shouted back and sent the two drivers to unbolt the gate. Outside there was a rabble of Wakhis with a dozen brown and chestnut horses, which stood with drooping heads and each with a back leg resting, the hoof on point. All had old saddle sores which had turned the hair white on their withers. Looking at them, I was glad that at least I knew how to ride. The men had travelled all night from a village further up the Wakhan. They eyed us briefly, and then began shouting at us, each man apparently imploring us to choose his horse to rent. They reminded me of the woman with the baby in Kabul demanding baksheesh. They were local peasants who scraped a bare subsistence. They were wearing, not any local dress, but cast-off street clothes from the towns: grey city jackets worn threadbare, and patched at cuff and elbow with scraps of linen and bits of wool sewn into the fabric. They all had filthy old white linen turbans, wound around the head with the ends tucked into the folds, which could be easily pulled out to wrap around their mouths to keep out the cold or the dust. They were a sorry-looking bunch.

But one man stayed apart. Pia murmured, 'The local headman.' He was a much younger man dressed in the correct and typical Wakhan clothes: a great-coat of a grey colour like slushy snow, woven from yak-hair and looking rather like fine tweed, and with a dark grey, almost black, herring-bone pattern, and with thick trousers to match. Talking about this to Pia later, he said that the clothes would have belonged to the man's grandfather, because that was the tradition.

First this man demanded to have all our details of name and country of origin and passport numbers, because we were entering his province. I kept my passport, visa and the travel permit from the Tourist Office in Kabul with other important papers in my jacket inside zipped pocket, and so produced them quickly. So did Don. But Pete had packed his away in the depths of his bag, thinking they would not be needed again, and could not find them. The young chief looked at us in scorn, and said we could go no further without the numbers. We realised that he was serious. Pia had moved off to talk to the Wakhis, and so was no help. I made a quick decision. I had noticed the man had written down my passport number on his scrap of paper with his pencil as I read them out to him, without checking in any way that this was accurate, so I just pretended to pull Pete's passport from his coat pocket, saying 'Here it is,' and opening my own passport again, seemingly read out another set of figures, actually repeating my telephone number from home, adding on a zero to make the required dozen. I had no idea what numbers American passports used, but the man seemed satisfied and I let out a breath of relief. This done, the head man got back on his own horse – far finer than those brought for our use – and cantered back up the track. To my surprise Pete never referred to or thanked me for getting him out of what could have been a sticky situation, although I suppose he would have found his passport eventually.

Next, we had to haggle a price for the hire of the horses. The motor road, if it could be called that, only continued for another couple of miles or so, and then we would transfer to horse-back. The men laid on quite a pantomime for our benefit. Pia did the bartering, shouting at the men, and then giving us a running commentary on what they were saying. He shouted a price and held his fingers up to show the amount: the Wakhi owners responded by putting their fingers to their mouths imitating eating, and begging a little more, otherwise they would starve to death and their families with them; they then tore at their hearts as well, to persuade us to have compassion for their terrible plight in these terrible con-ditions – Pia shouted to us that one had added, 'With winter coming on too'. In the end, the rental price was agreed: about one and a half dollars each horse, each day, which was about 200 afghanis, or just over £1 by my calculation. I privately thought it was all a bit of a game, a show put on for our benefit. We were obviously going to need all twelve of the horses – and I felt sure that this had all been pre-arranged.

But this was the local custom, and it was important to go along with it all. It wouldn't do to upset such people – we were too dependent on their good will.

Our bags, sleeping bags, the stores and petrol for cooking, together with five live goats, which were to be our main food supply, bleating unhappily, were loaded on to the six pack horses, which started walking on ahead, with the Wakhi men leading them together with the riding horses, while we rode in the Toyotas for the last mile or two to the end of the road. Here we were to leave the vehicles and change to the horses. I wasn't quite sure why we did this. It seemed far more sensible to have got straight on to horseback at the fort compound; and that is where, eventually, we found the Toyotas on our way back. I never learned who moved the trucks back to safety.

We shortly came to a place where two rivers met: the Pamir River that drained out of a Russian lake, and joined the old Oxus. This was the point at which we were to change to horseback. Looking around I noticed there was a Russian watchtower about a mile to the north. I got out my binoculars to have a look, but Pia grabbed hold of my arm.

'No – you put away. Do not look at Russians. They are watching us through very large telescopes. They know every detail about us. They know your passport numbers too.'

I was a bit taken aback. How could they? The only way was if the Head Man had reported to them. It was a possibility. But if they did, they would then probably know that we had given a false number. That could mean trouble. Pia was clearly very frightened of them. Pete said absolutely nothing, although he was right next to us, and I could see he was pretending not to hear what had been said. I was rather puzzled by his attitude. Saying 'OK' to Pia, I obediently put my binoculars back in my bag; but then secretly got out my camera and moving a little apart, when the Afghanis were not looking, surreptitiously took a picture of us getting ready to ride, with the Oxus, Russia, watchtower and all, in the background. But I felt I was a marked man from then on!

American-style saddles had been imported by the Klineburger travel firm for the use of their clients. They had a Spanish look about them, and I wondered if the design had originated long ago via the Conquistadors of the 17th century in South America. They were broader, longer, and more ornate than English saddles. The cantle or seat was tooled with decorations. The tree was wide on each of them and two horns were fixed either side of the pommel, to which you could either cling if your mount bucked, or to which you could wind your rope if you lassoed a steer. Pia fetched these saddles out of the Toyota: two of them, one for each American hunter on his trip.

As for myself and the three Afghans of our group, we had a crude wooden wedge with rope under the horse's belly to keep it, hopefully, in place. It was a horrible, primitive and unwieldy trap, into which one was wedged tightly and excruciatingly for hours at a time. I clambered aboard this contraption somewhat clumsily, feeling rather an idiot, as my horse stood with its ears back and eyes rolling around while it worked out what it had got on its back. Its owner cursed and shouted at it, and kept jerking the bridle up under its chin, making the animal even more nervous. I had ridden quite a lot of difficult horses in the past, but knew that this was going to be the worst ride that I would ever have. The saddle was as uncomfortable as it looked. Some of the Afghans were pointing and laughing, and I asked Pia irritably what they thought they were laughing at. He didn't really look at me, and said briefly, 'They are saying the saddle is called the balls-killer.'

'Tell them I've already discovered that.'

I moved my legs to stand up a little in the stirrups to get

comfortable and the horse seemed to think I wanted to move on, and it took off. Then I was very glad that I knew how to ride, otherwise I would have come off straight away. Luckily the horse knew which way to go, because it had just come from home and wanted to get back there, and as that was the only track, that was our route too. Another horse had already gone off ahead of us, and I just had the presence of mind to extricate my old Finetta 88 camera from my saddle-bag and snap a picture of the scene, as the horse ahead raised the dust.

After about half a mile my horse quietened down, and with head down just slogged on over the boulders, picking its way rather wearily towards its home fifty miles ahead. It was sure-footed and never stumbled, even though it had travelled through the previous night, and must have been tired and hungry. I was now going slowly enough to allow the others to catch up, for the pack horses could not travel quickly.

Looking about me, I wondered how many horses, camels, and donkeys had travelled this part of the Silk Road. Alexander the Great had been in this area in 328–327 BC, using Maracanda as his base, which we know now as Samarkand. I had read up bits of history in the brief time I had before I left England, and remembered that he had explored the mountain valleys west, east, north, and then south-east from that base, and returned west down the Wakhan to where we were now, completing his conquest of the Persian Empire, the area then named Sogdiana. Then he had gone south, up over the Hindu Kush and followed the river Kabul down to the river Indus, and then overland to the river Hydaspes. There he had defeated the Indian King Porus after an exacting battle against cavalry elephants, which had frightened Alexander's horses. His own favourite horse, Bucephalus, had died there. That horse had been tamed by the 12-year-old Alexander when no one else could ride him, and the two were devoted to one another; but it was then eighteen years old. Afterwards Alexander had gone back through Persia (Iran) to Arabia, where he himself died in 323 BC at Babylon.

I wondered whether distant descendants of Alexander today could ever make a substantiated claim to that ancient dynasty. I knew, from various books that I had read, that over the many years that had passed since then people claimed their horses had descended from the cavalry of his army. It was a nice thought, even now, as I rode east into the land that had once been at the extreme eastern end of his empire, that my horse might have a genetic connection back 2,300 years to the army of the Ancient Greeks, who had lived out their flaming sunset of civilisation with the heroic dynasty of Alexander. Then I thought wryly that my horse was no Bucephalus; nor was I exactly a heroic Alexander!

His cavalry was said to number five thousand horses at the start of his campaign to rule much of the known world, and although it must have been much depleted by the time he had reached here, it would still have been a large army; and with quadruple thudding hooves beneath them, the cavalrymen would have made an awesome sight as they swarmed down this valley towards India, raising a huge cloud of dust. I had seen one or two Afghans in Kabul, and there was one in this party today, who had the look of Alexander, with fair hair and green staring eyes that seemed focussed on something far away and unseen, and not seeing the immediately trivial and common place. They seemed separate somehow, not a part of the present time. I knew there was a culture of these slightly different ethnic types in Nuristan in the Hindu Kush. In the 1930s the Nazis had attempted to document them as true Aryans, a kind of blue-eyed master race, part of their delusional ideology. As I understood it, that race of people had come from long before Alexander's tempestuous escapades, and originated from the nomadic herders of the mountain valleys and plains of Mongolia. These herders had formed a confederacy of nomadic tribes called the Husiung-nu, which had harassed the Chinese of the Middle Kingdom in the 3rd century BC, who had been intent on keeping the lucrative trade routes open to the West along this Silk Road, and which the wild men of the mountains threatened.

In the days that followed I tried to find out as much as I could about the ancient history of this place. I winkled out fragments of ancient stories in desultory camp-fire conversations in the nights to come, as I tried to piece together what was being said through Pia. He could only give broken bits of the story, but some extraordinary beliefs and folklore did emerge, as I shall reveal later.

All these thoughts buzzing around in my head were dissipated when the others caught up with me, with their own swarm of noise. One of the men who had laughed at me earlier came up to me and slapped me on the back, now grinning in friendly fashion. I felt I had passed some kind of initiation test. At least I hadn't fallen off and made a complete fool of myself.

Not long after this I heard a strange noise which sounded like a human cry, some way off against the edge of the mountain. Then it came again, sounding like a woman wailing. I asked Pia what it could be. His reply amazed me.

'A woman is calling for help.'

'Why? What has happened?' I asked. 'Is she in some sort of trouble?'

'Yes, surely, I think so.'

'What sort of trouble? Why is she shouting?'

The horses did not stop. But Pete was now also looking across the valley to the noise coming from the rocky slopes about a quarter of a mile away.

'She has fallen down. I think she break leg.'

'Well, we must go and help her, we can't just leave her.' I

said and Pete agreed.

'No, I do not think so.'

'Of course we must', we both said.

But Pia was adamant. No one else took any notice at all.

'No. You are feranji, it is dangerous to interfere. The men here would not like. If they consider she should be helped they will go and get her in their own time. It may be punishment. It is local custom.'

I looked at the rest of the party. They were all stone-faced, and did not even look towards the stricken woman, but just kept riding forward. Pete said to me, 'Better leave it, Rich. We don't know what's going on. Do what the natives do. When in Rome, you know.'

I felt very confused. It was against nature to leave someone, especially a woman, to suffer, especially in this wild and remote place. I remembered reading that both Wilfred Thesiger and Eric Newby had administered to local people here and in Arabia, so it seemed a puzzle. But if it was to be ignored, then there was nothing I could do. I realised I knew nothing about local politics, and could not go against the decision of the locals' judgement, but I felt very bad about it.

We continued for about eighteen miles and stopped at a village, called Shelk, but also Sherk, and Sust, depending on who you were and where you came from, said Pia. We were not used to riding, and even the Americans with their luxury saddles were sore and stiff. I could hardly move when I dismounted. My crutch had gone to sleep and now tingled with pins-and-needles, which was a weird sensation that I had never experienced before. Even my old BSA motorbike that I had for many years had never done that to me, and I had ridden on it for long hours at a time, and in winter blizzards with the wind piercing my lungs.

The horses were unloaded and rested on a stubble field and

they started grazing with goats in a lawn of fine-cropped grass and herbs. Nearby there were small fields cleared of boulders that were growing tick beans, which Pia said they called barcola, and there were small fields of wheat as well.

The women of this collection of mud houses were not to be seen, but they had prepared hot crisp naan, which they had decorated with herring-bone patterns. I remembered seeing the same patterning on old-fashioned butter-pats as a child. It was strange how this pattern of alternate stripes had persisted through human culture. I had seen the same design on Bronze Age clay pots of the Beaker peoples in Sussex, where I now lived. It surrounded many church doors in stone-work of the Normans. And now I noticed that it had also been woven into the grey felt of the overcoats of the men of this village. As we were in a landscape of mainly 45-degree angles, with mountain peaks at the top of these equilateral triangles, I wondered if the people here related, had always related, automatically, to the horizon as their symbolic balance of cosmic order.

We went on our way, riding through the narrowing valley for hour after hour. I kept a little apart from the main group, and found my thoughts pondering the idea of symbols. My mind turned to what I had read in the past about the symbols adopted by mankind as he probed the meaning of life. It had always been so. One side of the mountain ascends to the sky as it were; the other descends. This was the rhythm of nature. Winter is darkness and cold: then the year climbs out of this pit and ascends to the zenith of warmth and plenty of mid-summer. Then the inevitable decline back to the shortest day. The ancients marked these events with ritual and ceremony. Making marks had a meaning, whether on stone walls, bread, butter, or clothes. It gave people a sense of their existence in the world, of belonging. Tribes would recognise one another by the marks on their bodies, and, later, clothes. I thought of

Arran sweaters, each area having its own pattern, and intensely proud of its own heritage. The Pharaohs took their emblems of everlasting life from the sun's pyramid of golden light as it flowed down from the heavens a few hours before sunset. It would be the same here, where life was not contaminated by the modern way of life: had not been overlaid by the conventions of 'polite society'.

I would have liked to have seen the simple tool these women kept for the making of marks on dough. Was it a special instrument that was handed down from generation to generation? Was it something special that she made herself? Or was it just any piece of twig snapped off a juniper or sea buckthorn bush nearby? Probably the latter. It was the mark that was important, not the means of making it. I wondered what other symbols, and even rituals, these people had in their daily life. It was too difficult to get past the various barriers, the language and suspicion. These people kept themselves to themselves. I was feranji. But I did later manage to photograph an important symbol from the past.

Meanwhile we were coming into the bottom edges of the 45-degree slopes of scree, which had formed as skirts to the solid mountains themselves. Looking at this scree, and getting really close to it, was daunting but gave a sense of excitement too. Where we were riding was at the very bottom of piles of boulders: and pretty big boulders too. Many must have weighed ten tonnes. Most were smoothed by either previous glacial drift or spring river floods. This was what we could hear falling in the night. The big ones would have enormous energy coming down from anything up to a mile above us, an avalanche gathering more on its way. Suppose one fell right now? We would be smashed to smithereens. I came past one which had recently rolled down, as it still had dust and broken pieces of rock covering it. My previous experience of scree was in the Scottish mountains, where perhaps the biggest boulders were the size of rugby balls. I had clambered across those slanting jumbles of broken mountain, and felt perfectly happy walking on its rough and tumble. This was very different. This held menace.

It had now warmed up. I checked my little Swedish thermometer, which was a comforting link to home. The temperature was now back up to 70°F so it was very pleasant. Yet overhead, snow clouds were draped around the peaks above, hanging their grey ropes of snow. The lovely clean air and spectacular void of this valley going into the far distance, with its capping of snow a mile above, gave me a sense of light-headed optimism. The feeling of dread had gone. Maybe that is the feeling mountaineers get as they work their way beyond the humdrum of ordinary life. Provided we did not break any bones or have altitude sickness, this life could go on for as long as it liked. Physically I now felt good. That was not to last.

The track we were on now had to cross the Oxus to its northern shore. It was still wide here, about twenty metres across. The water was like blue glass, and about a metre deep. Coming from the snow fields, it was perhaps a degree or two above freezing. I could see a shoal of large fish darting about, looking like grey phantoms, and I suppose just under a metre in length. I wondered what species they were – perhaps char, but I couldn't be sure. What was of more immediate concern was the river bed, which was a jumble of smooth and slippery boulders. These were not evenly spread like a paved road, bumpy but passable, but with deep gaps in between, into which I realised a horse's hoof could slip down, and become trapped or broken. But like previous problems, I now assumed that the Afghanis and their horses knew what they were doing.

Telling the noisy group of men who had accompanied us with the horses to stay back, and telling us to let the horses alone to find their own way, Pia went first to lead the way, the two Americans following. Just as my horse entered the water, peering down cautiously into the black chasms between boulders, with myself keeping as calm and still as possible so it didn't lose balance or get distracted, one of the camp followers leapt up behind me, making me jump and causing the horse to stumble slightly. Luckily, we were still near the edge and it recovered well. I cursed the man but only under my breath. I didn't want to make any enemies. Another camp follower just waded straight into the icy water, lifting up his clothes and showing his little brown arse before it was submerged. I managed to get a picture of that.

The water was a good metre deep for the most part, up to the horses' bellies, but somehow they all made the crossing without any real problems. You could see how hard these animals were concentrating. When we were all safely across, the horses seemed to look around at each other, catching each other's eyes, shaking their heads, and grinning through their teeth. They showed no camaraderie of this nature either with us or with their handlers.

The track east, continuing up the Wakhan by the side of the river we were now on, was virtually obliterated by boulders. Now for mile after mile we were picking our way and squeezing through gaps. Above us on the right was the mountain the Afghans called Barba Tangy, which was 22,000 feet high. Grey veils of cloud hung about its deep drifts of snow, partly enclosing them. Apparently, it had been climbed once: in 1968 by a Polish team of mountaineers.

9

The horses had brought us about 55 miles to perhaps the most beautiful village I have ever seen anywhere in the world. On the maps today its name is Sarhad, but Pia said it was called Sargass. Its collection of mud huts was perched on an ancient alluvial fan above the Oxus River. This place belonged to a time half a millennium ago, or even a whole thousand years before. It could have been biblical. The Oxus gleamed bright silver between its dark mountain walls, and the wooden cantilever bridge spanned the gorge like a huge fragile swan's wing.

It did not look possible that anything could cross that bridge, or had ever crossed it, because it was so delicate. My impression was that it was a decoration, perhaps for a ballet set, or a painting from the brush of a Chinese artist. It was almost dream-like.

I have always been glad that I saw it like that, because after the Russian invasion everything changed drastically. I heard that the bridge was rebuilt to a specification that would carry their armoured trucks through to defend their occupation of Wakhan up as far as the border with China. No doubt the village was greatly altered too. And ever since there has been fighting of some sort throughout the country. I feel I had a unique view of something special.

In the distance far down the valley to the south, above the Karamsar Pass into Gilgit, a mountain peak of snow was streaming a plume of ice vapour. This was Barba Tangy. This magnificent arena of white and blue and silver and black surrounded the village.

In the foreground, six men, women and children, with six bullocks, some donkeys, and a dog or two, were beating out wheat grain from the husks and stalks on a circular platform, and the faint breeze coming up the valley was winnowing the piles of chaff away into the air. Sheaves of short-stemmed wheat were neatly arranged in a pile by this winnowing platform. The afternoon sun highlighted the ancient harvest scene to a golden brown. The circle of flat ground was exactly like those I have since seen in Portugal and Spain, which were used until the late 1960s in remote rural areas. It was also similar to the flat circular places found where I live in Sussex, in the woodlands of the South Downs, where the ground has not been disturbed by modern agriculture for two millennia. Such places could have been winnowing platforms from the Bronze Age, when the whole of the South Downs dip-slope was virtually an agricultural zone, growing and even exporting surplus grain to lands across the Channel. We were truly in a time-warp.

Beyond the immediate harvest field, which looked to be about half a hectare, was a small building made of stones. It looked a little like the pillboxes left over from the Second World War in England, some of which are now protected monuments. Pia said it was the mill-house. It was fed by small streams of mountain water flowing in channels dug out and lined with hollowed poplar logs. There was a pile of long poplar branches nearby. I realised that they had to have been brought up from much further down the river. Nothing of that sort could grow up here. Even the simplest task involved hard labour.

Pia and the drivers were busy unloading our gear and preparing the mud huts set aside for our purpose. The horses were put out to graze, and our little herd of goats put into a shed and given food and water. Waiting for us here was the camp doctor, Dr Amin. He was a jolly, plump young Afghan, who had trained in America with NASA on treating the physical problems associated with extreme conditions of altitude. The Americans were clearly very glad to see him. Pia explained to them that the head guide of the hunting staff, Shahik, who lived in Sargass, had gone off to another village and so was not available. There would be another guide waiting for them when we reached the camp destination.

I wanted to get a closer look at the mill-house, and Pete came with me. We crawled in through a low doorway on all fours, and as the roof was only about four feet high we had to stay crouched when inside. Water funnelling through a log turned paddles on the mill-wheel, a circular lump of granite which was revolving at a furious pace and making a terrific grinding noise on top of another stone. Above the whirling wheel a conical goat-skin container filled with grain fed a trickle of wheat down into the central hole of the mill-wheel. A wooden trigger nudged the chute each time round to keep the trickle moving. A gritty coarse flour drifted out into a trough. Next to this was a bag-like container made of dog-skin into which the flour was emptied from time to time. The roof of the building was festooned with spiders' webs whitened by the flour dust.

Pete was impressed by this primitive machine. 'Say, that thing is automatic and low maintenance. No overhauling needed. All they have to do is provide a new mill-wheel now and then – what, every five years or so? Gee, that's great!'

I didn't contradict him but, although also impressed by the ingenuity of design, I thought that actually it was quite hard work. Any new stone would have to be shaped. And looking round, it seemed that all these villages had in the way of food was this flour and goat meat.

I went back to get my camera, and returned to try and get a photograph of the wheels, again crawling through the door.

Unfortunately, this time there was a woman inside, moving the flour into the bag. Luckily she didn't scream, but was so terrified by our encounter that she dragged a boulder out of the wall and squirmed through the hole to escape. It unnerved me a bit too. I told Pia so he could explain, in case there was trouble.

'Well, two things,' he said. 'One, you are feranji. The women are not allowed to be seen. Two, the camera. If you capture her image, you have power over her for ever. It is evil spirit. If her husband knew, then she would be beaten. That is the custom.'

Fortunately, no one had noticed me taking pictures of the harvesters on the winnowing platform, because that would not have gone down well either.

Pia had organised another lamb stew, or rather boiled meat with rice he had bought before we left, which we ate round a camp fire. In the last of the day before the piercing cold, and black sky which was obscured with high altitude snow, I had another quick look at the swan wing bridge. Pete and Don had had enough and got ready to turn in. It had been a long day and their focus was on the hunt ahead; all their energy had to be preserved for that. It was getting too dark for another photograph and so I didn't bother to take my camera. That was a pity, because an extraordinary thing happened.

A horse and rider suddenly appeared from the village. The rider had on a large white turban and a flowing dark grey cloak. He rode his chestnut gelding slowly across the bridge, and they were silhouetted against the white mountain beyond. It was like something out of Arabian Nights: the essence of romance.

Halfway across the bridge, the horse's front feet slipped through the slats. It stumbled forwards and its stomach crunched through the rotten wood. Horse and rider plunged straight down into the river. I had already noted that the water was very deep there, as a crater had been formed in the river bed by a swirl pool. I watched in horror as both vanished in a tremendous splash. Before I could even think about shouting for help, the horse's ears emerged out of the ripples; then the rider's head. Quickly horse and rider floated up together, and the horse swam for the shore, struggling out over the boulders. The rider remained seated. He must have been nearly frozen, for the water was icy and the air temperature was dropping rapidly. Together the pair clambered up the bank.

I expected him to return to the village, and I could hardly believe what happened next. The rider made his charge face the bridge again, and this time thrashed it into a canter. The pair leapt over the large hole and, reaching the far side safely, carried on along the mountain path. The man now looked like a dishevelled vagrant rather than the romantic Byronic figure that had started out.

Hardly believing what I had seen, I went back and told Pia, who was talking to the local men round the camp fire. He laughed, and told me they had seen the man leave, and had been making jokes about him.

'He is young. He has woman in the next village, Langor. She will warm him up.' He said something to the others, evidently repeating this with additions from the way they all laughed coarsely.

'But we have to cross that bridge tomorrow, Pia. It will have to be mended first.'

'No. Tomorrow we turn north. We do not use bridge.'

For that I was glad. Then I too got ready for the night in the mud hut. I noticed that on the beams were scratched the names of half a dozen American hunters who had, over the past two years since this scheme had been operating, come up here to shoot Marco Polo sheep. Pete and Don had already notched their names, and I added mine, wondering, as I did so, who was the last English person to come this far. I knew a party of plant hunters had visited the Wakhan in the past, also a few hunter-explorers, and I knew King George V had once been up here on a hunting trip. I wondered where he would have stayed. They probably brought splendid imperial tents and a royal silver service. With which thought I fell asleep.

In the morning I was awoken by alpine choughs whistling and calling *chak chak chak*, and there they were, hurtling by like black arrows. Vultures were circling out of their high roosts above. What I thought was a herring gull flew east along the route of the Oxus. I wondered where on earth it thought it was going, because it was heading to a distant water-shed over which was only the Gobi Desert. It was probably looking for a pass to the south, and India. I knew that Lake Ozero Karakul was about 120 miles to the north of us, so perhaps it had come from there – or even well beyond that, from the Aral Sea.

Pete and Don now had to 'zero' their rifles. At 15,000 feet bullets drop four inches less than they do at sea level, because there is less air resistance. The sights on the rifle barrels had to be adjusted to allow for this. They spread-eagled themselves on the ground and aimed carefully at targets 300 metres away, and each made groups of two inches which seemed to me brilliant. These guys were certainly out of the top drawer for accuracy.

The bullets bounced off the boulders somewhere into the sky, and the sound reverberated off the mountain walls for several seconds after. So did the whistling alarm calls of the alpine choughs, which scattered like police whistles in the streets of London in a 1920s movie. After about half an hour the Americans were satisfied with their performance. They had established dominance again in their own eyes, and that had assured this adventure for the rest of us. If they had dropped out now, I would have been side-lined and unable to go on. Everybody was happy: everything was going according to plan. Even Pia momentarily relaxed.

However, conscious that I was here to do a job, apart from my own enjoyment and satisfaction at being in such a place, I very much wanted to get out and do my own thing once we were really in the wilds – for that was where we were now heading. We were leaving the Silk Road and Marco Polo's footsteps, and were travelling into what was practically virgin territory for westerners. We were turning north, into the empty valleys along Russia's southern borders, an area which had been used by high-altitude sheep graziers on the alpine meadows for millennia, but was little known outside their closed community. And for that we were going to have to change from horses, which would not be able to cope with our loads in that difficult terrain, to yaks.

Word had been sent to the alpine graziers when we had arrived in the village, and they had arrived with a selection of the beasts while it was still dark. There had been considerable noisy confusion, and now Pia brought them forward. This started a shouting chorus of 'my yak is best', 'my yak is the strongest', 'my yak is the most comfortable that has ever been known'. Pia yelled out the translation of these claims above their own clamour, then gave up with a shrug and spread hands. Somebody might have claimed his yak had a direct blood-line to Alexander the Great's army for all I knew.

They were the most extraordinary looking beasts, almost primeval in their hunched stature, huge heads, and snorting nostrils. We had no idea, and just picked those that looked the strongest. Pia hired a total of ten yaks, each for about two dollars a day. Each yak hired came with its owner as well. There were curses and muttering from those owners who had not been chosen. But I suspected the money earned was pooled anyway and shared for the benefit of the whole community. This was their big investment for the year, and would ensure food for the winter. The horses would still be used for a part of the way, but only for some of the packs and stores. Pia had explained that the altitude was going to be too high for them to cope. Also, the track would be slippery with snow and loose scree, and was near vertical in places with precipitous drops. They had managed so far, but were now looking really tired out, and their breathing was a bit laboured.

Pia said the yaks were able to carry 100kg without any trouble. Later we saw one carrying at least double that, with a family of parents, three children, and their belongings all perched on one enormous animal. Pete remarked that the yaks were the Cadillac cars of this country: silent, sure-footed, powerful, and comfortable. Ours weren't very silent, I thought to myself. They were panting like wolves, wanting to get back up into the snow. It was far too hot for them here. Even by 9 a.m. the temperature had soared to 70°F. Their black tongues hung as they panted, for yaks can't sweat through their skins as can horses. This was about as low an altitude with which they could cope.

'Any lower and they die from pneumonia,' Pia informed us. That seemed a strange thought, turning our usual idea of that illness upside-down.

The yak is inbred from the original wild animal, *Bos grunniens*, of which a few may still remain in Western Tibet. Later, one of the Wakhis, who sometimes told stories around the evening camp fire, related a tale of folklore as to how the yak first appeared on the face of the earth. 'One day,' he said, 'one of the horses in the valley of the Oxus, an animal that likes to wander about and not do any work, asked an Indian buffalo if it could borrow the buffalo's coat as it wanted to go higher up into the mountain and explore. The buffalo grudgingly lent its coat and the horse disappeared, never to return, and lived for ever among the snowy peaks, where it was happy in its big thick coat.' That is the gist of what I managed to write down from Pia's translation – but the story was much more embroidered than those bare details. I was very interested in hearing a story which had been handed down from previous generations, but neither of the Americans seemed to care.

The shepherds from on high had also brought lambs and goats for us to choose, as we had finished up the last of the first batch the previous evening. Six were bought, and they snuggled into the packs and rode on the biggest yak the rest of the way to the camp ahead. Normally one goat is exchanged for one pound of tea in these villages. Pia had brought tea, but also handed over a few coins extra, for good will, he explained. I discovered, by asking questions with Pia patiently providing the answers, that these alpine herders use the yak for milk and meat, the cows being stimulated to give milk with brief suckling by the calves. This milk is three times richer in butterfat than the best Jersey milk in Europe.

The choughs had started whistling again when they saw the yaks. The village people cursed them with raised fists and shouting. When I asked why, the answer was that they had been known to steal the cheese and butter stored in sheds. I presumed this recognition of the yaks by the choughs was inbred, after perhaps thousands of years of interaction. Choughs are, after all, of the crow family, and intelligent and resourceful.

At last, everything was packed up and ready to go. Dr Amin had quietly got on with packing up his own gear and organising its bestowal on his yak. I saw that the yak saddles were the same amazing and crude design as those that had been on the horses, and I dropped unwillingly back into my crutch prison. My yak groaned horribly and so did I. They had a rope fixed to a ring in their nose with which to control and steer them. I must have pulled too hard, as it tried to buck me off and went hopping around like a young calf, kicking its back legs in the air. It was excruciatingly painful. Pete and Don grinned from the security of their soft saddles.

'Better than a rodeo show, Rich!' shouted Pete. Don added something to the effect that it was a good thing I had already got a couple of kids, as maybe I couldn't now expect any more.

'Show the critter who's boss!' continued Pete.

I guessed the two Americans had been given the most trusted quiescent beasts to ride because they were part of the whole valuable hunting facility. I was just a nobody, a spare part. I didn't mind: I was just glad to be having this experience, whatever discomforts it might bring.

The path into the mountains was steep all right. It felt like being in a cable car on that yak. I am not very good at heights, inherited from my father, who felt ill if he stood on the edge of a ten-foot Devon cliff. But I just had to make myself ignore the danger of slipping and hurtling down. I noticed Don's face had turned set and grey again, while Pete looked grim. Pia always had a shut-in look, even when he was talking directly to us. He was after all responsible for everything that happened. The main party with the stores had gone on ahead, I thought possibly to trample the track and make it easier for us to follow. Our two original drivers were behind: again as a safety check, I guessed. There was also a gaggle of walkers.

As we climbed, the wide Wakhan valley quickly became a narrow gulley far below, in which a silver thread ran into the far distance. I felt a growing excitement. We were rising into the land of the snow leopard at last! Perhaps, if I were really lucky, my childhood dream would actually be realised. I took my eyes off the falling slopes below and made myself look up into this new land of snow patches and hidden ledges that were at last coming into view. Some of these rocks were the colour of the animal itself, with their cryptic patterns of palest pink and brown and sienna. But as we went higher, so the rocks also changed, from mainly blackish-brown to more of a slush colour. I stared around at this new world of possibility, a world where very few humans normally ventured. It was all magnificent and rather overwhelming. The hunters were looking eagerly around as well.

'Keep your eyes skinned for a Marco Polo,' said Pete.

'Yep, sure will,' was Don's reply.

They were only interested in the thought of the trophy head they hoped to bag.

We passed an area of bare rock by the pathway that had crude drawings scratched on them, showing mountain animals being chased by dogs and being killed by humans. Pia explained that they had been there for as long as anyone could remember, and nobody knew who had drawn them or when, but many, many years before.

'Long time. Grandfathers' grandfathers – more,' he said.

They resembled the well-known primitive cave art paintings found in France. I managed to get off my yak to take a photograph. But this caused a problem, as my yak just walked on as I let go of its rope, and I had to run after it and get back on while it kept moving. I had by then just about mastered the technique of controlling the animal. Having ridden horses in Iraq and England, I was used to guiding the with my heels, a left heel nudge making them turn right, right heel to turn left. These animals had no idea of such etiquette. They just lumbered forward in a straight line. Of course, there was only one path for them to take, but occasionally they had to be steered by pulling the rope to left or right. I was wary of hurting the animal, knowing the nose to be very tender. The way to go faster was a sharp pointed stick, which was meant to be jabbed into the yak's neck. I could not bring myself to do this with any force, as Pete could. His impatient control indicated how he had been so successful in life.

However, even he was concerned about the cinches, a term I did not know, but which he told me was an old Mexican word for what I called saddle girths. Those on his saddle were a broad, tanned leather belt with curled edge to stop chafing. The local version had rawhide belts with sharp edges that cut badly into the yak's belly. I found it difficult to believe that the shepherds up here always used such poor harness material. There was nothing to be done, but it put Pete into a bad mood.

The sunlight became very fierce as our altitude increased, for we rose about 4,000 feet in one hour. The sky became a deep ocean blue. I had rolled my sleeves right up, but Dr Amin called out, advising me not to do so as I should get burnt. I am very dark-skinned and do not normally burn, but I complied. No point in antagonising anybody. The other discomfort was the large number of flea bites that I seemed to have gained from the previous night's sleep in the mud hut, and which I desperately wanted to scratch. Most were round my ribs and neck, and they lasted for several weeks. They were also making me feel a little unwell, but I thought that could have been the altitude. But the bites were so bad that when I did eventually get back home, I showed them to my doctor, and he thought I might have had chicken-pox.

We were supposed not to let our yaks lick the snow, but this became almost impossible as the hours went by, and soon they were sucking up snow like children eating ice-cream on a hot day. The horses stopped to drink at trickling streams, of which there were many.

We paused for lunch at a small meadow between the rocks. I saw that the plants were mainly sedges, not grasses, and they were now brown and withered, as autumn was about to turn into winter. It reminded me a little of pictures I had seen of mountains in Iceland. It was a relief to get off the yak. The air was still very warm and it was quite comfortable relaxing for a while. Then, without any warning, everything changed. First, the sun vanished, unexpectedly and abruptly, which took us all by surprise. Next there was a strange white vapour which seemed to hang around us like a shroud. It was very different from hill-fog back in Great Britain. It seemed to have a tangible feel to it. It was uncanny, but at the same time so different and so unlike anything I had experienced before that I found it briefly exhilarating. It became very cold in a very few seconds. We quickly put on our various items of cold-weather gear.

The yaks had had the heaviest loads removed to give them a rest, and tethered so they could graze on the sedges. They were quickly loaded up again, but with the loading came a problem which nearly stopped the whole expedition in its tracks. As the terrain was getting even more difficult, we were going to have to squeeze between rocks. Pete kept his rifle back, to load it on the yak in his own way, for although the rifle was secure in a fibre-glass case to stop it getting knocked about, he was worried that it would get banged and damaged if loaded, as previously, on to the side of the pack yak. He kept it separate to put on the top of the load. The yak's owner, a tall powerful man, disagreed, and he untied the rifle and put it back on the side. Pete ran forward and untied it. Then the man grabbed Pete's arm and pushed the rifle back on the side. Pete 'just got mad', as he recounted later, and swung his fist and cracked the man on the side of his head, knocking him down. The man jumped up screaming, and started to fumble in his clothes for his knife. Pia shouted at the man to stop, and forced himself between the pair of them. He told Pete to get on to his yak and keep quiet, and spoke loudly and firmly to the yak-man, who sullenly put the rifle where Pete wanted it. I was thinking that this was the last thing we wanted, for the local man would now be resentful and try to get even, and we were already in a difficult situation. I admired Pia's handling of what could have become very dangerous.

We set off again. Then suddenly it started to snow. It seemed impossible that the storm that followed had come out of that lovely warm blue sky which we had been enjoying a short while before. It was too cold to hold the rope to guide the yak, so I managed to tie it to the saddle. The animal had anyway been doing what it wanted all along, and knew far more than I did. I felt in the pockets of my specially bought snow-proof anorak for the balaclava I had brought with me that had once belonged to my grandfather, who had bought it in Harrods in the early 1900s, together with my old mitts, which leave the fingers uncovered but keep the hands warm, then pulled up the hood of the anorak and tied it down under my chin.

The snow quickly became a blizzard as we climbed despondently upwards. There was no longer any sign of where the path was, but the leader seemed to know, or rather his yak did, for I noticed the man's hands were in his pockets. We on the animals quickly became snowmen, but the half dozen or so Afghanis walking behind were very inadequately dressed, for the main part just wearing the same street clothes they had had back in the village, while their only footwear was those cut-down rubber-tyre shoes. Once again, I could only admire the durability of this race compared with us westerners. Looking back all these years later, it seems almost unbelievable. I know the Russians now organise similar hunts on their side of the border, very efficiently organised and equipped. No rubber-tyre shoes for them!

After several more hours, when the sun seemed about to set, we reached the top, or saddle, of the Sargass Pass. It was a height of about 16,000 feet. Breathing had become a bit difficult, but I buried my mouth and nose into my clothes, which seemed to help, for we weren't using any energy for walking. The snow was drifting and seemed just about at white-out. Because I had been letting my yak have its head and do as it pleased, it had become happier, and now charged ahead, taking the lead. I just sat tight. Everyone else was in their own shut-in world anyway. I thought the Americans might even had had their eyes closed. Pete had probably put himself into a sleep. Don had become very quiet on the way up, and I was not sure that he was feeling well. I had asked Pete when we had stopped for lunch, but he was totally dismissive of any problem, which was his way of dealing with life, it seemed.

'The Doc is keeping an eye on us. We don't have to think about anything like that,' was his response.

The walkers were now about one hundred metres behind, making use of the trenches the yaks were making through the snow. All at once the path dipped, and it was steep and slippery; I found myself almost sledging down on this strange prehistoric animal's back. Once or twice it slipped to its knees, but lumbered up again. On an easier place I stopped and turned, and took a photograph of Pete coming down behind me. I was beginning to think of him as very like that well-known American hunter and adventurer Ernest Hemingway. My animal trotted ahead for another two miles or so, down across a desolate slope of mountain snow into the valley, the beginning of the hunting area, and for me, at last, the beginning of the land of the elusive snow leopard. After a while I heard shouts behind me telling me to stop.

'We camp here for the night,' called Pia, catching up with me. I looked around at the drifts and wondered how this could make a camp. Pia pointed to a small stack of stones, half hidden by the snow, which seemed to be some kind of hut, or what in England, in medieval times, would have been a cold-harbour, and what my father knew as a 'linhay' – a rough and ready circular dwelling with branches and straw for a roof, for travellers and shepherds over the moors or downs; nothing more than a place to keep the winter wind away, and to light a fire perhaps.

We were stiff and cold. We had been in the saddle for seven hours. I jumped around a bit doing cabby-warms to get my circulation moving. We had to crawl on all fours through a gap in the stones to get inside, where we found that the roof of twigs and small branches of willow were too low to allow us to stand properly. We broke off some of these twigs and branches and with difficulty made a small fire. The smoke immediately made our eyes weep, and we coughed. One of the drivers got the primus going, made tea, and warmed up some rice which had been cooked the previous evening, together with some slices of goat meat, also left over from the previous night, hacked off the bone with a knife sharpened on the rocks. I think that probably made the knife even blunter than it had been, because some of the stringy bits failed to yield and were eventually torn apart on the sharp edges of the stones. We were too tired to care, and swallowed the food somehow. We were also given a handful of sultanas, which I thought afterwards must have come from a fly-blown stall in one of the village streets, judging by the effect they had on my guts in the coming night.

Small 'pup tents', as Pete called them, what I knew as bivouacs, were put upon the snow outside. We weighted the guy ropes with rocks. The sun had vanished, and our only light was the snow. It gave a dim background to everything around us. Perhaps it was capturing the light of the stars. It turned us all into black figures against its pallor: our bent slow figures bumbling on the ground with the tents, the soft outlines of the yaks huffing steams of breath around their heads, now seemingly turned to stone, and the drooping horses each with its lifted leg for rest.

Pete and Don were each given a cylinder of oxygen for the night by the doctor, but told not to use it unless their breathing became difficult. Apparently there was some danger, because we had travelled quite high and then descended several thousand feet too quickly for the body to adjust. Using oxygen at altitude changes the structure of the blood and bringing it down to what it is at sea level can cause problems. I was not given an oxygen cylinder.

The night ahead should have seemed daunting, but we were just too tired to care. Without even a word we turned in. Leaving my boots outside the tiny tent, I just took off trousers and jacket, clambered into my sleeping bag in shirt and sweaters and long johns, and immediately dropped into the underworld of unknowing.

10

It became a night never to be forgotten. About midnight I awoke with the worst headache I have ever had. The back of my neck felt as if I had slipped a disc. So this was what was called alpine sickness. I felt sick, and the Kabul Trots had struck once more. I had left my boots outside the tiny tent and they were frozen hard. I could only pull them half on as I staggered out on to the snow, which had become sheets of jagged spikes like broken glass. I could hear the howling of a pack of wolves, which seemed only about 400 yards away.

I crouched, half naked, and felt the cold strike into every bone in my body. I was too busy cleaning up with handfuls of snow to think about dying right there on the bare mountain or any other such fanciful thoughts, but what really took my mind off this predicament was the canopy of stars overhead.

They were extraordinarily large and brilliant. I forgot about my frozen feet and thumping head, and just crouched there looking up at Orion with his belt and dagger, and all the other familiar early winter stars. They were not the tiny twinkling pinpoints of white as seen at home, for they had magnified into a strange gloss of colour, as if starting to refract into their seven spectrum shades. These truly were the fire-folk described by Gerard Manley Hopkins in his poem:

Look at the stars! look, look up at the skies!
O look at all the fire-folk sitting in the air!

I wanted to stay and gaze but knew that would be fatal. It was vital to get back into my bedroll to survive, and I decided to pull all my clothes back on, especially my thick boot socks, and hoped I hadn't damaged my feet. This time I brought my boots inside and placed them under the sleeping bag to help thaw them. The night passed slowly and painfully, with shivering until dawn, and several more excursions out into that ice platform. I got as far away as I could under the circumstances, and presumed that something, perhaps the wolves, would find the remains of the eruptions from my stomach of stringy goats' meat and sultanas.

It seemed the Afghans had slept together in a great huddle, protected from the snow with a felt camel-hair rug, and covered by another. The local herders had been fine but a couple of the others had also suffered from alpine sickness. Pete had been tempted to have the oxygen, but had resisted. Don had taken some. Although only ten years older than me, and ten years younger than Pete, being in his mid-forties, he was prone to bronchitis, and right now did not seem happy at all. I had suffered from bronchitis myself for a few years: the result of riding long distances on my motorbike without any proper clothing. After this trip up into the Afghan mountains I never suffered with it again. I decided that if you survive, then mountain air is good for you.

Dr Amin was really employed for the benefit of the two Americans, and was a part of the Klineburger company deal. The large amount the Americans had paid included a fee for his services. The year before a forty-year-old American hunter had died while on a similar trip out here, from pulmonary oedema, and others had had difficulties. The doctor spent some time checking Pete and Don over but was very non-committal, just nodding his head and writing notes, and giving them the all clear. He included me in his responsibilities, and took my blood pressure and gave me six pills for my headache, one that was bright mauve and enormous. He did explain what they were for, but I didn't take that in. When I told him of the other problems, he just laughed and slapped me on the back.

I had already taken a couple of the aspirins out of the little medical store Anne had packed for me, together with a pill to stop the diarrhoea, which eased the situation. Although I felt a bit wary and didn't really want it, a cup of warmish tea and some naan bread filled the hole in my stomach. I knew I needed something to keep me going for the long day ahead.

The storm had blown itself out and now the icicles hanging off the rocks were dripping. A few yards away from the camp, with its noises of men and animals snorting, it was very quiet, with only the sound of the valley stream mumbling under the ice. The sun made the alpine meadows glow with bright yellow patches of sedges here and there as the snow began to melt, and with brown slurs that showed bare ground.

As we left, I looked back and saw ravens having their breakfast around our camp.

'The ravens are clearing up everything,' I remarked to Pia, who was riding past.

'Zarr,' was his short reply. He was not happy, lumbago having set in after the freezing night. His body was too used to having one of those American sleeping bags, and had softened away from the local hardiness. But I think he was also worried about his responsibilities. The snow-storm had not been expected, and he must have realised that Don was not really up to the rigours of the trip. I wondered what the doctor had reported.

The mountains of Russian Badakshan, with Mount Tagra Kakshi nearest, were a sullen dark grey to the north-west. Pia said it was forty miles off, but my photograph made it look much closer. The air was now razor sharp, so perhaps he was right. Most traces of vegetation seem to fade out at 15,000 feet, and after descending to 13,000 feet we rode into plains of quite dense dwarf sedges. We came to another stream bursting from the watershed, and turned at last into Toleibai valley, the centre of the hunting ground.

A group of strange, black, jagged rocks stuck out of the meadows, looking like the basalt giants of Easter Island. My yak was now going along quite smoothly, and needed no steering or goading. I felt a lot more confident; the air was easier to breathe, my headache was manageable and the pill for the trots had worked. I was even able to write up a few brief notes as reminders as we went along.

After about four hours travelling, I could see through my binoculars pinpoints of colour another two miles ahead in the otherwise empty wilderness. Pia said these were the tents and yurts of the camp where we would be staying for the next month. They were perched on a little plateau with distant views all around. We followed the small river along the bottom of its valley, most of the water gurgling under a frozen cover, with balloons of air slipping and elongating and sliding under the ice, making strange noises, like some modern ethereal symphony. Rills and cascades of crystal water broke out here and there, gurgling like the Devon trout streams I was familiar with, before vanishing once more into the grey opaque underworld with its pops and hisses.

I watched a small black bird bobbing about on the ice and suddenly lunging into the streaming water and vanishing for a few seconds underneath the surface before popping back out again. Drops of water slid like mercury off its back. It was obviously a dipper, but slightly different to the one I was familiar with. My mind searched its memory of the list I had read so carefully at the very beginning of this trip, and suddenly I remembered: Eurasian dipper. These chunky little birds, rather like demented blackbirds, hardly migrate, I knew, but this bird would not be able to exist here in another month, when the river would be totally submerged under winter ice and likely to be completely solid. It would have to move lower down – some way lower down, I presumed. I stopped my yak to watch the busy little creature. It vanished under the icy water again, insulated by the densest feathers of any land bird, hunting the larvae of insects, crustaceans, and perhaps even the eggs of small fish. I wondered what could be living in such cold conditions. Suddenly it bounced back out of a hole in the ice. It looked around, then took off with a low direct flight like a puffin, wings a blur as it struggled to lift its body mass on wings almost too small to overcome the flight wing-load.

My yak had become impatient at the delay, and wanted to re-join the herd. Pete was already half a mile ahead, having become impatient to set up in camp. I now gave my animal its head and soon caught everyone up. As we got closer a vulture swept over us, peering down with its dull orange head turned to look at us. It had straight, black wings finely pointed at the tips like a falcon, though it was far bigger than any falcon. This was the first time I had seen a lammergeier for sure, and so close as to be absolutely certain. It is one of the aerial mountain giants just about hanging on in Europe in the Pyrenees, and perhaps in Greece. I shouted to Don to look up.

'Sure, some kind of big buzzard, I guess. Course, we have bald eagles in the States. Guess it kinda looks like one of them.'

There was no point in trying to explain. I suddenly felt rather lonely. There was nobody to share the excitement of the amazing scenes around us. The bird stayed around, together with a youngster, all the time we were in this farthest point of our pilgrimage – for I thought of it as a pilgrimage: a visit not so much to a holy place but certainly to a very special place, a place that uplifted one above the ordinary, literally and metaphorically, a place I could never forget, and which I can see in my mind as clearly all these years later as I could when actually there.

Such birds of prey cleared up anything thrown out from the camp. There would be good pickings from the bones of the trophy animals that were shot. I had seen many other birds of prey as we travelled across these Pamir mountain meadows, but they had been circling high and were little more than specks, almost impossible to identify with any certainty. As the days went by, I did manage to name quite a few of the various vultures, hawks and falcons. Many birds, including waders, geese, and passerines, were migrating south to India, and so a good selection passed over or near the camp where we were based. They were all fleeing the winter, which made me a little uneasy as we stayed on while the weather closed in, with nothing but twigs and tumbleweed, as the Americans called them, to keep us warm and fed, using water that would boil at no higher than seventy-something centigrade. I also noticed, as the days went by, the aerial travellers going over numbering fewer by the day. It made me feel more and more vulnerable.

From a mile away the collection of yurts and bivouacs of the camp was a fragile sign of human life in the vast brown plain and rising slopes of mountains all around. As we came closer, so details began to emerge. I could make out a mud hut, the same colour as the ground all around, a yurt, a white tent, and about a dozen smaller tents. A substantial stream drained the rocky slopes above and ran past below the camp, a smaller trickle of water ran through the camp area. The Wakhis started to call out greetings, and then I could see what had looked like small boulders starting to move about and wave. These people had become imbued with the soil dust as if they were a living part of the scree and the empty brown space all around them.

And so we arrived at our destination.

As I came within a hundred metres, I could see a westerner sitting in a folding chair with a telescope in front of him. I guessed this must the man with whom I had been told to liaise, the Canadian zoologist Dr Ron Petocz, who was studying the biology of Marco Polo sheep. I was very glad to meet him at last, and as we got nearer I shouted a greeting:

'Dr Petocz, I presume?'

He stared at me and stood up, clearly startled.

'Who are you?' he shouted back. It was not the greeting I was expecting. He seemed astonished to see me. Surely he knew I was coming.

'I'm the man from the BBC – Richard Williamson.'

He shook his head in obvious amazement.

'Well, I don't know what's happened, but you're not supposed to be here. I sent a message over a month ago via the Tourist Authority to contact the BBC to cancel your trip, as it is now far too late in the season for you to sort anything out. You won't see much now. The season is closing in for winter. This place gets snowed in any day now. Then we have to get out fast.'

'No message got through to me,' I answered, feeling somewhat taken aback. 'Well, here I am, so we'll have to do the best we can.'

We shook hands. Christ, I thought, that was even before I had left England, let alone the three-week delay in Kabul. The Afghan Tourist Authority had said nothing to me when I was there. Presumably they thought that as I had arrived in the country I would muddle through somehow: that as I was there, I might as well join the last group to go up to the area. Nothing had been said to Pia either, who must have been quite horrified to find he had yet another person to cope with. He had not shown any emotion, just accepted that this was so. I had discovered this attitude in the Middle East, when in the RAF. The people accepted what life threw at them, without question. 'It is the Will of Allah!' I knew that it had once been like that in my own country – 'It's God's Will' covered everything, even the worst of tragedies. Modern civilisation has removed that comfort blanket; everything is questioned and blame apportioned to all and sundry. Stoicism, making the best of everything, is almost a lost ability. Well, stoicism was what I needed now.

I knew Petocz was a zoologist with a burning light in his mind to travel the rugged mountains of the world and to see how big mammals managed to live in such unlikely places. He was a committed conservationist, and dedicated to finding out exactly what they needed, and the impact of humans on their habitat. He had already studied the lives of Bighorn sheep in Canada before this study in the Wakhan. He was a thin, gaunt man of my age, and obviously very fit (though I learned he had suffered the usual illnesses from his winter sojourn in Kabul, including hepatitis), and he was clearly a man who did not suffer fools at all, never mind gladly. The BBC wanted to buy film from him for the film I was to write up. They knew he was cagey about selling material at any but the highest price. Nobody else was going to be able to film these elusive mountain animals (not at that time anyway). He knew that everyone up here, including himself, me, and the hunters, was already living on the edge of existence. Lugging a heavy camera around of the type then available at high altitude was almost impossible – and he knew it.

When we arrived, he had been staring up into distant mountain slopes through his telescope. With the naked eye, or even with my binoculars, I could see nothing more than grey scree reaching up for two miles beyond the camp as it sloped up into the sky. Above that the permanent snow fields began. Once the greetings and introductions were over, he went back to his task, and offered me a sighting. The scree came alive at once. Fifty-two Marco Polo ewes and their lambs were apparently grazing. It was an astonishing sight, though they were still only mere white dots with spindly legs, barely visible even under magnification. But they were the first real contact with the animal life on the roof of the world. Hardly any westerners have seen these animals, but here was a herd, out in the open, behaving without fear, and very much at home. They were not going to migrate away from these harsh and extreme conditions: they were in their element. This was their place on this planet, the place where they were happy to be, whatever the weather or the season. We humans, with all our luggage and support systems, were only just about coping with mere existence, and this in conditions that were still fairly reasonable.

Petocz told me that when the winter weather closed in, these sheep would want to descend to where we were now living. The camp would be closed by then. The only problem was that herders grazed the alpine meadows around us more and more intensively in summer and autumn, leaving less and less food for the wild sheep in the winter. Money from the hunters paid for the wages of two wardens who controlled local hunting, as well as supposedly subsidising graziers to stop their overgrazing to make a living. He was doubtful that this money ever got through, and later I was to see evidence of this. I had of course been told about this before I left and been asked to see what I could find out. The ewes and lambs were in view, so the hunting ban on the locals seemed to be working, at least while westerners were around.

I wondered where the rams were, and he said they were now in their own group, and had hidden away in nearby valleys out of sight. They were wary, because they were pursued and hunted almost continuously during the hunting season, and so they kept to the most difficult terrain. These were rocky, hidden valleys with large boulders where they could squeeze through gaps along ancient paths and partly hide themselves.

They were hunted in Russia to the north, and in West Pakistan to the south, and almost certainly in China to the east, although little was known about what went on there. These areas were so remote it was more or less impossible to impose rules about hunting. The Afghanistan government were publicly proud that they were leading a conservation project. Petocz shrugged his shoulders.

'At least some of the money gets through – but I think only a fraction. Much is backhanded into the wrong pockets.'

Little did any of us know of the tragedy that was about to fall on Afghanistan and its people. Conservation of animals fell by the wayside for many years, while the country struggled with the twin disasters of invasion and terrorism.

Pete and Don also came to look through the telescope, and exclaimed excitedly at the view of so many Marco Polo sheep. Petocz had a closed-in look on his face. They soon went off to check their rifles, and Petocz relaxed again. I sat there all afternoon watching the wild sheep. Petocz explained what I could see, which was that the ewes often kicked the hungrily persistent lambs away from their milk. He had been painstakingly recording every one of these interactions for weeks: how many seconds each lamb was allowed to suckle per time, per day, and so on. Few people would be patient enough just to sit there day after day recording pages of apparently trivial data, but here was the one in a million who would persist, in order to provide the evidence to encourage the politicians to allow the species to survive. Such work is how science discovers the truth. I told him about my own work in recording the numbers of the various species of butterfly, and mapping bird territories by marking down the singing males, plus counting and mapping plants, and all the other tasks associated with running the nature reserve that I managed back in England. Petocz and I had a similar outlook and appreciated the other's attitude.

I found that at 13,000 feet there was little one could do other than move around for a while and then sit and rest. The Afghanis sat down and rested much of the time too. One of their problems was lack of proper cold-weather clothing, although some had basic and rather smelly sheep-skin jerkins. Another problem was that they were smoking opium. Pete called them a 'miserable bunch of layabouts', which I thought was a little unfair. Despite all his hunting trips, he really only knew an American way of life.

We were quite comfortably lodged. The yurt had been erected especially to accommodate hunters for the season. It was very similar to those I had seen and lived in during my sojourn in Jordan in the RAF, as used by the Bedouins. The difference here was in the layers of covering, to take account of the altitude and temperature. Between the canvas layers was a four-inch-thick layer of Bactrian camel and goat hair insulation, matted together to make a basic felt, all propped up on willow sticks and bound around with basic hemp ropes. This was where we westerners slept. It meant our body heat was well contained on the inside, particularly necessary at night. Without this we would have been in severe frost. The daytime temperature was also plummeting fast now. Every day it was getting colder, but I couldn't record it, because it never even registered on my little Swedish thermometer. Even Petocz's official record had to stop after a day or two: at first it read 10°F by day, then disappeared into the peg and was never seen again. There was another tent for eating. The smaller tents were for those Afghanis officially with the group. The rest slept in the mud hut, all huddled together.

The main drawback was that there was no lavatorial arrangement, not even a pit. The ground was too hard for digging and there would have been no drainage anyway. We had to walk at least a hundred yards downstream and use the river, and adopt the Arab custom of using the left hand for washing oneself clean in the icy water: left hand, because the right hand is used for putting food into the mouth. I had learned many years before how terrible was the known punishment of 'cutting off the right hand', meted out at one time to offenders of even quite small crimes in the Arab world. Such a punishment was meant to be totally demeaning. I did not like the idea of polluting the river but the next habitation was many miles downstream, there were not that many of us, and the flow of water was tremendous.

A spring bubbled out of the ground near the camp, feeding into the stream lower down, and this was used for the tea and cooking. A round hole, three feet deep, had been dug into the softer ground between the spring and the tents. This was the oven for making bread. The inside was smooth, with recently plastered mud and clay which had baked hard. A young lad oversaw this important daily task. He spent every morning searching the surrounding area of small hills for what Pete called tumbleweed, but what was in fact a bushy perennial of the Artemisia family, which in the summer had made a ball of twigs bigger than a football and which by autumn had died and dried, and was an excellent, good, quick fuel.

The boy brought back a load of this shrubby material hoisted inside a blanket over his shoulder. Then he stuffed them into the pit-oven. When he lit them they flared up like petrol. The pit soon became very hot and the mud sides almost glowed red. In between tending his oven, he had crouched on the ground next to a flat rock, mixing up a batter of unleavened flour, ground on the millstone in Sargass, and carried here in a dog-skin bag. He pulled off handfuls of this mix and patted it into round lumps the size of footballs, then with his hands flattened them into pancakes on the stone, smeared one side with water and soused the other, then slapped them on to the oven walls where they stuck like glue.

The mingled scent of the artemisia and the fresh baked

naan bread wafted out into the bitingly cold blue gloom and mountain air of the autumn afternoon. It smelt wonderful and we were very hungry. After about five minutes the flat bread was prized off the sides of the oven with a knife and handed round, and gratefully received. It did not live up to its smell. We could have been eating wheat chaff or husks of barley. It was full of millstone grit, and was like chewing coarse sandpaper. There was no flavour: that was all in the smell. It was actually very unpleasant, and we ate in silence. I thought that one's teeth would disappear very shortly under such a diet, as they would be ground down to nothing. I saved some of mine, and dipped it later into my dish of stewed lamb which was being prepared by the cook. It didn't make much difference.

'I've eaten bread all over the world,' announced Pete. 'Some of the best was in France and Denmark.' He looked round. 'But this'll take some beating, I guess!'

The irony of his remark was fortunately lost on the group. Don was silent, and soon disappeared inside the yurt. Two lammergeiers flew low over us, no more than thirty metres over our heads. After the lamb stew, followed by tinned cheese and more of the baked naan, we all turned in for the night. The day-time temperature had seemed reasonably comfortable, with the reflected heat of the sun from the rocks warming our bodies, though it did not move the thermometers one little bit. The night became bitterly cold, our bodies not yet being accustomed to the glacial air. I made sure this time that my boots were tucked under my sleeping bag in my bivouac. I decided to wear both my pairs of long johns and long-sleeved vests all the time (put in at Anne's insistence, rather to my disdain at the time), just taking off the top layers of trousers and jacket and shirt, and then getting myself well down inside to try and get warm. Even so it took a long time.

Petocz and I watched Marco Polo sheep most of the next day. He lent me a spare telescope. Most of the time we discussed the film that the BBC hoped to make the next year. I desperately wanted to ask him about the presence of snow leopards in the area, but hardly dared. I was afraid that his answer might be in the negative. All the way here I had been thinking of them, and wishing and hoping. Now I was actually at the end of the trail I felt almost desperate to see one, even if only the tiniest glimpse. If his reply was 'none', then my personal dream would turn into a huge disappointment. Eventually I took the plunge.

'Are there any snow leopards in this area?'

He was staring through his telescope and did not answer. He was poised with his right hand hovering over his writing pad as he prepared to write down some small fact about what the ewes were doing, second by second. He had a stopwatch in his left hand and finally plunged its button; then wrote down the findings. Almost without looking up, he said: 'You could be looking at one through your telescope right now – but you won't see it. They are totally camouflaged and the darned things don't move much in the day, whether they've fed or not. If we get some more snow you will see their tracks alright.'

I let out my breath very slowly in a whistling sigh of relief. Petocz looked up then and grinned.

'I see. Got to you, have they?'

I shrugged. 'Well, you know, as I'm here . . .'

Later in the day an Afghan fur trader arrived, together with the ATA warden, whom Petocz introduced as Khasem. Khasem spoke good English. He was a graduate from Kabul University, his home town being Faizabad. He had always been interested in the wildlife of his country and was now employed by the Afghan Tourist Authority as a warden to manage and liaise with local people over the protection of the mountain animals of this area. He was wearing blue jeans, a body warmer and a black fur hat over his jet-black hair. I thought he was about 23 years old.

I thought it a bit odd that he was out with a fur trader, but when I later asked Petocz, he said it was sensible for two men to be out in the area together. One could then get help if necessary. Also, the trapper had been enlisted as the guide who would take the Americans out hunting. The main guide had gone back with the previous party. This current group was an extra, thrown in later than usual.

The trapper's name was Soufi-Kabouli. He was not the average herder of the area. They were all slow pastoralists, men who wandered about with their herds and lived life at the same pace as their sheep. This man was more alert. You could see it in his expression as he walked into the camp. His eyes were bright, he looked into your eyes, and there was an unusual smile in his greeting. He exchanged hand touches with us, touched his heart in welcome to me when Khasem told him who I was. Thinking about him later I decided that his name and manner indicated he was not a true-bred Afghani. He might have lived there all his life, and his parents perhaps, but I felt there was a distinct hint of Arab in his make-up. With Khasem's help in translating, I was able to ask him about his work. First he spoke about the mountains, almost poetically. Again, this was very different from the herders, who were only full of their own woes. I asked about his trade. Apparently in the last season he had bought 800 marmot skins, one wolf skin, two fox skins, but no snow leopard skins. I noted the marmot skins, thinking I must find out more about them later; but right now it was the illegal skins that I was interested in.

'What about Marco Polo skins?' I asked.

'Not allowed to take Marco Polo,' Petocz said, looking at Khasem for confirmation.

160

'No Marco Polo, not allowed,' Khasem replied.

There was no hint of secrecy in his expression. He was young, and he beamed almost continuously in that genial Asian manner, which can be very enigmatic and gives nothing away, whether honest friendliness or subterfuge. I decided he was honest, and so evidently had Petocz. A man who did not suffer fools gladly, he would have known what the truth was, and had dealt with Khasem for the whole season. Anyway, the fact that ewes and lambs were within a mile of the camp without fear showed they were not being molested for their skins. But I picked up on what the trader had said about the snow leopard.

'Are snow leopards being hunted secretly then, if the trader mentions that he hasn't bought any skins? That seems a bit of a give-away to me. Does he mean no one has been successful in trapping one?'

A slight shadow seemed to pass over Khasem's smile.

'No snow leopard allowed to be taken,' he replied firmly. He was clearly holding down his job on that one. Maybe he suspected that illegal hunting did take place. Snow leopards were not just 'skins': the beautiful fur on their backs was very valuable. Wealthy New Yorkers would proudly parade with such a fabled shoulder wrap, I knew. I had seen many in photographs, and read of the strident abuse by animal rights groups.

The trader then added, which made me suspect he understood what we were saying, although he hadn't let on, and Khasem repeated, that his last snow leopard skin had been bought nearly three years before. I decided that I had to take this at face value. To probe too much would cause animosity, and I couldn't afford to make enemies.

Petocz had made a collection of *Ovis poli* and ibex skulls and horns during the summer. These could be found scattered

161

over the mountains as I discovered later. Many were of magnificent size. We spent the day measuring these with stainless steel calipers, taking twenty-five measurements on each one. Slowly and methodically, science was probing the exact effect of altitude and habitat impinging on these animals, giving a database for future research records. They could then be compared to check how animals were coping with human intrusion into the mountains as well as with climate change. Age, general health and condition, comparison of one area to another affecting one herd from another, were some of the answers he was beginning to assemble. The record Marco Polo head for this area, within the country's borders, was a 64½-inch span, measured from tip to tip around the curl of the horns, not just across in a straight line.

Pete came along to see what we were doing. Don was not feeling too good, mainly because of the altitude, and stayed in bed until lunchtime. It wasn't looking too good for him. Dr Amin had reported that he was concerned, and giving him medication. But having come all this way, and spent perhaps $6,000 all in, Don was determined to carry on and achieve what he had set out to do. He turned up for lunch, looking quite cheerful, particularly as he was usually morose. I presumed that whatever it was that Dr Amin had given him had bucked him up, and he had probably also had oxygen.

But he didn't find what happened next very funny, although I'm afraid the rest of us did. He had decided to open a can of camembert cheese he had chosen to bring along from the Kabul superstore. Now looking decidedly cheerful, he prepared to pull the ring on the can.

'This is home from home, Rich,' he beamed at me, 'I just love camembert cheese. Something in it just agrees with me. I have this most nights at home and in many parts of the world on my hunting trips —'

As he was talking, he was fingering the can-pull to get a firm grip, and finally he ripped it open. What followed was quite spectacular. In brief, the cheese was living under its own pressure and just could not wait to get out into the low pressure of this mountain plateau. There was an explosion. Every delicious drop shot up into Don's face and over his clothes. His nose and eyes were covered with globs of cheese. His eyebrows turned cream and his special green tweed jacket was now mottled with yellow. There was even some on the tent roof.

'Son of a god-damn bastard!' He jumped up, throwing the tin down, stared down at himself for a moment and then stormed out of the tent, making for the stream to clean up.

'I did wonder if that might happen,' Petocz commented drily. I had noticed that Petocz closed up whenever the Americans were around. He did not particularly like the hunting men. They disturbed his territory and work, despite their money going towards conservation of the area. In addition, he was from Canada and they were American. I knew from my brother, who lived in Canada, that the two nationalities did not get on too well. We exchanged looks, trying not to laugh, as Pete was still sitting there.

To divert attention, I asked Petocz about the problems of the altitude.

'Well, the main thing is to watch out for blood in your spit,' he warned. 'That's one of the first signs that things are going wrong. It could happen at any time. It's downhill all the way then. And you guys are not getting enough time to acclimatise.'

No one had told us this, and ignorance had been bliss, as they say. Now I began to worry. Why hadn't Dr Amin told us what to look out for? Then I thought that perhaps Petocz was just being superior, and putting us in our place. He had been up here nearly five months and very possessive about the area;

and he took his work very seriously. The Americans were mere dilettantes in his book, and I was only passing through. He knew he could survive, so this was probably just one-upmanship.

Pete stared at him. I thought to myself that he hadn't got where he had without being able to suss things out.

'Well, I'm already acclimatised enough,' he stated shortly. 'I aim to start the hunt tomorrow morning.'

'How about Don,' I asked. 'Is he going to be fit enough to hunt?'

11

The two hunters got up at 0230, three hours before daylight, and were soon on their way, accompanied by the trapper guide, Soufi Kabouli, and a couple of men to act as porters. It was now 9 October. I was not allowed to go with them. They took five yaks between them, while the other five rested up for the next day. I went back to sleep until dawn. After breakfast, knowing they would be then be well out of the way and I would not be disturbing their trip, I had a look around the area, feeling slightly breathless as I climbed up the boulders four or five hundred metres away. There were patches of snow in the shadows but no animal tracks to see at all. I settled myself against a rock in the sun and scanned the sides of the mountains through my binoculars, spending an hour peering into every crevice and ledge. As Petocz had suggested, somewhere up there a snow leopard could be peering back down at me.

Suddenly I heard a strange clamour high above. A chevron of geese was flying south. They were bar-headed geese, the first I had ever seen in their wild and true element, although I knew them from wildfowl collections. They would have bred somewhere in Tibet, on the edges of that vast plateau, and were now heading south to spend the winter in India. They were so far above that I could hardly see their necks with the naked eye. I thought they must have been about half a mile high, making them at about 18,000 feet. I counted forty-two.

These charming geese were introduced into Europe in 1888, and are a familiar sight for visitors to wildfowl reserves.

But in the wild they have a difficult time. They breed among the lakes of the high plateau that stretches from Russian Badakshan, the Tadzhik Pamirs, right across through to China, where their eggs are taken for eating. In the moulting season the flightless birds are caught and frozen in the ground, for winter eating. Survivors fly to India where they are shot. They are regarded as pests, feeding on agricultural crops.

I had seen tame birds at Slimbridge, in Peter Scott's wildfowl collection, when on a visit with my father to see his friend. (Scott was also a rival glider pilot of my brother John: they both had turns at being British Champion.) To see these birds now, in the wild, struggling to get above the peaks of the Hindu Kush was thrilling. I could see their silvery plumage, bright and almost glittering in the powerful sunlight, but had to imagine those two chocolate stripes over eye and cheek, with that cryptic banding also running down their necks. That is how they camouflage themselves on the mountain lakes, when they lay their necks along the water surface and become hidden by water ripples and flecks of ice.

When I excitedly told Petocz what I had seen, he said that he had seen cranes migrating too, over a month previously, on 5 September. They had been targeted by a pair of golden eagles, which singled out a bird at the rear of the flight chevron and forced it down between them. I would have given anything to have seen that.

'You should have been here earlier,' was his parting shot. Well, I thought, it was hardly my fault that I wasn't.

Petocz was busy with his recording and did not want disturbance, so I wandered around the camp. Nothing much was happening and very few of the men were visible. I wondered where they were. I came across a small stone hut that I hadn't noticed before, hidden among the natural boulders. Peering inside I made out a Wakhi sitting alone in

166

the deep gloom enjoying a pipe of opium. There was a small crucible of flame burning at his side as he lay curled up as in the womb, drawing in smoke from a long thin pipe. Bleary eyed, he observed me vaguely. He wasn't really aware that I was there. He looked old, but might have been only thirty. The hard mountain life wears these people down at an early age. The women lose their looks – the warm, soft, eager looks of youth – in their early twenties. Petocz had told me that nine out of ten Wakhis were terminally hooked on opium.

I noticed there was an ancient iron stove in the middle of the hut. From behind that I heard a brief sound, whimpering, coming from another dark corner of the hut. The man was not alone. A boy was huddled in the gloom, looking much like a heap of rubbish, his filthy coat of grey yak hair in shreds about his tiny body. He had a grey skull cap pulled down over his ears. He appeared to be in a state of some misery. He wasn't smoking, I was glad to see, but I wondered what had happened to him. I found out later.

Hearing noises, I went back outside. The cook appeared from behind the camp area with a lamb, led by some kind of twine round its neck. He was calling it forward with quiet sounds, like a father making first contact with his new born child. When they got to the rill, he got out a large folding knife from his pocket and slit the animal's throat as he held it down on the soft sedge meadow. This was tonight's supper. The lamb did not struggle, or appear to feel any pain, or make any sound. It just seemed to accept the inevitable. This was how things were. This was very unlike the pig-killings I had seen on our farm in my childhood, when the animal made the most unearthly screams and took a very long time to die, firmly tied and held down by two or three strong men. The calm ritual scene here reminded me of a TV news flash I had once seen of a Tibetan villager setting fire to himself after dowsing himself in petrol, in protest against the Chinese invasion of his country. He had held his arms out with fingers pointing to the sky and remained as motionless as a statue. He must have put himself into some sort of religious trance. He had not moved as the flames took hold and quickly turned his body to a burnt cinder, when he then fell over and broke into brittle pieces.

The man swiftly skinned the animal and spread the skin out to dry on a rock. Then he cut the flesh up into small pieces on a flattish stone kept for the purpose, placing the meat into a large metal pan with clean water. I rather wished for a clay pot in keeping with the feeling of an ancient ritual. I could see the 'fire-pit' boy in the distance, returning with his large bundle of artemisia. I thought he must be the cook's son.

At 1430, nearly twelve hours after they had set out, the hunters returned. There was great excitement among the group of men who were part of our entourage, most of whom were shouting 'Marco Polo! Marco Polo!' I noted that they had learnt the English word. I was surprised they were so excited. Pia said, 'They do not like this place. It is cold and uncomfortable. They want to be getting home. They are from the town. As soon as the hunt is successful, with trophy head, it will all be finished. They then get paid the rest of their money. That is why they are excited. The yak owners, though, are paid by the day for their services, so they want it to go on longer.'

But it soon became evident as they approached the camp that the hunt had not been successful, and even worse, Don was not at all well. The exertions of the day had been too much for him, and stupidly he had taken off his coat and hat on a glacier because the sun was hot; he had then suddenly got very cold and was suffering from a severe sinus pain. But there was also worse news: he had fired at a ram nine times altogether but only wounded it, and it had escaped leaving a blood trail. He was in no state to go after it, and as it was getting late and they needed to get him back to the camp before he collapsed, the ram had been left. This was highly disapproved of by the authorities, and by the guides.

Pete and Pia helped Don into the yurt where he was examined by Dr Amin, who gave him some oxygen, which seemed to be an action of last resort. But as he was coughing some blood there was no choice. Pete went for a lie-down also. He had not had a sighting, let alone a shot. The man assigned to look after him took him in some tea and some fresh naan bread. He had hardly said anything on their return, just shrugged his shoulders and headed for the yurt, saying he would be there for supper.

The trapper guide explained to Pia what had happened, who then told me the gist of it. Soufi Kabouli thought the wounded animal would soon be taken by wolves. He knew there was a pack in the area. In fact, they had been heard close to the camp as the men had left that morning. I had heard nothing, nor seen any signs of wolves on my walk around, but they were too clever and crafty to give their presence away in daylight so near to human habitation. And there was not enough snow for footprints, except in the shadows right next to the larger boulders where they were not likely to run.

In the late afternoon a herd of forty-three ibex passed the camp along the lower slopes of the northern mountain, about 1,500 metres away. I watched them through the telescope. Most were very big animals with horns that looked to be about forty-eight inches in length. Petocz said they were about thirteen years old. The oldest had pale 'saddles' which looked like white blankets across their backs, and beards about eight inches long. They had white rumps and short black tails. They fed as a herd, though within the herd the age groups were slightly separated. The oldest animals, five or six of them, stayed together higher up the slope.

'It's 1705,' said Petocz, looking at his watch. 'I predict that they will bed down right now. They're on a time clock. They know they have to conserve their heat to survive the night. This is coming up to their rut, and they need every ounce of fat on their ribs to be able to fight to get the females.'

Sure enough, the main group did lower themselves to the ground and became practically hidden. But it wasn't quite so simple as that. The young ones did not bed down, but kept on feeding, and the little group of grandfathers followed them on their bony black legs, and slogged on along that bleak dusty rocky hillside with its scarce stalks of plant life. They had not eaten quite enough, and it was difficult to see how they would get enough tallow round their ribs to manage to raise that crucial burst of energy and stamina they would need to fight and maintain any dominance in the rut.

These were Siberian ibex, *Capra sibirica*, one of seven forms of high mountain wild goat. The other six are scattered west of the Himalayas as far as Spain. It seems they may all have evolved from the true wild goat, or bezoar, which lives in the hilly deserts of Arabia. Those are smaller animals, as they do not need the sustaining bulk of high mountain species, not needing to conserve heat as these ibex did at this altitude. I wondered if the scimitar shape of their horns had given the Arabs inspiration for their curved daggers. The curved swords of Chinese warriors seemed exact copies of what was being paraded in front of me at that moment.

The largest of all the various Siberian ibex are found where we were, in the Pamirs. Petocz said they could weigh up to 290 pounds. But to be that weight, they would need access to meadows such as those we were now camped on, and which these days are overgrazed by the herds of domestic sheep and goats. This was what the income from the hunting contracts was supposed to alleviate. I could see how such money would help with scientific conservation, but wasn't convinced that it would alleviate over-grazing. I suspected the men would take the extra money and continue grazing just how they liked.

Now that it was too dark for Petocz to continue his recording he was quite happy to answer my questions and tell me all the background, and so he continued while I made notes.

'Siberian ibex can live up to 20,000 feet in the Pamirs. No one seems sure at exactly what altitude they differ. There seems to be a slight lack of clarity as to where the races diverge, if at all. Some scientists think the different races interbreed. They are conducting breeding experiments on captive animals to try and find out. I'm not sure that will prove anything either way. Animals in captivity are almost bound to react differently from those in the wild. Different races would breed together because they would be fully fed, and have nothing to do for their actual daily survival. Therefore they would have nothing to do except breed. There is also proof that during the last Ice Age, the Spanish ibex (*Capra pyrenaica*) did not interbreed with Alpine ibex (*Capra ibex*) even though they were living together in the same area. Cave paintings of the Stone Age show both as separate species with no hybrid. That seems to me to be proof.'

During the day I had heard some thunderous booms from across the mountains to the north, and during supper I mentioned that, wondering what it had been. Petocz said he had heard the same noise several times previously and thought it was ice-falls in the glaciers, or extra-large rock falls.

'OK, that's possible – but I thought it sounded more like quarry blasting coming from Russia. We are quite near the border after all. What – about a dozen kilometres? You know, I was very puzzled by that tarmac road way back running along the border at the entrance to the Wakhan. It seemed very odd to me. What's it for? What are the Russians up to? And that noise – the Russians could easily be building something up here, couldn't they? I remember how the Nazis had secret tunnels, and underground towns practically, where they were building V2 rockets, and other deadly weapons. The Russians could be doing anything up here in this totally isolated situation and no one would know about it.'

Pete looked up. 'The CIA would. I bet this place is overflown by the TR2 spy plane, or satellite spy rockets. If there's something going on, then I guess it's known about. I should be careful about saying anything about that when you get back, young Rich. You could find yourself in trouble. Anyway, it's nothing to do with us. Probably just getting rock for their roads, I guess. As long as no one interferes with my shooting, I don't care what they are up to.'

'I agree,' Petocz added. 'Best all left alone. I certainly don't want people up here poking around and interfering with my work. This is the roof of the world and as near to primal habitat that one can get. I want it kept that way.'

I dropped the subject, but it did puzzle me, and when the Russians invaded Afghanistan some few months after I returned from this great adventure, I was not surprised.

Petocz then reminded me that if I was worried about safety then we had our own soldier assigned to protect us from any invasion. I laughed. Our 'soldier' was a bit of a joke. He was a young lad and looked about fifteen years old, but had to be a bit older than that. He had marched forward when we first arrived, and saluted us. He was very proud of his uniform, his rank, his importance. He was somebody, and his bearing indicated his pride. He stood with a straight back at all times, while the rest of his compatriots mooched around humped up by the cold. He was dressed in blue fatigues, as they were known, a soft thick woollen cloth of trousers and jacket, with a red epaulette of some rank or other at his collar.

He looked us straight in the eye, unlike the other camp workers, who were rather sly and looked sideways at us, and seemed to rather despise us; but were belligerent at the same time because we were so very much richer than them, and so must look down on them. Although I tried to make friends and talk to them, it was impossible. This soldier lad was the only one of his battalion within a hundred miles of this place. We understood he had trained in Kabul, but he too spoke no English so I couldn't communicate.

He was there to guard us against attack. He had the best quality armament. It was a stick. It was a very good straight stick and he kept it well polished. He held it by his side when I took his photograph, and was very proud of it. I wondered if he would present arms with it, or slope arms, or otherwise do the drill of a rifleman. He did not interact with any of the kitchen or utility business of the camp, but kept guard all the time, often standing to attention, marching up and down along an invisible line, and staring steadfastly towards Russia. It was just like an episode of 'Dad's Army', and would have been laughable except that it was actually rather sad. He must have felt very lonely.

He obviously longed for one of the hunters' rifles, but I doubted he knew how to fire one. He stared at them when they were cleaning them, and when they came back from the hunt had come close, and stretched out his hand to touch one; then followed them with his eyes as they were put away inside the yurt. The Americans kept them chained to the central pole in their travelling cases.

Pete was worried about Don's health, mainly, I thought, in case it affected his own stay in this difficult place. The doctor had been giving diuretics to them both, to remove urine. I was not being treated, and felt fine enough except for breathlessness when walking up slopes. But I supposed that was only to be expected. After all, I told myself, I was higher than Mont Blanc all the time, and had only been at this altitude for a couple of days or so. Once I was acclimatised, I expected to be as active as Petocz. Pia had kept in the background since we had arrived, mainly checking that we were all right in the mornings and at night. I saw him going round talking to the various people, presumably checking that they had done the job allocated to them. I gathered that he relieved the young boy soldier from time to time so that the lad could sleep, but Pia's idea of guard duty was to sit down behind a rock out of sight of the rest of us.

While we sat there in the dusk after supper, chatting desultorily, I noticed a woodcock fly into the camp and settle by the small stream. Pete said he was going to turn in, and Petocz went off to check something with the trapper guide. The bird did not move, and when they had gone I lifted my binoculars to get a better look at it. It was beautiful to watch, but I could see that it was quite exhausted. It sat very still by the wobble of water that was still unfrozen and glinting like an old glass bottle rolling between the sedge banks. Then after a while, it dipped its long brown knitting-needle beak into the stream, and then settled back on to its folded legs. It was of course migrating, out of Siberia and onwards to India. A long hard journey, and I thought it must have been caught out by snow north of here. It could have been an old bird and so reaching the end of its life.

I could see that it was paler than any I had ever seen in England. Normally the plumage is a mixture of the colours of dead oak leaves and reddish shadows, and fallen long leaves of sweet chestnut lying haphazardly on the forest floor, with shadows and small patches of sunlight filtering through the canopy giving its own mix of bars of light and shade. When the bird sits on its nest on the forest floor in England it becomes invisible. Even the dead stalks of leaves are replicated on its feathers, and leaf veins are copied, so that every part of a forest floor is repainted into the bird's camouflage.

But this bird here in the Pamirs had been camouflaged with

the grey ice and withered winter stems of herbs and sedges and the minute shadows formed amongst stones and dust. That is the great secret of *Scolopax rusticola*. Right across its temperate and boreal breeding range of old world distribution, quite separate from its moult and change of plumage, its feathers can alter colour to greyer colours, depending on where it has to breed. In this case I was probably looking at a bird of that narrow breeding range along the edge of the Himalayan range which, like ptarmigan in the Scottish Highlands, adapt to snow cover for protection, even though this change is made without the normal moulting of feathers.

I wondered whether it could possibly be a great snipe, which breeds in western Siberia, and winters among other places just south of the Himalayas. I knew that bird had a paler underside, though flecked with blackish striations like the catspaws made by a breeze on the surface of water, the places where it likes to wade and search for worms. I carefully moved a little closer and then stood dead still. I was at the wrong angle to be able to check the markings on the forehead, which differ enough to be the absolute identification. Was that crown stripe segmented into five brown blocks as in the woodcock, or was it one continuous stripe with a yellowish band above?

I couldn't decide, and ever since I have wondered if I had indeed had a sighting of that fabled bird, the great snipe. It is simple for those who know about such things to claim that size is the determining factor and so I should have known easily. But there I was in the rapidly darkening dusk, and with nothing with which to compare it. It is straightforward when one is looking at the pictures side by side in a book. Once in the hand the difference would have been obvious enough. Back in Victorian times, in England they were shot without thought and often set up in a glass case as a trophy of family history. Even nowadays one is sometimes shot in mistake by a hasty wild-fowler.

As a young man still living at home with my mother on the bank of the river Waveney bounding Norfolk and Suffolk, we were neighbours to the Turner family, where two of three brothers had won the Victoria Cross: one in the First World War, the other in the Second, in the Western Desert. They were superb shots, with various large animal heads hung in their hallway and on the landing of the stairs. One treasure which I coveted was the fabled great snipe set up in a glass case. It may have faded with age of course, and perhaps that was why I thought it was paler. I always hoped that they would give it to me, but that never happened. But it was for me one of those vivid pictures that stay with one for ever.

Eventually, fearing that this bird, with night approaching and several people around who would find it a very tasty addition to the daily fare, was in more danger staying within the camp than if it moved on into the wilderness around us, I walked towards it to put it up. As I hoped, it fluttered away downstream and was lost against the blackness of the rocks. At least it had gone in the right direction – to the south.

But it did not fly out of my mind, and not just because of the reason I have given: it triggered an even deeper response within me. I was struck by the extreme difficulty of every creature in this bleak landscape. Everything was living on the brink of existence. The animals and birds were almost like phantoms, hardly seen at all, and if seen, then vanishing again like a ghost. Everything was so much more on the alert. It heightened my senses and I too felt more on the alert, more strung up, more in need than ever to respond to the environment. One could not relax. Nothing here could afford that luxury. The environment was an ever-changing kaleidoscope: every colour, every shape, lurked with danger. The eyes of every living thing were darting about every second of their lives, otherwise they could have but seconds to live, even though in the prime of life and condition to escape.

And at the peak of this food chain – because that is all it was – here in this continuously uplifting mountain range, towered the snow leopard: the ghost cat, the shadow in the clouds. Their life was the most precarious of all. Left to themselves, they had the power and the innate skills to exist in total harmony within the niche into which they had evolved. It was humans who were their worst enemy, as is the case with all creatures. Hunters snared them, shot them at long range, caused their early deaths by manipulating their habitat. We humans could never be their equal. We could not outwit the animal on equal terms of face-to-face encounter, which was creation's natural method of dominance or existence. The snow leopard was supreme in its own environment. There was nothing that could outshine this elusive creature. That was its attraction of course: something to attain to.

I wondered again what the chances were of my ever seeing one. My excitement when I had first comprehended the actuality of this incredible opportunity of coming to the Pamirs, where this almost mythical animal lived, was still potent. But it was now highly modified by the realisation of the practicalities and difficulties of the terrain. To see one, to perhaps even get a photograph: that would be an experience never to be forgotten. Or would it be better not to see one, to keep the dream, the hope of the unattainable alive? Once such an ambition is achieved, does it become captured, commonplace? I was so nearly within reach of my dream, but I could see that a great effort would be needed to realise it. The snow leopard would not come to me: I would have to go to it. And therein lay the problem. I couldn't see how I was going to be able to get into the area where they lived. And meanwhile, I wasn't really making any progress on the job I had been sent here to do.

It was completely dark now, and I made my way back to the yurt, quietly hunkering down in the blackness of night. For some time I mulled over these thoughts, and told myself that if I did not see a snow leopard then I mustn't get downhearted. It would then remain the apogee of the unattainable. It would be enough to have been this near. At least I now understood, and had experienced to some extent, the territory over which the creature had dominion. It was a wonderful goal for the mind to imagine. It would remain the shadow in the clouds that never gave up its mystery.

12

I got up the next morning knowing that at last I was going to be able to get out of the camp. I wrote the date down in my notebook: 10 October. The days were slipping past and it was difficult to remember, without the reference point of newspapers or television. I had told Pia the day before that there would be no BBC film if I could not explore beyond the confines of the camp and its human world, and experience the true wilderness. That was part of the truth, but also of course I needed to go for my own urgent need to see what lay beyond. There was little I could do within the camp confines and immediate terrain. I knew it was going to be tough going. Don's condition was proof of that, although I knew I was far fitter than he had ever been, and he was of course a few years older than me. He was now confined to bed for the foreseeable future, and understandably not in the best of moods. There seemed to be some question of whether he was actually going to survive. He was not fit enough in the first place, then had not given himself time to acclimatise; the altitude and exertion had been too much for him. Pete was different: his whole attitude was different. He had made sure he had kept fit before embarking on this adventure, and he had far more respect for the animals he shot – he made it clear that if he hadn't got a clean shot for a kill he did not pull the trigger, even if that led to disappointment. He had again gone off just before dawn with Soufi-Kabouli and two bearers.

Remembering the problems of the Sargass Pass, I felt a

little fearful of going up high again, but I had had time now for my body to get acclimatised. There was also the problem of straying unwittingly into Russia. We were very close to the border here and could quite easily cross into Russia without knowing, because it was not clear where that border was when on the ground. It was not marked as such on the enlarged photocopy map that Pia had. There was a vague idea that it was 'somewhere here', as he drew his finger along the map. Mountain ranges and valleys were in place but the photocopying ink was blurred, and the whole picture looked like a grey blancmange.

I was to be accompanied by Khasem. He had arranged for three yaks for this trip. I had asked for the same one I had had on the way up, as I felt we were used to each other. One of the yak-men was the young boy I had found crying in the stone hut. The yaks had been tethered to rocks and not fed at all overnight and not been allowed to bed down or rest. The claim was that this harsh treatment made them perform better the next day. Pete had already had a row about this.

'This crazy idea sticks in my craw. How can it be right? It's a tough show out here but these guys make everything worse.'

I thought that these people must surely know their own animals better than our outsider ideas. The men did not seem to be deliberately cruel. They had been working these animals for centuries now. A yak with a full belly would probably not perform so well, would be drowsy perhaps, like some humans are. To get over this terrain in the dark needed every bit of alert care and attention. Besides I did not think it very sensible to complain about such things. We were in their hands and they could take their revenge in all sorts of ways.

The Americans had brought sun-bloc cream along with them which they had been smearing liberally over their foreheads and cheeks, noses, and chins every day. This was something I had not thought about, and Petocz had given me a tube for my own use from the first day.

When the two yak drivers arrived just after dawn they too had, unusually, their cheeks plastered with white cream. The trouble was – it was not sun-bloc. I knew immediately what it was, because my tube of toothpaste had disappeared from beside my sleeping bag, where I had placed my washing gear. I knew too that my bag had been gone through, but I was too canny a traveller to have left anything of value lying loose. My money was always strapped round my middle, under my sweater, and I never took my watch off. The loss of the toothpaste was not enough to make a fuss about. I didn't want a confrontation which would put the men on the defensive against me. And anyway, it was too good a joke to spoil.

There was already something of a problem. Much of the time the Wakhis were sullen, not so much with me but with the Americans. It had started with Pete slugging the tall driver when he lost his temper over his rifle on the way up. Although Pia kept the two apart, making sure the man was never on Pete's team, neither the man himself nor his compatriots were going to forget that. And out on the hunt the previous day, Pete had felt they were grumbling all the time and unwilling to co-operate with his wishes. At supper he had complained to Pia about this.

'These Wakhis are acting kind of belligerent all the time. And no one speaks our language.'

Pia had muttered to himself to the effect that, 'It's a good thing you don't understand their language or you might not sleep too well at night.' But he had then explained that the men were concerned about getting snowed in. The Sargass Pass had to be negotiated to get out of the area, and if that got blocked with snowdrifts twenty feet deep, we would be totally marooned and that would be serious.

'We are usually finished by now. Your trip was a late addition. They worry. They want to get home. So the sooner you get your trophy head the better for all of us. Soufi-Kabouli is good man. He knows where animals are. Today you were unlucky. Also, if you speak simple words, he can understand. More than perhaps you think.'

I had been right: the fur trader did understand some English. I hoped Pete would appreciate the hidden warning. It was at that point he went off to bed, and Pia had gone off to talk to Soufi-Kabouli, no doubt with a few words about not offending the American. He did not have an easy job, I had decided.

We had waited for a while, to give Pete and his little group time to get away so that we would not interfere with their objective. In any case Khasem intended to go to a different area. I levered myself back into the saddle from hell and we set off. The yak-man and the boy were together on one animal, the boy holding on behind the man. Khasem was self-evidently pleased to be able to show me 'his' reserve. The hunters were never interested in the conservation of the area, other than how it related to their chance of a shot at the biggest animal. I was a fellow warden and knew what the work meant, and asked the right questions, which satisfied his pride in his work.

There was a crystal light shining from sky, and hard snow all around us as we climbed towards Munjalak Pass. High above, three Egyptian vultures were circling, their wings almost silver-white as the dawn sky lit them from below, the black of wing tips and outer flight feathers alone showing the outline of these sails. A hobby falcon then passed high over, with that long straight purposeful flight that all falcons have, which shows their deadly intent, the uninterruptable flight of an arrow homing on its target. It was on its way to India, following the route of swallows and pipits, buntings and finches that were but a fraction of flight time ahead for the falcon, but what would be for us many miles and hours of slog among the boulders and scree.

My yak trundled on without my guidance as before. I had twisted its rope on to the saddle pommel, but if necessary I could quickly grab it to steer the beast. I tried to write some notes as we went along, but had to keep them as short one-worders just as an aide-memoire for later. The bouncing about wasn't too bad, but the cold was intense. My fingers quickly became frozen, my toes were frozen, my torso was also beginning to complain, although the constant adjusting to the yak's lurches at least kept the blood stirred. My crutch was cramped and squashed within the saddle of this sluggard, but the rarified air and clarity of vision made me forget all the intense discomforts. There was no dust, no vapour, no scum of human existence up here, three miles above sea level. Now and then I hauled the yak to a stop so that I could use the binoculars and find out what was in the sky above. This was the moment one could wish to be a bird, and use this fine air. To be a vulture or an eagle on those soaring wings, with nothing but blue above and the land crawling far beneath as you circled! Of course, there was a downside. They had to descend to eat, and my mind saw the filth and old bones and rotting flesh that the vultures were heir to, but what an uplift there would be against those mountain walls when that necessity of feeding was done.

While I do not romanticise nature, I am sure all these birds must enjoy flight. Much of their day needs to be spent hunting for food, but that flight must also be a pleasure. Sunlight warmed the valley meadows far below and created warm air that rose, and held them with little effort on their part. All they had to do was open their wings and soar. They knew exactly where to find the thermals, or rising columns of warm air.

Once at height they rested on the sky, circling, and seeing

a continuous panorama below. How many times had I watched buzzards back in England playing together, dipping and feinting as they pretended to joust, sometimes touching their claws together in mid-air, often rolling on their backs and calling with a wild skirl as they talked excitedly, perhaps claiming a point in all this play. So it was here, as I scanned back and forth across the sky, making my yak stand the while. Through binoculars I could see a continuous speckle of vultures, hawks, harriers and falcons on all sides to infinity. With eight times magnification I suppose I had a range of perhaps four miles to the faintest dot, and within this compass I could make out about forty contacts. Most of these appeared to be following the southern migration of passerines on which they fed. Such sights have long left England and even much of Europe, although I had read in the bird magazines that Gibraltar was still a good place to watch the autumn migration.

Suddenly I heard a strange whistle. I looked around at Khasem, thinking he was trying to attract my attention, but it was not him. It was a mellow call, what we tend to describe as 'flute-like'. It was coming from somewhere ahead at ground level, but there was nothing to see and no idea as to how far away the caller was. We were coming to the head of the pass, and as we breasted this we were faced with brilliant eye-scorching sun reflections coming off the snow, which had melted and refrozen several times. My eyes were so dazzled I had to almost shut them, and I was unable look round at ground level to find the source of the strange call. Then I noticed that both the yak driver and Khasem had tied some sort of black cloth with rope around their heads to cover their eyes. I recalled with some panic that one could easily suffer from snow blindness in such conditions. I felt in my pockets for my old RAF sunglasses that Anne had insisted I bring (which again I had equally insisted I would not need), only to remember that I had left them in my bag.

I was wearing my grandfather's balaclava again. It was made of camel hair, and sand-coloured, thick and excellent camouflage. He had used it for duck shooting. It had been so invisible that he once had a wigeon come in to land on his head. His diary records (in his usual laconic style) 'I got it anyway,' as it flew away in fright. This historic garment became even more useful now as I pulled it right down over my eyes and hid the painful sun glare.

I heard the odd whistle again, and peering through the camel-hair fringe saw black dots ahead on the deep snow drifts in Muntjalak valley. There were three of them. I told the yak drivers to stop as I wanted to see them properly, to check what they were. Surely not marmots? But they should have gone down into deep burrows by now to hibernate. They must be birds. Perhaps vultures down on a carcass. Don's Marco Polo ram had not been found, after all, and its body would be the same colour as the snow. They were half a mile ahead, but once I got the binoculars on to them it was obvious what they were. They were chunky birds, almost round as they huddled on the snow-ice. There was a grey and white crag near them. All at once this crag, or part of it, began to move and then, to my astonishment, most of this rock broke up into small pieces and began to travel rapidly across the snowdrift.

I knew then straight away what they were: the way they ran gave them away. I had seen that so many times at home, when a covey of partridges ran along with their bouncy, toddling little run. But these were not partridges, although they were in the same family, as were grouse, ptarmigan, quail, prairie chicken, see-see partridge and sand partridge. My mind ran over them all in a flash as it found the right species. I was enjoying my first sight of snowcock (*Tetraogallus*), but exactly which of the several closely related subspecies I had no idea. They range across mountainous regions from the Caspian Sea east across Tibet and north to the Russian Altai range. Science thinks that they were a single species that retreated into the mountains after the last ice age, and then began to split up into sub- species as they adapted to the slight differences in climate and vegetation and altitude of these various mountain areas.

We then heard them whistling and squawking. I could see they were flicking their tails, holding their heads high and walking away, finally springing up to flee away down-slope at great speed hugging the contours. At half a mile away we were getting too close. When we got to the place where they had been, we found they had left no footprints, the snow being crusty ice. It was almost as if we had imagined them, for they had now totally vanished. But I did find a single feather on the ground, one that I treasure, the closest physical link to one of the most difficult birds to see on the planet.

There were, though, plenty of footprints of ibex and Marco Polo sheep. They were heavy enough to have broken through the ice crust, and their prints were embalmed. But not a single animal was to be seen. We carried on towards Russia. The young boy driver was continuously whining to himself. Khasem ignored him, except for a few curt remarks made sotto voce. He looked physically strong enough, even though he was little more than skin and bone wrapped up in rags. I presumed he was not feeling very well, but couldn't think what his problem could be, other than alpine sickness, and I felt it couldn't be that. I must admit that I ignored him. There was little I could do. I knew my own children whined sometimes for no reason. I was far too interested in what was going on around me to worry about a boy who was not my responsibility. Later, I was sorry for my indifference.

I had seen how Pete concentrated solely on his own goal – the goal of getting a trophy head of a difficult species. For him the hunt was paramount and nothing else mattered. Only that way would he succeed. He was far superior to me in his abilities in this hostile place, able to ignore his own bodily discomforts and needs, and those of others too. He had shown that to succeed here needed the same resolve that was needed to climb Everest, or to win gold in the Winter Olympics. That of course applied to everything in life: to succeed, to get to the top, one needed to be totally ruthless. I tried to think myself into that same mindset. Although I was here to write a film script for the BBC, I was now determined that I would see a snow leopard, and that nothing would get in my way. It had become a quest. Time was the problem. There was the threat of winter snow closing in and the possibility that the camp would break at any time. But the sudden encounter with the snowcocks and the tracks of the mountain animals had made me very hopeful. Overhead the raptors were still there on their passage south. That was also a good omen! Anything could happen now.

And it did. We had been in the saddle for about four hours and were at about 15,000 feet. Suddenly Khasem stopped his yak a hundred metres ahead of me, turned in his saddle, jabbing his finger down and ahead, indicating silence with his other hand. He pulled his yak round and came back towards me with a big grin on his face, again indicating silence.

'Is Marco Polo ram,' he whispered. We dismounted, and he told the driver and the boy to hold the yak ropes and to remain still and quiet. He and I crept forward on foot. The snow crackled and crunched alarmingly under our boots, although in fact we made less noise than the yaks. I could feel my heart racing. Nearing the lip of ground leading into the valley ahead, we crept forward, almost bent double. Then we crouched on all fours and peered over. There he was, less than five hundred metres away. Khasem whispered, 'Sixty inch.'

That made it a top trophy animal in the eyes of world hunters. It was an extraordinary sight. The triangular white head with massive curling horns encircling around looked like something prehistoric, not of this time. The ram was asleep, enjoying the brief heat of the sun on his white body. I was looking at the king of this whole principality, and he was wearing his crown. For that moment I forgot the snow leopard. There could be no more majestic sight than this prime ram to be found in these mountains on top of the world, or indeed anywhere.

Beside me Khasem was grinning like the happiest of men; his eyes had completely vanished, his brilliant teeth shone in this bright sun. This was his animal, and nothing to do with the hunters and their Wakhi guides. He had known it was here, and he had led me to it. He told me later that this animal was for conservation only, not killing, and he had brought me because I was here to conserve, not just to kill, and I was, with Dr Petocz, the first people here for that reason; and I was the first from England to see it. The world was changing, he was to say later, and we must see these animals for beauty, not just for meat or trophy. For this moment, he was silent. We both were, as we watched and wondered at this grand spectacle.

I felt rather ignorant and stupid. Before this trek, only a month or so ago, I had not realised that such an animal could exist. Although I had seen pictures of American big-horn and Argali sheep, and had heard of the Marco Polo, those artists' impressions and photographs of the giants had not sunk in. I don't think anyone could comprehend how magnificent the animal actually is, without having seen one in its natural habitat. There was far more than any picture could ever convey. The animal was surrounded by the cold air, the snow, the silence, the vastness of the distant white peaks beyond this twelve-mile valley. After a minute or two, Khasem nudged me: he had spotted four more rams. The king had an entourage, it seemed. But the four others were minors in comparison.

The old ram woke up, turned its head, showing its twin

corkscrews to right and to left. Each horn curled through one and a half spirals. It seemed to be holding an unbelievable weight, like an Olympiad weight-lifter holding the weighted bar in a pose above his head before letting it crash to the ground. But the old ram sprang to his feet, holding his crown up high, and we could see clearly the thickness at the base of each horn where it joined its head. This was as thick as a man's thigh. The creature started to walk slowly along the side of the scree, merging perfectly in its off-white coat with all the snow and the slabs of grey rock and stone.

One of the younger rams immediately got up and settled itself into grandfather's bed. Perhaps it was the most comfortable patch on the slope, but more likely it was still warm; or perhaps the youngster fancied himself taking on the mantle of the king for a few moments and impregnating its own coat with the old animal's smell and scent of urine. But soon all four stood up and wandered slowly down the slope, feeding on the minute fragments of plant life that still remained along their path, following their leader. Below them were seven ewes and three lambs, keeping their place. While we were watching, a piercingly cold wind suddenly sprang up, yet the blaze of the sun still warmed one side of our faces. We were too absorbed to bother.

The leading youngster stopped, and looked back along the path. This made the second stop, and look behind, then the third, and finally the fourth. They were, it seemed, walking in order of seniority, each checking that its sub-dominant was keeping its place in the line of princes. It reminded me of the white-robed clergy in surplices and their servers in High Church ascendancy of rank. Or, more appropriately for this region, the rams resembled the hierarchical order of Arabian sheiks and princes in their robes that I had witnessed in the Middle East. Women and children were kept at a distance of course.

189

Then, out of the blue and without any warning, a veil of snow descended. This curtain shrouded the old ram first, then his followers. It seemed as thin as muslin, falling first from a dry clear sky, then thickening abruptly, and within half a minute all the sheep had vanished and the mountain side became nothing more than frozen vapour. It was an uncanny moment, and seemed unreal. Where had that frozen moisture come from? Russia had been hidden in thick metal-grey clouds for half an hour, which I had noticed, but been too absorbed in watching the rams to take heed.

Khasem was galvanised into action. 'Is snow coming too quick. Must hurry now, no good now.'

We climbed back on to the yaks and began the long climb back over the pass. Khasem pulled a blanket out of his saddle bag and handed it to the boy who wrapped it round himself, covering his head as well. His clothes were totally inadequate for the conditions. The wind was blowing hard sharp crystals of ice into our faces like diamond dust. It was too hard to settle; it was not soft snow, more like grains of glass, and it skittered along in twists and eddies, forming miniature plumes behind whatever obstruction the wind came upon. It was then that I saw my first sign of the snow leopard. We had seen footprints all the way of sheep and ibex, but this was quite different. I shouted to Khasem to look.

'I think that's the track of a snow leopard?' I hoped he would confirm my observation.

'Yes, is snow leopard running, last night.'

The pad marks were as wide as a smallish hand would make; each nearly a metre apart, each cluster of four pads separated by over another metre. The snow had been soft enough at that time for the cat to sink in a few millimetres and now these were filling up with ice crystals and forming plumes in the craters. I stopped the yak and got off and stared at the imprints, felt with my fingers the outline of the pads and splayed claws, looked for the smallest trace of fur, feeling the creature was so near, and yet any hope of contact evaporating before my eyes. It had loped across this icy terrain on exactly the same route that we were taking, only twelve hours or so ahead of us. Where was it now?

'Is no good to stop,' Khasem was saying urgently, but I hardly heard him. 'Must go, or we will be trapped here.'

The young lad began to cry again. He was frightened. But I was so focussed on the idea of the snow leopard that I took no notice. As I got back on my yak, so the others had gone ahead while I made the yak follow the line of the footprints. Within a couple of minutes I had lost contact with them. After only a short distance the snow had filled up the footprints of the elusive snow leopard, and I suddenly realised I had been extremely stupid.

Fortunately, my yak had more sense than I did. As I tried to force it to the left, where I was sure Khasem would be, the animal dragged its head to the right, trotted forward quite purposefully, and within a few minutes had joined back up with the others. Khasem grinned, but was obviously shaken up. To have lost me would have meant big trouble. My own relief was extreme. I had nearly lost the whole thing in just a few seconds of madness; and the realisation that I had completely lost my sense of direction was terrifying. With no horizon, a traveller in snow or fog can wander in circles until exhausted. I should have known better. I had once experienced that on the marshes in Norfolk, and had been nearly drowned by a rising tide.

13

We returned to luxury. It hadn't snowed on the camp side of the pass, but it had made the air colder than ever, and the cook had abandoned his outside fire and retreated to the mud hut, lighting the iron stove. We huddled round this ancient monstrosity with its meagre fire of twigs and small branches and dried yak dung, and watched the wisps of steam beginning to wander out of the kettle. There was quite a fug, with the smoke and the number of people who crammed in. We didn't care. We had got back safely and were slowly thawing out.

After a while, the young lad who had been with us all day and had been so frightened came close to my side and looked up at me, saying something in Pashto. He really looked a pathetic little creature, his clothes little more than rags and his bare legs scarcely thicker than the small branches in the stove. I wondered how he had survived the cold, even with the help of Khasem's blanket. I had no idea what he was saying and shook my head and spread my hands to try and indicate this. His young eyes were huge in his thin face, and he tugged my coat and repeated his message again, this time almost in a whisper. Khasem noticed the little exchange, and came over and laid his hand on the boy's shoulders.

'The boy say he is sorry. He is sorry he was frightened today. He is ashamed that he cried. His mother and father died two weeks ago and he does not feel good.'

That was all. It was very dignified and I was much moved. I shook the boy's hand and patted him on the shoulder, and asked Khasem to tell him how sorry I was to hear this, and that he had been very brave. The boy smiled, settled down by the fire in his rags and went straight to sleep on his filthy sheep-skin. I asked Khasem the boy's name.

'Raschid.'

'What happened to his parents?'

He shrugged. 'Some fever. Bad water perhaps. Very quick. It happens often.'

'What will happen to him?'

'The people here will look after him. He has other family. But everyone very poor, no money. He can earn a little by work with the hunt, like today.'

After about half an hour the kettle boiled as best it could at this altitude and tea was made. Although it was weak and not very hot, it was extremely welcome. I was also handed hot fresh naan bread. Once I was warmer, I went back outside. Suddenly everyone started shouting. A yak was approaching, a piebald animal. Khasem said the rider was the guide Shahik, from Sargass. Shahik shouted a reply. Everyone groaned. I asked Khasem what was going on, what they had shouted.

'Oh – is custom. When hunter returns, we call to ask "Do you return as a fox or a lion?" Lion is successful, fox is not. He answered "as a fox". That is bad.'

Shahik had been out all day, hunting for the animal that Don had wounded. A message had been sent to him when it was known that a wounded animal had escaped. He had been on its trail since well before daybreak. Everyone crowded round as tea was thrust into his hands, and they all listened to what he had to say. Khasem translated for my benefit. Don's wounded ram had left a blood trail for several miles over three glaciers. Shahik had abandoned the trail when the animal had climbed into a set of ravines and towering precipices above Sargass. Later I was to go into this labyrinth and see one of the most thrilling and spectacular battles of mountain animals imaginable. Shahik had also seen twenty-five 'nursery' rams on the way, all in a sort of crèche, I gathered, though he hadn't used that word.

Shahik was the head guide of the Wakhan and had worked as a hunter for twenty-two years, living all his life in Sargass. In that time he had shot 300 Marco Polo sheep, and many ibex, wolf and snow leopard. He was now about thirty-five, a wiry, muscular man, with a grin showing quite shamelessly bad teeth, and given, it was hinted by Khasem, to moments of morose silence as well as sudden and extreme cheerfulness. Despite the cold he was dressed in the kind of clothes Mallory had worn for his attempt on Everest in 1924: shirt, pullover, and tweed jacket. I suspected these had been given to him by one of the hunters he had taken out in the past. They were quite astonishingly Western. Right now, despite his lack of success over the wounded ram, he was in a cheerful mood.

There was a further excitement. Somebody spotted a small column of yaks approaching in the dusk. These animals were loaded up with bundles of wood. Pia had sent off a messenger to buy wood for the cooking fire from a group of herders somewhere along the Russian border, who had access to this valuable commodity.

'OK now if snowed in,' Pia said, beaming with pride at his organisational powers.

'Yes, great, well done,' I replied; but finding it rather ominous. Certainly, if we got snowed in fuel would be in desperate need. But if we got snowed in, that amount would not last the winter. If we got snowed in, then I didn't really want to think about what would happen. However, in the short term it was very welcome.

Once the sun set at about 5.30 p.m. everyone became even more cheerful, because at sunset the daily Ramadan fast ended. It had been a long and cold day, and it was not allowed to let food or drink pass their lips. It added just another layer of difficulty to their lives. It was one of the causes of the bad tempers. They were not allowed to eat during the hours of daylight, and due to the altitude and the cold they were very low on blood sugar. Only those who had travelled were allowed food and drink. Our party and Shahik had been allowed tea because they had travelled all day. Now tea and naan were handed round to everyone. Then they prepared for their evening prayer session, and I made myself scarce.

Pete had returned, again as a 'fox', and after the obligatory tea and naan had gone to bed, asking to be woken up for the evening meal if he hadn't reappeared. I had looked in on Don earlier, but he was not really up to talking. So I went off to seek out Petocz.

Although there had been considerable talk about the various Marco Polo rams, there had been no mention of 'our' ram. I did rather feel that our little group had returned as a 'lion'. We had captured that unbelievable sighting of the king ram. It was our trophy. Khasem the conservationist, young orphaned vulnerable Raschid, and myself, a stranger here with minimal knowledge of the area, had found and seen what was probably the finest animal in the Wakhan – in Afghanistan itself. It was all due to Khasem's skill and knowledge, of course, but I was honoured and thrilled to have been part of this grand occasion. Most importantly, 'our' animal was alive. It was not beheaded so it horns could be displayed on a wall in America, or anywhere else. With luck it would live the winter through. It was getting old, I knew, but next spring it would perhaps sire for one last time another member of this race of superlative giants.

I was longing to share my thoughts and excitement, and so told Petocz about our sighting. He said he knew about the beast from Khasem, but had not seen it. He understood how I felt, but his attitude was very matter-of-fact and scientific. He concentrated solely on his work: there was no room for romance or sentiment in his mind. I understood that also. His passion was to be the one to find evidence, hard facts, and so to oversee the establishment of nature reserves in this remote and hostile area. His dedication was very admirable.

Over the evening meal, I heard Petocz asking Khasem about the sighting, and they discussed it quite openly in English. Pete sat nursing his bowl of stew and chappati, chewing morosely and seemingly not listening. But I could see that he had heard every word, and now and then he looked hard at me when he thought I wasn't looking. He was, I had decided, quite a secretive person, although seemingly amiable and open. He was shrewd enough to keep quiet. His face now took on a steely look of intent.

Young Raschid was also talking animatedly to the older men, and I could tell from his gestures that he too was telling them about the big ram. He looked at me from time to time, and I knew he was saying something about me. He seemed to have recovered his spirits for the first time, and I hoped he was over the most intense stage of grief.

I had noticed earlier that the two lammergeier vultures had been cruising continually around the camp, and the local men had been shaking their fists and raising imaginary guns towards them, even shouting and jumping up and down to scare them off. I asked Pia why they were so annoyed with the birds.

'Oh, they think birds know something,' he said dismissively. 'They think these birds bring death. Sometimes people die in the mountains, the vultures arrive of course. They do not like to be reminded. But really the birds know that where there are people there is food, they just hope for bones and meat scraps. That is all.'

As vultures gathered round dead animals, this was very understandable. It reminded me of our own superstition, not so very long in the past, about white owls bringing death.

Dr Amin had heard us, and being a doctor, knew that his part in proceedings was to keep everyone cheerful. A cheerful person is a healthy person. He had a fund of cheerful stories, always relating to his own experiences, which he would relate whenever he thought it necessary. Talk of death and vultures feeding on carrion was not a cheerful subject. He had noticed Pete was very quiet. The man was tired, and unsuccessful in his hunting. This was not good. He already had one American patient, and did not want the second one to succumb. I could almost read his thoughts chasing across his face. And so he now launched into yet another little episode in his life to change the subject and make us laugh. It was his earnest manner and flowery language that made his stories always amusing, rather than their actual content. He now spoke loudly to get everyone's attention.

'Mr. Williamson. This is the special place for you and for the BBC. I know. I can see. But I can tell you, the special place for me is not exactly here! It is very nice place I know. But where do you think is the special place for me?'

I shrugged and smiled, and spread my hands.

'I will tell you. It is America. Yes, America! I would like to go back there again sometime, because, can you guess why? Because when I was there, I was pumpkin! Believe me! Believe me!'

With this exclamation he was looking round, smiling cheerfully, and looking for our reactions. I found the idea of him as a pumpkin very funny, and was grinning broadly. Pete was also grinning. The herders were staring blankly at us all. Dr Amin continued.

'I see plenty nice girls in Miami, not like here of course, very American girls, bare arms and legs. But all my friends call me pumpkin! Do you know pumpkin? It is, how would you say, empty! It means somebody who does not drink or smoke or chase girls! I would like to be pumpkin again in America!'

He laughed and slapped his thigh at his own joke, satisfied that he had achieved his purpose. But he also looked a little sad. He was clearly remembering that life in America had been very different from life in Afghanistan. We all laughed with him, though the joke did not seem to have any point.

It snowed in the night, but around the camp this had melted by ten o'clock. Don remained confined to his sleeping bag, but Pete had gone out again at 2.30 a.m. There were no yaks available for myself to use. They worked one day and then rested the next, so Pete had taken the only ones available. Those that had brought in the faggots had gone back with their owners, who were not impressed with the scant feed in this valley meadow, Pia said. Khasem went off to check something, and took young Raschid with him.

Later in the morning a flock of about seventy domestic sheep and goats grazed past the camp, which denuded the last of the vegetation. They were not supposed to do this, as they had been compensated by the Afghan Tourist Authority to leave these meadows for wild animals. But they were herders who had a licence for meadows further up, and they were now moving the flock down to the much lower pastures, as winter was coming and they did not want to be snowed in. Pia was very anxious that I should understand that this was not really a violation of the agreement. The men had no choice. I was more concerned that these herders with their age-old knowledge of the mountains were getting out in a bit of a hurry! It made me feel that we were in a rather precarious situation. It worried the camp staff, too, and it was obvious that they were grumbling again. I wondered if they would take the law into their own hands and just clear out. It seemed a distinct possibility and was an unsettling thought.

I asked Petocz for his opinion. He just carried on staring through his telescope and said it should be all right for a few more days. I thought to myself that he had only been up here for this single season; he had not experienced how winter weather actually worked. I suspected he just wanted to stay up here doing his job, and did not want to return to Kabul.

Pia wasn't much help either. His responsibility was with the hunters and he knew that Pete was not going to give up until he had his trophy head. If this did not happen then he could, and no doubt would, give a bad report when he got back to America, which might affect future hunting trips. And he, Pia, might lose his job. So he was not going to be the one to say we must leave, perhaps until it was too late. I felt very anxious about getting snowed in. If that happened and we were stuck for the whole winter, there was the question of survival, and I would certainly lose my own job; and how on earth would Anne and the children then cope?

I knew nothing about how to read the weather up here, other than to look at the sky. I have always been interested in clouds, and at home in England knew roughly what would happen a short while ahead from the way the clouds formed and progressed in any twenty-four hours. My brother John had considerable knowledge from his experience representing Britain in the World Gliding Championships in various different countries, and I had learned much from him. Here, each day seemed to threaten storms. These showed as alto cirrus coming up from the south. There was no barometer at the camp which would have shown how close and how strong the Indian weather fronts actually were. When they met the freezing mountain air, precipitation would be snow – but how much and for how long? I could only guess and fear the worst. The trouble was, I had no control over the situation and was at the mercy of the others. No one else watched the sky: not even Petocz, which surprised me since he was a scientist. I thought the weather might affect the behaviour of the animals, but he was only interested in his actual records of movement. He was dismissive of the Afghans' behaviour and wary of their motives for wanting to leave. If he was all right – then so should they be.

We sat together all that day just looking at ibex two miles away on the far slopes to the north. These were mainly females and nursery youngsters. There was a lot of activity. Petocz remonstrated me, because I called one of the females 'mother': that was not scientific and just stupid. So I called it 'nanny', which he said was a good name for me in that case. But I thought 'a goat is a goat, and they are billy goat and nanny goat', and stuck to my guns. The nanny was playing games with her offspring. They faced each other while standing on a little hillock, and the nanny lowered her head towards her kid when it made a mock threat to her. They clashed heads, not so gently either. She was teaching the youngster 'pretty good', as Pete would have said. After this she allowed the kid to suckle, as Petocz called it, 'long and hard'. Long and hard was thirty seconds.

Nearby two young males seemed inspired by this brief encounter to try their luck against each other. The two young males had each chosen a rock just a couple of feet apart. These two small pillars were about five feet higher than the surrounding scree. They could have been ancient jousting pillars and were perhaps worn smooth with the horny cleaves of a thousand hopefuls over as many years. The two were just close enough to touch their horns. The knurled lumps on the front of these curved horns probably engaged like cogs in a gearbox, although they were too far off to see such details. Each male pushed and clattered the horns together gently. After a while they rested one against the other, and may even have gone half asleep, Petocz told me.

All at once they woke up from this reverie, clambered down from their vantage points, and, rather to my surprise, set to with proper head clashing. They walked back a pace or two after each contact, stared at their opponent's horns, then leapt forward again to meet head-on with a crack which we could not hear at that distance. This seemed to make them even more lustfully angry and in need of closer contact, so they stood up on their hind legs and started thrashing out with their front legs like mad March hares. When I called this boxing, Petocz said drily, 'It's actually called threat-jumping. You should read more scientific papers and learn the correct presentation.'

'Right.'

But I thought to myself that I was a writer as well as a conservationist, and probably had more idea of what would be acceptable to readers; but I didn't want to argue with him. The BBC would need his co-operation for the filming in due course. I was used to these technical codes of language, which excluded outsiders with their insider boundaries of speech and behaviour, which the cliques concerned considered so important, but which were often rather laughable. Also, I had been through military service which broke down such barriers when several cultures were forced to live together, and had to find common bonds. I got on with writing up my notes and ideas for the proposed film.

'What will be the best time for the filming?' I asked Petocz.

'Not as late as this,' he replied. 'Well, not before mid-June, because when the winter snows melt there is a lot of flooding. You must make all the difficulties clear. They must be very well organised. They must be fit. You have seen what it is like up here.'

There were seven mother ibex and seven kids in the group we watched that day, and there was often brief playing between mothers and their young. Petocz pointed out a group of Marco Polo sheep resting. Looking like the ground around them, they were almost invisible, and it took me a moment to latch on to them through the glasses. He said their behaviour was very different from that of the ibex. There were fewer young than there should be, and the young lambs hardly ever played.

'I've only seen the youngsters play once, in the whole five months I have been up here, when two lambs butted their heads together just one time. What I do see a lot of is the lambs licking the maternal ewe's faces, hoping this will make them stand up so they can suckle. But the ewe threatens its offspring if it suckles too long. All a bit worrying. Lack of grazing means fewer young and then little milk.'

At 11 a.m. the group of ten Marco Polo ewes and four lambs stood up, Petocz recording seventy-five minutes of rest. After stretching, each of the four mothers was ready for its young and allowed suckling: the time ranged between 11.2 and 11.5 seconds by his stopwatch, which I thought a remarkable similarity. Petocz was fitting together every detail of the life up here, bit by bit. It was like doing a jigsaw puzzle. Every last piece had to be in place before the full picture emerged, and one could say that one could predict how and why populations of animals and plants, insects, birds, were able to exist; and also, what they needed to go on existing, and indeed whether they could go on existing. The balance of the general ecosystem was vital. Nature conservation is like farming: the farmer knows exactly how to grow a crop of wheat or maintain a herd of milking cows. Understanding and providing the needs of animals and plants in their natural habitat was akin to farming, but on a truly vaster scale. And there is so much that is still not known even about what is known, let alone what is still unknown.

Thinking of the unknown and the unseen brought me back to the snow leopard. I told Petocz about seeing the footprints the previous day, but not the actual animal.

'You probably won't,' he replied dismissively. 'You can't expect everything, especially in such a short time. You've seen more than most – your ram yesterday was just about the best of the mountain animals. Snow leopards are even more elusive than Marco Polo rams. Snow leopards are not dopey herbivores, having to graze fodder all the time to get enough nutrients into their system to deal with the conditions here. Snow leopards watch and wait out of sight. They can go for days without eating. The best time to see them is when they make a kill, but that means being lucky enough to be in the right place at the right time. Look for a sickly or lame ibex up high in some inaccessible place – that's your best bet.'

Pete came back soon after midday. He was not in a good mood. When I asked him how he had got on, he just grunted. 'A group of small rams in the western valley, none with horns of more than forty-five inches.' I noticed he didn't look at me when he spoke, and I wondered why, but presumed that he was tired and disappointed. Soufi Kabouli had told him to shoot one of those.

'That guide said it would be better than nothing,' he told me grimly. 'I didn't come here for that. I'm staying until I get what I want. Right now, I'm going to get some sleep.'

He gave no inkling then of what had actually happened that morning, and it was only a couple of days later that I heard the full story from him. What I did notice was that the Afghans stayed huddled together, muttering ominously. They got paid for the trip however long or short it might be, and they wanted it finished. They had no interest in the size of the trophy secured by the hunters, except that a big trophy might mean a bigger tip. Pia was looking worried, and arguing with the men. I admired Pete's resolve. Much though I wanted to see a snow leopard, I too wanted to be getting out of this place. A very cold wind had started up, much colder than before. It made the wind-chill factor almost unbearable. Glaciers rumbled throughout the day, unless it was the

Russians being busy again.

I had got enough information now, more or less, to write a rough shooting script for the proposed film, and knew the chance of seeing my phantom of the clouds was fairly remote. But I was also aware that new stories and details turned up every day. The longer I stayed here, the more information I would have, and so be able to make a more interesting write-up. So that when Pia, hoping for my support, asked me what I thought, I told him, rather perversely against my own will, that I agreed with Pete and wanted to stay as long as was humanly possible.

He was silent for a minute, just staring at the leaping flames in the bread-oven hole. Then he turned to the Afghanis, and by the way he indicated me, was translating what I had said. There was a brief murmur among them, and what I can only call a deep sense of malevolence settled over them all. It was palpable and chilling. Young Raschid had appeared amongst them and he now began to cry again, putting his arm up over his face so no one would see. That shook me. I didn't want to be responsible for his unhappiness or even, if the worst happened, for his demise.

It was so cold that Pia said we should have our supper in a nearby cave, and so at sunset we all crowded in. It was only a hundred metres from us but I had not known it was there, for its entrance was hidden by a massive boulder. I suspected this decision was as much to cause a diversion as anything, for the men seemed to regard the mud hut as their domain, and for us westerners to have invaded it that evening might have caused trouble. Pete had got up and joined us but was even quieter than usual, keeping his head down and shoulders hunched.

The cave was really just a deep hole in the side of the hill. On its roof were enormous scratch marks. I guessed immediately that they had been made by *Ursus horribilis* – the grizzly bear. It meant that bears used this hide-out as a winter retreat as soon as the humans moved out. When they stretched themselves they reached up and ran their claws over the roof, which, about four metres above ground level, was way above our reach.

It reminded me of the German legend of Siegfried and the dragon's caves, where he is supposed to have killed the dragon. One such place was the Drachenfels in the Sieben Gebirge. These caves were excavated after the First World War for the thick deposits of guano left by bats roosting there over millennia. Agriculture was in need of any help it could get at that desperate time. Embedded in this free fertiliser were the skeletons of hundreds of bears, and they were a much bigger animal than the brown bear of today. These giant herbivores even pre-dated the cave paintings made by Stone Age artists, as they had copied the likenesses of brown, or grizzly, bears.

I asked Petocz which species of *Ursa horribilis* was present here in the Pamirs. He told me that it was probably the same species as found in America, known as Kodiaks. They were the biggest bears, weighing up to 1,650 pounds, but these were probably more similar to the smallest brown bear, the Syrian, weighing in at 550 pounds. These are the bears which we have in zoos in England, which in years gone by had been imported for bear-baiting and dancing. Petocz said zoologists disagreed over whether there were subspecies or just different races.

'Over fifty subspecies of grizzly bears have been named. The main difference is in the colour of the fur. In some cases they are reddish, and in others, very dark. Difference in fur colour is even found between bears in Sweden and Norway, while the Russian animals could be almost black.'

I forbore to point out that he hadn't really answered my question. His pontification led me to suppose that he hadn't actually seen one of the bears himself, and I didn't want to push him into a corner. I asked Pete if he had ever shot a bear in America. He looked at me and shook his head briefly. He seemed extremely tired and morose. But then he said, 'Yep – I got one in Alaska on Kodiak Island – about twenty years ago, I guess. That was one big animal. One front leg was about as big as my whole body. I had the skin and head made into a rug, but then it got stolen from the repair shop. That man put it in the window for advertisement. Next day there was no window and no bear. That trip cost me a lot of dollars – three times more than for here, as we had to hire a plane for the whole time there. Then the insurance on that bear was peanuts. So, I ain't got a good memory of that critter.'

As soon as he had finished his meal he went off to bed.

There was a heavy fug of fermented milk, opium smoke, fire smoke, belching bodies and boiled mutton that evening. A sick yak had been brought into the cave as well, so there was little room to sit comfortably on the mattress of old dung and ashes. The opium encouraged one of the Wakhis to tell what seemed to be a legend, passed down by goodness knows how many of his forebears in this cul-de-sac at the end of the world.

As the man told his story, Pia translated for me in a whisper so as not to interrupt, and I managed to write down the gist of the tale. This was the folklore of these mountain people passed down over many, many years about 'spirit men', which I presumed were shamans. Travellers through these terrifyingly hostile mountains had met these spirit people, who had to be placated and virtually worshipped. All travellers were desperate for whatever help they could get, but having to ride with supernatural demons required great courage and great knowledge. You had to know what to say to them, how to behave, and most of all, how not to antagonise them. I smiled to myself – not much different from today then! I wondered how much of their origin lay in opiate dreams, or even high-altitude light-headedness, but I knew that shamans had once wielded great power over ancient tribes, and possibly still did so. After all, most religions have the same effect.

Our story-teller said that these spirits guarded the ways over the mountains. I presumed this meant the passes. Travellers must take gifts, money, food, something of value. If they arrived without due humility and homage, the spirits would send storms, or snow and ice, and the traveller would be lucky to survive. As he looked straight at us westerners at that point, I felt he was making a point that we were supposed to note. After a while he stopped and closed his eyes, and became silent. I thought of how these stories had been passed down the ladder from one story-teller to another over many centuries. The story-teller was once one of the most important people in a tribe, not only as an entertainer but, more importantly, he carried their history in his head. Indeed, I understood the story-teller was often a woman, and she wielded much power.

Khasem took over with a tale of more plausible historic reality, talking first to the Wakhis and then translating for me, Pete having gone off to bed. He said that the Chinese had compiled a handbook of instruction on many of these problems for the traveller. Special emissaries had been sent to deal with the Hsiung-nu warlords of very long time ago – 'This is Bronze Age, Reeshard' – and one of the most important, Chang Chi'en, had been captured by the tribes in the desert just east of the Wakhan, and had lived with them for many years. He had even married one of their women and had children. He was a tough, fearless, yet fair-minded man capable of getting on with everybody, and able to bide his time. For twenty years he watched and waited, never forgetting his mission. At last, he saw his chance and escaped, teamed up with a local guide and continued his exploration westward. He became the first known Chinese person to enter the areas of Samarkand and Bactria. He is regarded by history as one of the greatest explorers, comparable with Marco Polo.

He tracked down the core contingent of the Hsuing-nu, who had formed their base on the north-west frontier provinces of India and become settled; and possibly complacently aloof to their enemies. Chang Chi'en returned home, reporting on the wealth of the area. This gave the Han army the information they needed, and they quickly marched west, far as Sogdiana. Thus the great Han dynasty was established.

'I read this at university,' he told me, 'It is interesting part of the story of this area, you think?'

'Indeed, Khasem. It is obvious that many clever people have come through here in years past. I am interested in everything to do with this place.'

Khasem replied, 'I will tell the men what you said. They will like that.'

He did, and there were low grunts of approval and nodding of heads. I had regained my brownie points. Khasem continued in the same vein. He said how the opening up of the route that we now know as the Silk Road meant all kinds of useful products, plants and raw materials became available from the East to the West and from the West to the East. Grapes were introduced, and also alfalfa seeds which were then grown as crops for animals. As he always spoke to the men first, so they chipped in with bits of information, which Khasem then included as he turned to me; but mainly it was information he had learned while at university. Borax from the soda salt lakes was used in medicine, alum for glazing fine paper, and curing animal skins – the men knew about that – ammonium chloride from volcanic ash used as a catalyst when soldering gold ornaments. The Chinese bartered their silk for these. Apparently, the men sneered at silk. They had no use for such delicate cloth – no use for yak riding, they snorted.

The list started to get wild, the men shouting out words and Khasem translating for me: jasmine, date palms, saffron, water lilies, spinach, tapestry, woollen rugs, lapis lazuli, almonds, slaves, camels, and cabbages, and even women and children, were all rattled off.

Khasem said to me, 'Well, of course, a lot of this is from medieval times, under the Chinese T'ang Dynasty. Today is different. For many years here is cut off from such trade. It is all too difficult. Today there are easier ways for trade to move.'

I nodded. I knew most of what he told me anyway, but did not say so. Anyway, it was interesting to hear this first-hand, as it were. The story-teller man now woke up again and continued with tales of ghosts and spirits and terrible things that happened. When this seemed to be petering out, Pia said, 'There is one story that might interest you, Reeshard. It is about the Tsar of Russia. The men know this. It is true tale. I will tell them and you, you'll see – they will agree.'

He launched into a tale that was almost bizarre. Apparently Russian tribes from just across the border had witnessed the burial of the bodies of the late Tsar and his wife and children, all of whom had been murdered at a time when there was great trouble in Russia and the West – '1917,' Pia grinned at me – and their bodies had been brought all the way across southern Russia and buried up here in the mountains, very near here, just over the border with Russia, or perhaps even in Afghanistan itself, so they would not be found. The men had nodded and grunted and chipped in with information during this story, and it was clear that they all knew and believed this. I asked Pia if it was known exactly where this burial place was. He nodded, and waved his hand around the general area of the Tulabai valley.

'They all know, but they will not tell you. But they see the ghosts of them sometimes, wandering through the mists. It is not a good omen.'

I had heard about this theory before, and knew that many scholars at that time had thought that this is what had actually happened to the bodies of the Russian royal family. However, in the many years since my visit it has been proved not to be so, although I suspect that the men of that isolated valley still believe that the Black Lord of Russia is buried there, and still see the restless spirits of the homeless ghosts of those hellish murders wandering in the mists and clouds in this valley at the end of the world.

So ended our night of story-telling in a cave that was used for several months of the year by the brown bears of the Wakhan.

14

It wasn't until after he was successful in his quest that Pete told me what had actually happened that day. All I knew was that he had come back early and in a bad mood. When I heard his tale, it reinforced my thought that he was a very secretive bloke who played his cards very close to his chest.

For the first time, he said, he had been frightened by an incident that had happened. He was frustrated by the day's events, but nevertheless excited by what he had seen, and even more determined to achieve his goal. His guide had taken him into the Tulabai valley, a wild and difficult area that is twelve miles long. They had blundered about for over three hours in the dark of the early hours before it got light.

'How those yaks found their way I have no idea. I could see nothin' – no moon, no stars, heavy clouds covering the sky and no light at all. I just didn't know where I was or where we were goin'. When it got light, we were miles up this valley,' he went on. 'After a bit we saw nine rams in a bunch, but they weren't the calibre I was after. The guide kept telling me to take one: it might be fifty-two inches. He kept saying "Shoot! Shoot!" But I knew those horns were not that big – I thought only forty-five or so, and so my reply was no.

'We made a careful detour around these animals, and stayed above them, and got by without them knowing we were there. You know, it is pretty difficult out there, and these men don't speak much of my language. That's not good. I'm goin' to complain about that to Klineburger back home. Anyway, I decided we should leave the yaks and creep forward, because that way we could hide ourselves better behind rocks. So we left those critters with their tender and went on, on foot, and we came to a ridge with a wide basin below it. We crept on to this ridge and looked over, and there they were. Twenty-two rams. The smallest one was probably just a bit less than fifty inches. That was some picture, I can tell you. Twenty-two Marco Polo, ranging from say forty-five into the upper fifties. I doubt many hunters have seen a sight that good. I felt pretty excited, this was more like what I had been expecting.

'We huddled together behind those boulders, figuring out what to do. I had the spotting scope – the Afghans had only binoculars. All the rams were bedded down. I looked at each one in turn, assessing its quality. I can tell you my blood was churning and I felt warm for the first time on this trip. Then as I was adjusting the scope, I touched it by accident so it moved an inch, and as I looked again at what seemed at first just to be the mountain side above the rams, I could hardly believe what I was seeing as I focussed. Right there in front of me was a ram with horns of around sixty inches. I was looking straight at him! I moved over and left the scope steady, and indicated to the guide to look at what I had seen. He told the two bearer fellas and they got their glasses on to it.

'Well, they were pretty amazed I can tell you. There those animals all were, bedded down, and this one big ram lording it over them. It all seemed great. Too great, of course. They were over half a mile away, and in a wide open basin. The boulders below us were not big enough for me to hide behind, there was no cover for me to get any closer. I couldn't get round the basin because there were sheer cliffs on each side. We all knew it was hopeless. The guide kept pointing at various impossible routes. I shook my head. "No good." They understand what you say if you keep it simple.

'Y'know, that canyon was like the end of the world. I had

to make the toughest decision of my whole hunting career. There was a real trophy head right in front of me, and I couldn't get a shot at it. I indicated we retreat. "Back now. Tomorrow. Find ram tomorrow."

'Well, I had been crouched down there for an hour glassing. When I stood up, I fell over backwards. Both of my feet were frozen, I had no feeling in them at all. That scared the hell out of me. I was so engrossed that I hadn't felt cold. It took me an hour before I got any feelin' back in my feet. That bothered me, I didn't like that one bit.

'Then on the way back, we were riding down a very steep icy slope when my yak slipped and slammed into a boulder, pinning my leg with its thousand pounds of weight. The Wakhis managed to pull it off. Luckily, I hadn't broken anything, but I had a badly bruised thigh and it hurt pretty bad. When I got back and looked at it, it was grazed and bloodshot, a huge bruise forming. Goddamn thing kept me awake most of the night, but I got up the usual time to get back to that place.'

We were now at 12 October. Pete had again left just after 0230 hours. There was a buzz going around that he was on to something. I wondered what. I hadn't yet heard any of the above story of course, and couldn't see what could have happened between him going to bed and getting up again to cause any excitement. However, I was not allowed to go out myself, which annoyed me but reinforced the feeling that something was afoot.

Overnight snow had threatened a blizzard, but it cleared up at dawn, and the air had become like ice. It had a feeling of being white hot, searing into the lungs. It was not totally unpleasant. I felt as though my lungs were being thoroughly cleaned out and all past bugs and problems would be gone forever: no more bronchitis, I thought to myself. And that proved to be correct. I only wished Don could have enjoyed the same sensation. If he hadn't gone down with his alpine sickness, I was sure his bronchitis would also have been cured. If only he had had the sense to wait until he had adjusted to the altitude before rushing into a hunt. He was coughing blood, but wasn't getting worse. He was taking oxygen every so often which perked him up, and Dr Amin said he wasn't over-worried about him. He appeared at lunch and ate a little tinned cheese and naan and some tea. I asked him if he knew what Pete was up to.

'Nope – didn't speak to me really. And I couldn't be bothered with him. Well, I'm going back to lie down.'

During the morning I had wandered about along the stream below the camp, getting well below the place where everyone went to relieve their bowels. The water was freezing over, much more so than it had been when we first arrived, and I wondered how long it would be before it became totally frozen, a mini glacier. Meanwhile I watched the big bubble of air under the ice looping and elongating, looking like grey jellyfish or cuttlefish sliding into their hideouts, only to appear again farther down. I was sitting quietly on a boulder when I noticed some movement out of the corner of my eye over to the right, maybe twenty yards away. I turned my head very slowly and carefully so as not to frighten away whatever it was, but there was nothing there. I knew there was something there though. I just had to be patient for a few moments and it would reveal itself.

Sure enough, after five minutes, when I thought my behind would be welded by ice on to the granite rock, the thing did move. It was the woodcock again. I was hoping to see the bird feed, and sure enough, because I kept dead still, it eventually trundled along the edge of the ice on its short little legs, searching for something to eat. With its two-and-a-half-inch beak it picked here and there, finding perhaps larvae of butterflies and moths or even seeds of sedges. But I became so uncomfortable that I had to move, and it immediately rose with a faint clatter of broad wings, and twisted away in rapid flight, giving a brief but welcome resonance of a Scottish moor, or even a Devon tor.

I was very frustrated at not being able to ride out further afield, due to the lack of yak transport. The animals were suffering from lack of food and over-use, and could only work alternate days, I had been told. I wanted to explore further away from the camp, to get into real wilderness, but it was impossible to walk far at this altitude, and the clutter of boulders everywhere made the going extremely difficult. It was also impossible to remain still for long and wait for animals to move and reveal their presence.

However, I did have one other special sighting as I circled the camp from about seven hundred metres away: another of those key-hole side-glimpses, this time of something white, the briefest flicker of movement on the ground a dozen metres away among the boulders. I had been walking as fast as possible and climbing rocks, so was warm enough to keep still again for a few minutes. I stopped and half-sat myself on to a rock so I would blend into its shape. Nothing happened for a while, and again my buttocks froze; but I knew this was the only way I was going to see anything. I stared over at the crags where I had seen the movement, where small crevices made miniature caves, and into which any small creature no bigger than a rabbit could creep and just peep out at this human enemy loitering with intent. My patience had its reward.

Within a couple of minutes an ermine popped out of a hole ten metres away and sniffed the air. It was completely white, or rather just off-white, and I could see its tiny black eyes glistening like wet ebony. It rippled like a snake along a platform of rock and, as it vanished into another hole, its black-tipped tail flipped, reminding me of those tassels made up from its European cousins which end their days on the ceremonial capes of Lords. Say twenty skins to adorn a single cape, multiplied by what, three hundred peers, and double that to include their spouses: twelve thousand ermine stoats. It was a quite staggering thought.

Petocz had not told me to expect these little animals, and indeed, when I related my sighting, said he had not seen one at all. Of course, in the summer they would have been in brown pelage. He concentrated so hard on the big animals that he was quite capable of not noticing anything smaller than a goat. The change into its winter white coat can be achieved in only a few days, and turns a stoat into an ermine. This one did not appear again, even though I nearly froze to the boulder. I thought it would have had quite a good food supply, as I knew they would take ground-nesting birds and their eggs, and that there was a Himalayan mountain vole, *Clithreonomes*, and also the pika, or rock rabbit. Marmots were too big for stoats to tackle.

Marmots had plenty of predators though. The brown bear would dig them out, and so would foxes, and sometimes eagles caught them. Shahik had trapped and cured the skins of hundreds in these valleys. Petocz said that they could weigh as much as 18 pounds. I had hoped to see these large, plump grey animals, but they had already been hibernating for a fortnight before I had got to the valley. All I had seen were their holes, which went deep underground, and were centuries old, perhaps even millennia. All the colony had to do was to graze the alpine pastures for half the year – and sleep the other half.

Here they were right on the southern edge of their Asian range which stretched from the Caspian Sea to the Pacific coast. Petocz had told me that this species were Himalayan or steppe marmots, *Marmota bobak*, while those in North

America are hoary marmots, *Marmot caligata*. The alpine species is *Marmota marmota*, and further, that subspecies have been isolated across these ranges.

He went on, 'They gather bunches of dead grass and sedges to make their winter nests under the ground. Then to survive the extreme cold at this temperature they close off the entrance burrow.'

I wondered how they survived without oxygen, but presumed enough air got in through a port-hole crack in the rocks, and in hibernatory mode they would not use up much air anyway.

Petocz was continuing: 'Breeding begins as soon as spring arrives but their first job is to remove the winter bedding. The 2–4 young are born after 42 days pregnancy in June. In good conditions a marmot can live 20 years.'

Rather to tease him after this scientific spiel, I had asked him if he had ever seen one of these animals performing the famous hay-carting trick, when one animal gathers armfuls of dead grass, lies on its back holding this truss in its arms, and is then pulled backwards by its tail by another marmot to its den, where the hay is easily transported underground for winter fodder. I had read in a book that Swiss farmers had sworn that they had seen this unlikely activity, and another similar tale that rats held hen's eggs in their arms and were towed back to base by another. Another fallacy I had read was that swallows hibernated underwater in ponds and lakes, in tight bunches, clinging claw to claw, beak to beak, for the whole winter, emerging in the spring. Even Gilbert White, one of our great naturalists, seemed to believe that tale.

Petocz had derided me for repeating such twaddle. He seemed to think I believed these stories myself, rather than that I appreciated them for what they were: folklore.

'Well, you never know with nature, do you?' I said. 'Some individuals of a species are more adaptive, intelligent, and entrepreneurial than others, just like us humans.'

The ermine did not reappear, and I needed to move to get my circulation going again so, as it was time for lunch and I was hungry, I made my way back to the camp. Just as I arrived back there was a hubbub of noise, and everyone pointing into the distance with excited shouts of 'Marco Polo! Marco Polo!' In the distance I could just see a party of yaks returning. Through binoculars it became clear that one was loaded with the great head and horns and white body of a ram. Everyone was jumping up and down, hugging and slapping each other on the back, and shouting and laughing. A successful hunt at last, and they could now go home!

As he came into camp Pete dismounted, looking happy for the first time, grinning like a schoolboy who had just won the Victor Ludorum at the end-of-term sports day. The animal he had shot was of phenomenal size, with an unbelievable set of horns curling away on either side of its head, way beyond its ears.

I had the only camera that was working, and so was designated photographer-in-chief. The first picture had to be of the Toyota driver/guide, Ahmed, who wanted to be part of the victory drama, and held the mighty head in his hands. The body had already been skinned, and another yak carried the carcass meat, which would be cooked in due course.

The head was then lifted on to a smooth boulder and I took the standard photographs of hunter and hunted, eyeball to eyeball, head to head, the victor cradling the defeated between his arms. But the big black eyes were now glazed and half-closed, no longer alert, and the long black lashes had begun to drop. Its soft sensitive nose, the size of a rugby ball, which had kept it safe from dangerous intruders for thirteen years by testing a million scents on the air, was now a little bloody.

It was the horns, though, which captured all the attention. Truly the ram wore a crown, or diadem. They curled outwards for one and a half coils, encircling a space five feet across its head. They were corrugated at their base with ripples of horn like those of fossilised sand in an ancient seabed. Such basic patterns are repeated throughout nature: in the clouds, the sand, in fungi and other plants, and, if we could see them, in the wind and air. Such structures are surely an essential part of the evolutionary process. Everything on this planet has its likeness somewhere else, and the connecting thread has its own beauty and expands our human minds.

Certainly, these horns gave humans an emblem of design to magnify their own sense of greatness, however misplaced that might be. It was evident that Pete respected his quarry, but also that it enhanced his own status. Was this the triumph of Zeus over the Gorgon, or was it the other way round?

It was a moment of crossroads for me. One part of me was thrilled to see the triumph that had been played out by an epic battle between two mountain contestants. Another side wished that the perfection before me on the boulder, an animal of almost mythical proportion and ability, had not had to die before its proper time, merely to satisfy the whim and vanity of a human being. Was it acceptable to kill big game? Despite their own skills, the odds were loaded against them: a determined man had weapons that an animal could never outwit. The problem was further confused in this case, as the money paid for that trophy head was going to aid the protection of all the other animals – in theory. In human terms, the leader had died in order that others might live.

I was wondering if this was 'my' ram. I murmured to Khasem. He replied equally quietly, 'I do not think so – he was in a different area – but it is possible. I hope not.'

I hoped not too. Thank God it was not a snow leopard, anyway.

Pete was now keen to take down measurements of his trophy, a record of this triumph, that his satisfaction might be further enhanced. The measurement 'around the curl', as it is termed, that is to say, along the outside diameters, was 60½ inches. The measurement round the base of each horn, the circumference, was 14½ inches. It was truly a trophy head. Pete fished out a couple of cans of beer which he had brought along for just this occasion, and we westerners drank to his success. That evening, when we had eaten, he told us the story of his marathon hunt. I recorded it on my tape-recorder – luckily, like my camera, still working – and transcribed it on my return.

'Well, we took off as usual, soon after two-thirty this morning. I thought the hunt was going nowhere, with snow and sleet blowing and a blizzard mounting. We blundered about again in the dark, so I just sat tight and let the yak do the thinking. Like you said, Rich, that works. We got to the back of that canyon as day started to break, and sure enough there were the same nine young rams still in almost the same place.

'We carried on beyond them, and searched for the twenty-three big rams again, but they had evaporated. I felt pretty bad about that, so sick I felt like vomiting. I had walked away from a world-class ram the day before, after a week of nothing, and now the place was empty. I couldn't understand it. There was no place those critters could go – there's only glaciers at the end of that canyon. I couldn't think they had climbed out, but that was a possibility. So I figured I'd push on into even higher elevation in search of those rams.

'That guide fella was not keen, he kept saying "the end here, nothing further, no ram further". But I got to thinking. They didn't know what was beyond where we were standing. I could tell they had not been any further along that ridge. This was their standard viewing point. It was like Columbus sailing round the globe, and his men frightened they would fall of the edge of the world. I had spotted a bit back on the path a track made by animals that I thought I could follow. So I grabbed my gun, and told them to keep the yaks back, and I just walked on.

'I worked my way uphill for a mile or so, and sure enough, there was a little bench of rock up there that we could not see from where we had been. I crawled on my hands and knees across this bench. Right at that point I got to see those twenty-three rams again. But just as I was getting into position for a shot, the wind changed and was at my back, and taking my scent towards them. Must have been something to do with this goddamn blizzard going over. So they knew I was there, and they were bolting down that hillside with the big one joining in among them. They resembled a bunch of cattle on a ranch when they're bein' rounded up, I can tell you. They were in some hurry, and bunching up, and even jumping over each other.

'I leaned back against a rock about as high as my shoulder, and had my safety off trying to keep the rams in my sights in case I got a break and got an open shot. Then would you believe it, I had trouble that I've never had before. The heat from my face fogged up the lens on my scope, and it iced instantly. I grabbed at my shirt collar and scraped the ice off the damned lens, but it was partly cleared and partly fogged.

'There were boulders all over that slope, so those rams had to separate from one another to get round them. That big ram swung round to the right, separating himself from the remainder of the herd. I happened to be right on him with my scope as he broke around a number of boulders. He was looking small but I guessed he was somewhere between two hundred and three hundred yards by the time I shot, and he was running directly away from me. I cut loose and shot him in the spine in front of his hams. He just went end over end.

When we examined him, I saw the bullet had travelled through his body and come out of his brisket. That bullet hit exactly the right place, shattering his liver, lungs and heart. There was a lot of luck in that shot. He was dead three different ways before he hit the ground.'

Pete stopped for breath, looking around at us all listening intently to his story. He hesitated, and I thought he was waiting for praise. I knew enough about shooting to know that it was more than a 'lucky shot'. It had been a brilliant piece of co-ordination of brain and skill. To have shot an animal clean dead in those circumstances would have been extremely difficult. The man was obviously a superb shot, and I said so.

'Yeh, well, I guess I know what I'm doing. Anyway, I've had enough, I'm for bed.'

The next morning while we were still on our own, he told me the rest of the story, starting with his tale of the first day. Then he continued: 'There was a bit of trouble out there yesterday. I didn't want to say in front of those Afghanis, though I expect they're full of it. I damn well came near to hitting one of them again.'

Apparently, the guide, Soufi Kabouli, and the two bearers on hearing the shot had erupted in great excitement, and had started to 'whoop and holler' and wave their arms about. The yak owners had mistaken the calls for them to hurry up with the animals, and everyone had rushed forward. When they saw the dead beast, the two bearers had pulled out their knives and rushed towards it. Pete had shouted to the guide to ask what the hell they were doing.

'Cut throat,' shouted Soufi Kabouli.

'No! No! I screamed at them, but they were wild and out of control. I got between them and the animal and defended it, but they were all shouting, "Cut throat, cut throat! Is custom!" over and over again. Suddenly I remembered it was the Muslim religious requirement to cut the throat and bleed the animal. Blood is unclean to them. "Hold on, Soufi," I shouted, "stop, we talk." I got them to calm down a bit, and tried to make them understand, first I skin the animal, then they could cut throat. For a while I felt pretty scared, I can tell you. I was alone with what seemed like a bunch of madmen. Me against a gang of wild Wakhis, all armed with knives. There was a lot of muttering, but Soufi Kabouli got them under control, and we got on with it. Strange lot, once they handled the huge size of that ram, they changed completely, and suddenly I was a hero, slapped on the back, and cheered. Mind you, it was pretty hard work, getting that animal bagged up on to the yaks. I'll have to give them a hefty tip, I suppose – but it was worth it. You wait till they see this in the club back home.'

I wondered why he had been so bothered about skinning the animal before they bled it. I was sure they would have been careful to let the blood drain away from the animal and not to soil the skin. They knew what the hunters wanted; and also they would not have wanted to be trampling in the unclean, and to them unholy, mess. Pete did seem to get set in his own ideas, and lost his temper too easily when frustrated. He was used to getting his own way.

Later that afternoon there was another shout of 'Marco Polo! Marco Polo!' as a couple of yaks approached. Sure enough, on the back of one of them was another ram. Shahik had tracked Don's wounded ram across three glaciers, and at one time had crossed the Chinese border, he claimed, though I wasn't so sure that that could have been so. The Russian border, perhaps. This place was such a crossroads of ancient world powers that without satellite navigation one could have been in any of several countries without knowing it. But Shahik had not been challenged by any border guards; not that any seemed to exist among these mountains.

This ram was smaller than Pete's, but with a measurement

of 55 inches around the curve of its horns it was big enough, and Don seemed pretty pleased with it. He turned out in his hunting clothes for a photograph in the last of the daylight, and even managed a kind of grin for this trophy statement. The fact that he had not actually been the one to kill it did not seem to register, nor the skill and persistence that had been involved in dealing with the wounded animal, tracking it for miles. I thought Shahik had done a good job, and made sure he knew I thought that.

The incident brought home to me the blatant and un-necessary need of men to prove dominance over the animal kingdom and its royalty. Once it had been necessary for man to kill such creatures for their own sustenance, either to protect themselves against wild animals or to hunt for food. Now, surely, in our civilised world it is time to celebrate our intellect and show how we have become guardians of the planet and its occupants. But that, unhappily, is wishful thinking.

15

Don left the next morning, accompanied by Dr Amin. He was in a bad way, but satisfied over his 'kill'. He said the briefest of farewells as dawn broke, and frankly we wondered whether he would get out alive. They were transporting him back by stretcher along what they said was the quick route to Qual-y-panja, very close to the Russian border. There was much bitter muttering and shaking of fists among the men after he had gone, because he had not tipped enough. But that might have been standard practice for any reward in this hostile place: they did grumble most of the time. After all, the 'ground crew', as Pete called the Afghan workers, had to suffer the same difficulties and discomfort of living as we did, but with the extra burden of doing all the work, and without that vital spark of interest in the surroundings: for the Americans the lure of the hunt; for myself, the excitement of the magnificent scenery and chance to see a new habitat and new creatures – and especially the tantalising and now totally absorbing thoughts of the snow leopard.

Shahik had gone back to Sargass, his task completed. Soufi Kabouli had already left. I gathered that he had had enough of Pete and his behaviour over the prize Marco Polo. His farewell had seemed rather curt, but Pete told me he had given the man a good tip.

I had assumed that once Pete had shot the trophy Marco Polo head that he had sought so obsessively, that the camp would break up and we would all make our way back down from this high hostile place. But he still had an ambition to get a trophy ibex head, and before going off to bed the previous evening had decreed that we stay put.

'I've paid out a helluva lot of dollars to this set-up, and I ain't goin' to leave until I've got what I want.'

That day, 13 October, he was going to have a rest and stay in the camp, and so it was arranged that Petocz, Khasem, and myself would have a trip out. We were accompanied by the young orphaned Raschid, who rode on the yak behind Khasem. The plan was to explore the farthest reaches of Afghanistan's most northern border with Russia. We set out a little after dawn for an area that Petocz wanted to check. It was a day that was nearly to bring disaster for me, but also the most thrilling encounter so far with what I was longing to see.

We rode for three hours northward through the valleys and then over a pass of about 14,000 feet towards the source of the Dry-y-Panja, the Pamir River. There were patches of crisp snow in the shadows of boulders along our way which the yaks tried to lick in passing, but we all knew by now that they had to be stopped or 'they would become lazy and not travel so fast'. I personally thought that they might get colic, but knew better than to say it aloud. Snow covered all the scree slopes on the northern and eastern sides right down to our level, and then the mountains reared high above that scree to about 16,000 feet or more. It was all quite magnificent and I knew how lucky I was to be part of it all. We were somewhere near Concord Peak, which presumably had been named in the Victorian era, in those days when all the rulers were either brothers or cousins, as part of an agreement over territory between Britain and Russia.

The air was warm enough in this sheltered valley for us to shed our thick winter-weather coats, although Khasem kept his red windcheater tightly buttoned to his neck, with a black sweater beneath that. Petocz seemed warm enough in his grey sweater with its white zig-zag pattern across the chest and his usual blue jeans. Both wore their enormous wide, black astrakhan hats, which kept the chill out of their heads. I was glad to see young Raschid had been kitted out with warm garments from somewhere, including a white turban which had probably belonged to his father. I wondered how Don was getting on: if he had dressed a bit more sensibly he might not have got so ill – a warm hat would have kept the cold out of his sinus tubes for a start. I remembered that the French hunter we had briefly met as we came up had been wearing a thick woollen peaked cap, and he had not suffered. But then, he was probably pretty fit in the first place. I was glad again of grandfather's Harrods' camel-hair balaclava, which I kept clamped to my head both day and night. It seemed to be adequate for the purpose.

We came across a pretty sight after crossing the pass, when the ground sloped gently downwards towards two large blue glittering lakes in the valley a mile or more ahead. These were near the source of the Pamir River and a little downstream of Lake Zor Kol, as far as Khasem and Petocz knew. Beyond them, brilliant white snow slopes with blue shadows rose into white cumulus clouds, which at times became part of the mountains, as though both land and sky were floating serenely above the surface of the lake and changing their shapes second by second. High above them, the sun beat down and its reflection hammered the lake into a million sparks.

'As far as Petocz and Khasem knew' – but in truth they didn't really know where we actually were. I had thought we were on a routine tour of the district as far as the others were concerned, but it now turned out that neither of them had ever been in the area before. I had presumed they knew it well. They discussed the situation a little uneasily, Petocz showing apprehension at trespassing over the Russian border. Looking at the maps much later, back in the camp, it seemed that the lake was indeed on the border between Russia and Afghanistan, but it was not clear as to which shore this border ran along: north or south. Again, back in camp, some of the Wakhis were convinced that the mountains were in Chinese territory. But at that moment, up there, totally away from any sign of so-called civilisation, I didn't really care where we were, or what country we were in. I was seized with a euphoria of spirit, and just wanted to get down to that lake and see what was the temperature of the water, and whether there were any birds on it, or plants in it, or maybe just to enjoy being next to such an extraordinary and surprising scene.

However, Petocz insisted on checking out the area first for his own records, and so we lay up behind a boulder which was facing the sun and reflecting the heat, so that we warmed up for a while. Then we glassed the whole area to see if there was anything about. But it was too bright and exposed for anything to dare to move, whether sheep, ibex, or leopard. They would easily be seen in that clear air. Yet there was an Egyptian vulture circling around on the other side of the lake. Although it was quite high, perhaps something had died out there. My mind immediately began to roam over the possibilities of a snow leopard kill. The sun was on our right side, and we were looking north into what would appear to be Russia. I searched for any sign of human life. If we were on the Russian border, surely there would be a watchtower. We had seen them lower down. I even imagined a patrol of soldiers or a vehicle, but there was no hint that any human had ever been there, or ever would, and the thought evaporated. This was real wilderness, and apparently untouched. For the first time I felt completely relaxed.

The others seemed to have dozed off. Raschid curled up at my feet like a dog. He was an only child and now totally alone, and his behaviour was like any stray animal. He needed to feel he belonged. Such moments of companionship were giving him a rock to cling to. He didn't speak much, but when he wanted my attention he would grab my coat, and with his eyes wide open, would say urgently, 'Meesta Reesha!'.

In that short moment of total silence, with the others asleep, the universe seemed poised and timeless, as though we were suspended on an earth that was totally benign and without conflict. Nothing had ever sullied this valley. Nothing modern had ever been anywhere near it. It was pristine and primeval. Throughout Europe the mountains, however majestic, had cable cars to take noisy skiers to their summits. Even in the seemingly remotest Himalayas, climbers had documented every known finger and foot hold, and today it is all on computer and can be looked up on intrusive websites. I knew I too was an intruder, and felt guilty about that, but mainly I felt very lucky to be able to sit and look at the scene before me. I breathed the cold clear air. This was my own garden of Eden, a paradise to hold in the mind; an experience to sustain me for the rest of my life.

The others stirred, and we decided to explore a little further. The yaks had been grazing the sedges and had wandered a little distance away, but Raschid soon gathered them up and, holding on to their reins, led them for us while we walked to the shore of the lake. We came across a couple of large Marco Polo skulls with their horns attached, which were lying on the meadow. They had been there some long time, years perhaps, and the skulls were bleached as white as the moon. I took a photograph of them together on a smooth white glacial boulder. Petocz examined them and declared that they had both been seven years of age, and I noticed their horns had developed in totally different ways. One had begun its third spiral, and was long and thin with blade-like edges to the horns, and very sharp points at the extremities, like daggers. The base of these was only as thick as a man's forearm. Petocz got out his tape measure, finding the measurement around the spiral from tip to tip was fifty-two inches. The other skull was only thirty inches, but with much thicker base measurements, as thick as a man's thigh. We found ibex horns too, one enormous set which had curled right back over the animal's head and would have almost touched its back. Each was forty-seven inches long. Petocz said this animal was thirteen years of age. Its molars were worn down almost to the bone, so it probably died of old age.

We had brought cheese and naan, and ate that right at the edge of the lake. A hundred-yard-wide stream bed led off westwards, the water little more than a trickle flowing haphazardly through huge smooth boulders formed over many years by glacial flow, and in recent times by spring floods caused by winter snow melt. Petocz said that this was the border with Russia. It was very cold. The sun had warmed to exactly one degree centigrade above freezing, as measured on my little Swedish thermometer. The lake would certainly freeze hard at night. I had not washed properly or removed my clothes for a fortnight, and longed to feel clean again. I wished I was strong enough to swim in that icy fresh water and feel the exhilaration that I had felt as a boy at school having a cold shower every morning, before the rest of the school was awake. When I said this, Khasem just grinned in disbelief and Petocz said I was an idiot. Khasem told Raschid what I had said, and he looked at me in amazement before hiding his face in the side of the yak.

I had a good look into the lake, but could see nothing growing there, no plants, fish or even insects. Petocz told me he had been told that back in the Victorian days a British army officer had explored these lakes and had brought along a plumb line of 100 metres to determine the bottom of the lake at the end of the Wakhan Corridor. He had portaged a skin boat up here by yak and gone out to the middle of the lake, and begun to drop his line. He had bottomed after only about four metres. That was all.

'Was it this actual lake?'

Petocz pursed his lips and shrugged his shoulders. 'Possibly – I'm not totally sure.'

There were no feathers to be seen of birds that might have dipped in here for a wash and brush up while on migration, which I thought rather odd. Wild duck, such as ruddy shelduck, would surely have dropped in for a rest and preen, as this was the time of the autumn migration to India out of Russia, and left at least one feather for me to see on this windward shore. But then I realised I was being rather stupid. That big ginger-coloured duck, looking almost goose-like, would already have been through its late summer moult on its Tibetan lakes, where it also bred, at a height of 17,000 feet, in the same way that its similar cousin, the common shelduck, moults in the Baltic, becoming totally flightless for six weeks until new feathers allow it to become airborne again, and ready for the southward flight for the winter.

I had first seen ruddy shelduck on Lake Habbaniya in Iraq, when stationed there in the RAF. I had been amazed when an ancient fowler I met on the Suffolk marshes, when I was sixteen, told me he had shot a pair one night during a moonless flight. 'But that were a long time ago, boy,' he had said as he looked up into the sky, remaining silent for a few moments. 'Ah – that were when I were your age, too.' Hardly believing him, I had looked them up in one of my grandfather's books, to find that occasionally the birds had been known to erupt westwards, spectacularly so in 1892, to Britain and even the USA.

I knew that another duck that would possibly migrate over this lake on its way to India was wigeon. I longed to find a feather, as I had often searched for them on the marshes at home in England, just to have a link with its journey. I suppose that this is the same as a dedicated trainspotter, or 'anorak' as they were dismissively called, collecting the engine numbers of those giants vanishing in clouds of steam on their journeys to far places, and leaving only a moment of brief encounter: but a memory that would last for ever.

What was this need to connect with such objects? To relate to something bigger than oneself? Is that why people flocked to see the great and the good; why they made pilgrimages to Rome, or lined the route of a royal procession? I realised, in these last weeks, that the snow leopard had for many years been my 'royal personage', my Flying Scotsman; or, I thought now rather wryly, actually my Mallard, since I was searching for wildfowl feathers along their rail track journey towards the south. Mallard was the engine that had broken, and still held, the world speed record for steam. I had seen it once, at rest in its museum, with a carapace of latent energy and presence. It had been named together with most of the other A4 Pacific class locomotives after the evocative names of birds – Merlin, Eagle, Wild Swan, Peregrine, Osprey, Kingfisher, Golden Plover were those that I could remember of the list. But all conjured up those grand qualities of strength and speed and beauty.

The snow leopard had all those qualities in abundance. I wished now that I had seen the creature in the zoo in Kabul. At least I would have seen it, despite the miserable surroundings in which it had been housed. But I knew that would not really have assuaged the need that had grown within my mind. It would have been too depressing. No – the snow leopard belonged to the impossibly wild places on the edge of civilisation – no, more, beyond civilisation. And so I kept watch on the sky to the north where I had seen the Egyptian vulture circling, and decided I had to go and have a look there. Remounting my yak, I set off.

Petocz and Khasem followed half-heartedly for fifty yards, then stopped. Petocz shouted that we must be at the Russian border. Young Raschid ran after me and tugged at my coat, looking very worried, and said something in Pashto with the inevitable 'Meesta Reesha', trying to stop me from going on. But, feeling supremely confident and strong in mind, I brushed him off, determined to see more. I urged my yak through the stream flowing out of the lake – Petocz's 'probable Russian border' – and continued.

The boulders were very smooth along that river bed, having been embedded and worn down for centuries by glaciers and winter floods. The yak did not like them. They must have felt slippery under its feet, and after a hundred yards or so it stopped and refused to move. But I had seen the Egyptian vulture drop down, and was determined to find the spot. I got off the obstinate beast and walked ahead, leading – pulling – it by the rope attached to its nose. I could see Petocz and Khasem watching me, and young Raschid jumping up and down, throwing his hands up in the air and shouting something back at the others as he sat down on a boulder and watched me leave.

I stepped carefully from boulder to boulder, waiting each time for the yak to make its little jump behind me. I felt very free and adventurous at leaving the others and being on my own in this vast landscape. I wanted to get completely away, out of sight: to be totally alone – to find the vulture and the snow leopard kill I was now sure it was feasting on; and, I was also sure, to see at last the creature itself, which had to be nearby.

The yak however had its own ideas. After another hundred yards it became more hesitant, staring down at the gaps and the deep drops between the boulders. Then finally, on the top of a huge boulder as big as a hippopotamus, which was completely isolated from the others, the animal stopped dead and refused to budge. I found myself pulling its head forward as hard as I could. The animal snorted wildly, but stayed put.

Afterwards I wondered why the nostril bridge hadn't given way and whether I had perhaps permanently damaged it. It was of course a crazy thing to do, but at the time my only thought was to get forward into the unknown area ahead, because I knew the snow leopard was there and would show itself to me. The place where the vulture had gone down on to something – and that could only be the remains of a kill carcass – was only a couple of hundred metres ahead. I was sure there would be tracks all around and that the leopard would be close by, even asleep in its den.

I thought of going on alone and leaving the yak to find its way back to the others. But it was marooned on this blasted rock, and would not go either backwards or forwards, and seemed completely helpless. The other two men were some way back, and showed no sign of having noticed there was a problem. There was nothing to do but to try and get the yak back the way we had come. Somehow, I would have to get it to turn round.

But Raschid had seen there was a problem, and he now came forward, jumping over the gaps where he could and sometimes climbing down, when he vanished from sight, so deep were the holes between some of the boulders. Eventually he was next to me, grinning like a little pixie, pulling my coat with his 'Meesta Reesha', and, taking hold of the nose rope, started to coax the yak, which responded more willingly to his hushed tones of reassurance. Once he had got it turned round, he eventually got it to jump back the way it had come, on to the next boulder, and then the next, where he waited for me to follow. I had no intention of going back, and told him I was going on; but of course, he had no idea what I was saying. I pointed to my chest and then flung my arm to the north, while waving my other hand at him to say go back. He understood that and looked very worried, saying something in an urgent tone, obviously some kind of warning as he waved his hands towards where the others were resting, showing he wanted me to go back to them.

I could see Petocz shouting and waving his hand backwards, and then he crossed his arms in a kind of semaphore signal, meaning 'no go'. He was clearly worried and agitated. I ignored him, and went forward, leaving Raschid and the yak to make their way back. I knew he could cope. It was only that last boulder that had been too difficult for the yak. I wended my way across and round the boulder maze until I came to smaller boulders, and then level scree with patches of snow in the shadows. I thought, just a little further and I'll see what is out there, and then I'll hurry back.

The sun was still up, and I had completely forgotten about the three-hour journey back to base camp. The vulture had not flown up, so it must still be feeding. I crouched low and crept forward a couple of hundred yards to where I thought it should be. My feet crunched in hard snow lying in the shadows, and occasionally clattered on dry pebbles lying in warm sun when I slipped slightly. It sounded alarmingly loud to me, and would surely alert any wild creature that danger was afoot. I slowed right down and moved, as I hoped, more like Grey Owl of the famous Canadian stories of the 1930s. I rested for a minute or two, because I had begun to get short of breath and my heart was pumping fast.

Then I stood up very slowly, and peered between the boulders where a snow drift was lying in deep shadow ahead. Every sense went on breath-stopping alert. I knew there was something there. Whether I had heard a faint sound, or whether there was a shadow movement to one side my eyes had not quite caught, I don't know; but I knew something was just around the boulder, twenty paces or so ahead. My heart was pounding even more, and I had to sit down and let the adrenalin flow through my body while I rested a minute.

My mind raced even faster than my heart. What if it was a

bear right next to me? What could I do if I was face to face with it and maybe its cub? I had no weapon, not even a stick. If it was a snow leopard it would run off: no, it would have known I was there and already have vanished. It had to be a vulture. It could only be a vulture. I wanted to see, but found I couldn't move. I didn't know if I was being indecisive or cautious. Neither, this is reconnaissance, I told myself. General Montgomery had said 'Time spent in reconnaissance is not time wasted.' But it wasn't any of those; I literally couldn't move.

Then I really heard a noise. Some sort of dull tearing, or perhaps a big stone being moved. I felt instinctively for my camera in my pocket, and realised that it was in my backpack tied on to the saddle of the yak. The noise and my own slight movement unlocked my body, and I felt the taut tension disappear. I moved forward slowly, hoping to get a glimpse of whatever it was, and prepared to move back equally carefully if it was unfriendly. But I had hardly started forward when there came a violent thrashing of wings, and the black and white vulture, with its piggy little eyes and scrawny neck and pale grappling beak gaping a squawk, was taking off in great alarm from a mere ten paces ahead.

I was rather pleased with myself that I had got so close to it. This was a creature as wild as they get, and it had not known I was there. Later Petocz said it was likely only a camp follower and no doubt used to humans, and probably fed on the scraps at our base. I didn't think so, and felt he was just trying to put me down. Now it had flown I could get a good look at what it had been feeding on. A shoulder of the snow drift told the story which must have started during the previous night, or certainly in the very early daylight hours, and showed me there had been a tremendous drama – or so it seemed to me. The remains of a young ibex were scattered across the disturbed pebbled scree. Its body was in deep shadow from the overhang, which hid it from above and explained why every vulture in the area had not been present at such a feast.

I could see it had been killed without much of a struggle. The lower neck had been gripped to kill it, and the organs from the pleural cavity had been eaten. Perhaps the animal was already wounded, and had couched there in hiding and had been surprised. I examined its legs and they were not broken or wounded. It had to be a snow leopard kill – but why hadn't the animal dragged the carcass to safety, as would have been its usual behaviour? Although perhaps out here there was no need for 'usual behaviour'. Perhaps the animal had eaten its fill and would return later for more. Perhaps I had disturbed it when clattering about on the boulders nearer the lake: there was a lot of noise, and it was only a few hundred yards away. Perhaps it had hidden up nearby, and was watching me. That seemed unlikely; but I got a sudden frisson of possible contact and nearness of this elusive creature. I scouted around, feeling terribly excited, and quite forgetting everything else about the day's plan.

Then I saw the tracks: the tracks of the snow leopard where it had touched the snow. There was no mistaking those again, and they had slight smears of blood from the kill. I tried to follow the departing tracks, but they gave out with the last tiny drops of blood on the snow, and then nothing more on the dry pebbles beyond. As a boy I had read the account by Sir Henry Rider Haggard of how a bushman in Africa had followed the track of a wounded animal for hundreds of yards across dry stony ground by creeping forward on hands and knees, blowing the ground very gently to find which stones had been invisibly touched by the animal's feet, which had knocked off fragments of dust, which could be seen when blown. That kind of skill is gained over a lifetime, and was totally beyond me. But I found an area of dried sedge heavily grazed around, which would have been a feeding place of the ibex. It was a young animal, probably weak for some reason, and the snow leopard would have singled it out and made its kill. The herd would have fled in terror. Then I realised that the overhang where I had found the body was actually the cache site. I needed to look for where it had been killed.

Standing up to look around to get my bearings, I became aware of shouting, and with a jolt suddenly realised where I was. Looking round with a certain amount of fear, I was glad to realise it was young Raschid coming to find me. The adventure, my second close encounter with the shadow, was over. Third time lucky, I said to myself.

16

That night we had a splendid supper cooked by Pete, which we ate in the bear cave to make it more ceremonial. The main dish was steaks trimmed off his Marco Polo ram, but to our amazement he produced some treats bought from the one and only Kabul supermarket we had visited just before we left town. These he had hoarded for a month, packed at the bottom of his gear out of sight of everyone, and kept secret for the special night of celebration that he had dreamed of for twenty-five years. It was only for our small group. The Afghani men ate their usual fare of meat and rice, but with very generous helpings of meat from his beast. We started with oxtail soup. Macaroni cheese accompanied the steaks. Tinned ham and a dish of beans followed. Then we had biscuits and cream cheese. Tinned peaches and pears almost finished us off. Our stomachs had shrunk during the past weeks on boiled lamb and rice, but there was now another very special treat to follow.

It was some sort of tea that his wife had made herself, apparently mainly out of rosehips and some special herbs, but he wouldn't tell us which. This tea had already caused resentment by the local Afghanis, as Pete refused to drink their brew and always insisted on hot water, to which he added one of his own home-made 'tea' bags. It was not the sort of brew I was used to and, frankly, it tasted rather weird; but I drank most of my mugful with feigned enthusiasm. Pete watched each of us carefully as we drank. He wanted his wife's love and devotion to be given full credit and not sullied by indifference or frivolous remarks.

'Mmm – delicious, very refreshing. Just what we needed. Like a hot toddy. How very clever of your wife to make it,' I said, between mouthfuls.

'Yeh, I allus take some with me on my hunting trips. It keeps me going.'

I nearly laughed – thinking that it would no doubt keep me going with the 'reply of the tea' in the middle of the night. Still, having a pee at forty below was not too much of a problem now, not like the dreadful night or two when alpine sickness had struck. I had become accustomed to the altitude and the intensity of the cold, while the stars were always an incredible sight.

We were huddled around the fire in the cave, reluctant to break up this special moment, which we all realised meant a great deal to Pete, before turning in for the night. In a moment of silence something strange happened. There was the sudden sound of wolves howling, very briefly, like someone tuning an instrument before a concert, but they sounded quite close.

'They can smell the meat,' Khasem said.

'Well, they won't get any,' Pete replied. 'Not till we've done with it anyway.'

The Kabul Afghans looked nervous, and muttered among themselves. I imagined they had probably been raised on mythic tales of wolves which ate babies and old people, and even perhaps had magic powers. The local men were completely indifferent, and showed no reaction. They were oblivious by then anyway, with their pipe dreams. I remembered what I had read in the books of the American writer and film-maker Lois Crisler who, with her husband, had lived with wolves in Alaska. The titles of the books jumped into my mind – *Arctic Wild* and *Captive Wild*. They had revealed what wolves were really like, dispelling the ancient mythic tales. They had found the animals caring, communicative, and always ready to please and forgive. I remembered she wrote that she had once howled with them, and had a strange response. I thought I would try it, and see what happened. I said as much to our group, and Khasem raised his voice and told the others.

I went to the cave entrance and stepped out into the silent night, with its vast panoply of stars. My brothers and I had used wolf howls as a contact when we were children, copying from our father, who had once been a boy scout in Wolf Patrol – one of Baden Powell's first ever, he was fond of telling us. Now taking a deep breath, I opened my mouth and howled into the night. Instantly there was a single high long howl in reply.

I turned back into the cave. Everyone was looking at me. I could see eyes wide open, Petocz grinning sardonically, and the Afghanis frozen with horror. Raschid had hidden his face with his arm. Even the dazed local herders seemed to wake from their torpid indifference. A few seconds of silence, then a chorus of howls broke out and echoed round the cave. The pack must have been only a couple of hundred yards or so from us, perhaps less. The howls changed from a high yodel to a low moan, and I could hear individual animals singing, or nearly growling, different long-drawn notes across almost the whole octave range. Nobody said a word, but everyone was alert and tense. I could sense they were all feeling somewhere deep inside themselves that same primeval urge to hunt, that we were a pack, and that this was a part of life on the precipice of existence. For myself, I felt a sense of elation. We had communicated. I had spoken to wolves and they had replied. I felt closer than ever to the natural world.

The howling suddenly stopped: the silence seemed almost as eerie as the noise. I looked outside again and thought I could see shadowy creatures moving off and out into the snowy landscape. I suddenly realised what I had done, and the effect it might have on these rather superstitious men in this primitive place. I turned back inside.

'They've gone,' I said loudly, knowing Khasem would relay my words to the men. 'Off hunting. That was the pack call to gather together and go. I've heard it before. They won't be back.'

Khasem duly obliged, and with some relief I saw the men relax and revert to normal. Raschid lifted his head and looked at me. I hadn't meant to frighten him. I smiled and winked, and he grinned back

'That was one hell of a moment, Rich,' said Pete. 'You know something? This place has given me one of the great moments of all my life, perhaps the greatest moment.' He was silent for a second, then continued, 'And boy, that's sure saying something.'

'Worth all the cold and the hardship?'

'You bet.'

'Me too.'

I stood shoulder to shoulder with this taciturn adventurer, who, it seemed, had had more stories to tell than Ernest Hemingway, but all of them completely true. We shook hands.

'Better turn in, Rich, I wanna be off first thing to have a last go for an ibex.'

I lingered outside, looking up at the mountain peaks soaring in stark shadows up to the sky. I thought of my father and his scaling of all those peaks of his life, which required as much courage of mental conflict as this mere physical conflict with bodily discomfort. He had experienced that in the trenches of the First World War, and overcome it, and the rest of his life had fought to explain what he called 'Truth'; really, I thought, the meaning and purpose of life, real life. My mind went back to that night in Regent's Park Zoo in the great winter of 1963, when Father had held his own against the academic literati and titled big names. He knew and understood things far beyond mere facts. That night at the zoo, I had had a magical moment with the wolves out in the dark, which Father would dearly like to have experienced instead of talking business with publishers. Tonight had far surpassed that. What would Father had made of this close encounter, this communion, with wolves under an icy moon? I thought of the Great Winter chapter in *Tarka*, which always took me to that faraway, almost unattainable place of the mind's apogee, and always left me moved to tears. Would I be able to do that? I ruefully reminded myself that I had come here to write a working script for a film, and that I already had a full time, 24/7 job. Apart from his time as a farmer in the Second World War, Father had written full time – that had been his 24/7 job. My tale will probably have to wait, I thought. But I promised myself then, as I stared up at the stars, that one day I would write of this adventure. And now, rather more years later than I had ever envisaged, I have.

I know my adventure cannot compare with those of climbing Everest for the first time, or reaching the South Pole, or forging the North-West passage, or crossing the Empty Quarter with Burton or Lawrence, or surviving on the remote Russian island of Kolguev, as had Trevor Battye. I had travelled to all those places in my imagination, as I read the stories of those grand adventures, where hardship and self-reliance and skill had been tested to extremes. But this unexpected, almost accidental trip to the remote wilderness of the Wakhan had given me the chance to experience the reality of the edgy excitement and danger that was involved; to experience in some measure the hardships of the lives of the people who lived here. Above all it gave me the chance to see for myself what it was really like, to watch animals and birds I had never thought to see. I would never forget those wolves, yet I still had not achieved my real heart's desire – to see the creature I most wanted – that elusive shadow of the clouds, the snow leopard. And I was not going to: my dream must remain just a dream.

I suddenly realised how cold I was getting, standing still lost in my own thoughts. Everyone else had vanished. A final pee to get rid of Pete's special tea-brew, and I crept into my sleeping bag.

The next morning grey clouds of falling snow obscured the hills every half hour or so, to be followed by moments of warm sunshine. Pete had gone out at dawn, accompanied by Khasem, for one last search for a prize-head ibex. Petocz and I watched some yearling ibex in the distance playing a game of butting and leaping, their small black tails flicking in excitement, just like the older animals a day or so before. Farther along the hills three larger males were clashing, exciting another crowd of yearlings and females which came to watch, stimulating those young to clash as well.

'Rather like a football crowd,' I remarked.

Petocz's only reply was a sardonic sotto voce 'Hmmm.' I knew he still considered my remarks facetious and stupid. To him I was not a true scientist, while I thought he missed the wider picture. Even though we were about to leave, he was still making notes and keeping records with as much concentration as ever. After a while the old males lay down. Petocz watched them through his telescope, and then offered it to me. I could see their black beards moving rhythmically up and down, and realised they were chewing the cud. After a while they rested their heads on the ground.

'Taking off the weight of their horns. Those big ones weigh 20 pounds or so, and are too heavy to hold upright all day. I've seen that a lot,' Petocz said, as he continued to make marks in his notebook.

It became so cold our toes felt frozen, literally, despite sudden glares of hot sun from the sky, from stone and snow

244

reflections. The air felt different, and I had a feeling of being suspended, almost dangling in space on an invisible thread of unreality, and it was unsettling. I wondered if my brother had felt this, when, ascending in his glider, he rose up fast and suddenly through the ice and occlusion of that pyramid of cloud, reaching the height of almost thirty thousand feet, a record, suddenly popping out at the top into brilliant light and incredible icy cold, as he had told me.

'I'm going for a walk round to get warm,' I told Petocz. He just nodded.

I trudged around the camp as far out as I could safely go, hoping, ever hoping, for that sighting of a snow leopard, but knowing it wouldn't happen, certainly not here. Unless, of course, the young ibex attracted them. I found the remains of a snowcock, which had been caught by an eagle and pulled to bits on the snow, leaving only a few of its grey feathers, speckled with black, mimicking all the mixture of colours in the granite rocks. Every part had been eaten. I looked at the marks on the ground. Strangely there were no signs of vultures having landed, which they would have done if any part of the bird had been left, so the eagle had carried the remains of the bird away. It had left impressions of its enormous feet and claws as ice-casts, where the trampled snow had melted momentarily and frozen again. I picked up the feathers for my collection, as I had on previous occasions.

Later in the afternoon, as I arrived back at the camp, another guide appeared, having, I learned, ridden over an alternative pass from Sargass, as that was now impassable. He had come to find out what the situation was: time was running out and everyone was getting edgy. When I first saw him, he had dismounted and was standing still by a boulder. I only noticed he was there because part of the boulder suddenly seemed to tumble away, giving me quite a start. He came forward grinning away like a schoolboy, apparently not in the least cold despite the journey and his lack of suitable clothing. He had no overcoat or other high mountain equipment, except for a balaclava and a pair of alpine goggles. What he did have was a tweed jacket of exactly the same blend of colours as those feathers on the snowcock, which seemed a remarkable and happy coincidence, or a brilliant piece of teleology. The jacket was frayed at the cuffs through years of wear, and probably had been his father's before him.

He introduced himself as Ahmaddin Nangyyar. I told him my name. He nodded: he had heard about me. We exchanged a few remarks as we sized each other up. I explained that I was from the BBC and preparing the ground for a film to be made the next summer. He discussed the animals we could hopefully film. There was nothing new, nothing that I had not already noted and decided, but as a matter of form these pleasantries were exchanged. Then he said something that thrilled me, and almost made me jump out of my skin, although for him it was only a remark in passing. He said that he had seen a snow leopard that morning as he came through the pass.

'Really?' I almost yelled. 'Tell me more – tell me exactly what you saw!'

While we had been talking young Raschid had sidled forward. He had been scrubbing cooking dishes in the stream. He noticed my reaction, knew something had excited me and spoke to Ahmaddin. The lad was very bright and alert, and aware of everything that went on. I could tell from his expression that he had asked what the man had said, and Ahmaddin told him. Raschid looked at me, beaming, was silent for a moment, then tugging at my coat as he often did, burst out with a torrent of words. I caught the occasional 'Meesta Reesha'. When he had finished, he stood silently, looking at me anxiously, then at Ahmaddin, who also looked from the boy to me.

'He has just told me that you have been looking for a snow leopard, that you and he have had a bit of an adventure, trying to track one. That this is very important to you. Yes?'

I nodded. Ahmaddin put his hand on the boy's head and ruffled his hair and laughed and said, 'OK. We find the snow leopard to show Mr. Richard. OK. OK.' And turning back to me, 'We go back through the same pass, there is good chance.'

Raschid could not have understood the words, but he understood their meaning. He clapped his hands together, laughed, and then rushed off to collect his pots.

To me, Ahmaddin's words seemed a statement of fact, not speculation. I had heard the men speaking about him with respect. The man knew the area better than anyone else. I felt a sense of relief and confidence. I was very aware that time was running out. We were supposed to have left already. But tough old Pete was determined to get his prize ibex at whatever cost. He had returned as a fox, and insisted on yet another day. I gathered Ahmaddin had been sent for as the best chance to find him a good trophy. However, while he stayed on, there was still also a chance for me to achieve my dream, and now it had new purpose.

We had some more Marco Polo steak that night. Pete suddenly said, rather lugubriously, 'Waal, that'll run out in a day or so, and we don't have any jerky to keep us going. If you get snowed in any place, Rich, you need jerky to see you through.'

He had mentioned this iron ration frequently, but although I knew what it was, I didn't know how it was made.

'What exactly is jerky Pete? How do you make it?'

'It's what keeps you alive when you got nothin' else. It's simple enough to make. I've brought a little, enough for myself for days out as it were, but not enough for the winter out here. Especially if we had to share it.'

He didn't seem to realise the import of his words. Would

he really make everyone stay on to the point of no return, just so he could get his prize?

'It's easy enough to make. I do it as a routine every autumn, just like my wife makes her tea, and pickle.'

Then he explained what he did. He cut strips of meat from the shoulder and neck of a deer or other herbivore. This was soaked in a 50/50 mixture of salt and sugar, and black and white pepper. This was then piled criss-cross and left for three days, then dried in the oven at 100 degrees or in a smoke house. Then it was wrapped in cloth and paper 'so's it can breathe'.

'Doesn't it ever go mouldy?' I asked.

'You can get rid of that with vinegar,' he said shortly.

He also made what he called real iron-ration jerky, which was the meat sliced 'real fine' and mixed with raisins, prunes, and nuts, which had also been sliced 'real fine'. He then heated tallow, which was entrail fat, and poured the resulting liquid over the jerky to bind it, and let it all set in tins to mould as blocks.

'I guess we could do somethin' like that up here if we need to,' he ended.

He was then silent and stuck his head down low into his shoulders. I felt a bit worried. Had he realised that he had misjudged things, and that there was a possibility that we might get stuck up here? He had always relied on his jerky to keep him going on his hunting trips, it was almost a talisman. But he had only a little left, enough for, what, a couple of days, just for himself and perhaps some for me? If we got stuck here, then we were talking months, and I doubted if we could survive. But none of the Afghan guides seemed to be unduly worried. I looked at Pia, who had been keeping very quiet and out of the way in recent days. He caught my eye and shrugged.

The expression on Pete's face changed. He had that far-away look that he had when he first arrived, when he was planning the next move. So I was not surprised to hear him say, 'I'll go out again before dawn, Rich, and get us an ibex, then at least —'

He didn't complete the sentence, but I finished it off in my own mind: 'then at least we'll have something to eat if we get snowed up'. It was not a comforting thought, and rang hollow in my head.

Pete got to his feet. 'I'll get my head down then. Night all.' And he left.

As I also got up, Pia stood up and came over to me. 'We've been talking, Khasem and Ahmaddin and me,' he said. 'Tomorrow *has* to be the last day. The season is closed in, and we cannot stay here any longer. Too dangerous. So you can go out with him to Toleibai if you want. Ahmaddin will go with you, he has much experience – and the boy insists on going with you. Starting at 3 a.m.'

I nodded my thanks and shook his hand. This was the chance I had waited for. Nothing would have stopped me from going, now it had been offered. So, in the middle of the night, I left the warmish cocoon of the bedroll for the bitter black of a 3 a.m. winter night sky, that had no stars and only the bleak pallor of grey snow on the ground. Despite my excitement, it was not a good moment. It was snowing and the cold was almost sickening. I was glad I did not have to put on any clothes, as I had been wearing all of them all night, including my long white thick sea-boot socks that naval personnel wore on Arctic patrols in the war. At least, I thought, I haven't got to hack ice off the ship like they had to, in case it became top heavy and rolled. A couple of Afghani men had brought the yaks forward already saddled, and with a bag of small provisions. Young Raschid was waiting for us, hopping from one foot to the other, very cheerful but very cold. Tea was handed round, and naan bread with a lump of almost inedible cheese. Pete was very taciturn. I thought he was probably annoyed at the presence of myself and Raschid. A hunt has to be a solitary affair if it is to be successful, and he was set on getting his ibex. Ahmaddin said something to Raschid which made him cower slightly. I presumed he had said something like, 'Behave yourself and keep quiet – or else.'

We all set off, Ahmaddin leading the way, then Pete, telling me to stay behind and to keep very quiet. I indicated to Raschid to get up on the yak behind me, putting my finger on my lips to indicate silence. He looked as pleased and happy at that as if I had given him a fortune. I felt sorry for him, but also a great deal of affection. He was so unassuming, like a young puppy that just wanted a pat on the head and to be told it was a good dog. He clung to my back and tucked himself in as close as possible, despite my wooden saddle sticking into him. He reminded me of my own son, still much younger than this lad, only seven years old, but already with much the same 'ready-for-anything' attitude. Bonding between a father and his children at a young age is very important, what Pete called being 'buddies'. My own father had tried on occasions, times which remained a precious, though fragmentary, memory for me. I hoped my own children would have good memories of me. This lad had lost his father, but it was evident, by the way he had transferred his attention to me, that they had got on well together.

As we trudged out of the camp on our three yaks it began to snow. Soon it seemed to me to be a white-out. I had a sudden fear of being hopelessly lost. How could anyone know which way we were going? Suppose we got separated? I felt like turning back. But that would be certain disaster. We had already been travelling for over an hour and, looking back, I could see our tracks were already disappearing behind us. I was in a catch-22 situation. I did not want to frighten Raschid, so kept quiet and just sat in the saddle, feeling completely empty. Perhaps Ahmaddin could tell our direction from the wind. I noted it was blowing on our right quarter. We trudged on for over another hour. Then we halted. The driving snow had stopped and small areas of stars appeared above, as the clouds moved across the sky, revealing glimpses of constellations I thought I recognised, including Polaris, the North Star. We dismounted, and Ahmaddin very quietly told me and Raschid to stay put while he and Pete progressed forward to what looked like a craggy lip above a valley. The dawn was just beginning to turn the gaps in the clouds a pale green, and the stars were fading.

I felt a great sense of relief, because Ahmaddin clearly knew exactly what he was doing and where we were. Pete had loaded his rifle, and the pair of them crept forward. Their feet crunched into the snow with a muffled sound that soon faded. The outline of their bodies faded as well, as another swirl of snow began to fall like a shroud. They disappeared. Raschid and I were left alone in a total wilderness. Raschid had hunched his shoulders and was shaking his head. His mouth was turned down. There was no happy excitement now. He looked very vulnerable, worried and frightened.

I was a bit worried myself, and felt completely out of my depth. The wind changed direction while we stood sheltering next to the yaks, and we had to move round to their other side. I realised I wouldn't be able to use the wind direction as a guide after all. The sky had closed over again and all the pre-dawn dusky light had vanished.

We stood huddled against the yaks. I could see the snow was beginning to fill the footprints of the other two. Those footprints were their only link back to us, and although they were still visible, they soon wouldn't be. I thought if I kept them open everything would be all right. But how to make Raschid understand what I was doing? I walked a few steps forward, and then back, making a definite track. Then I went a bit further forward and did the same. I got hold of Raschid's arm and pointed. 'Your turn.' He understood, 'OK Meesta Reesha,' and copied what I had done. I thought, if nothing else it will keep us occupied and a bit warmer. We took it in turns to extend the path forwards while the other held the yak ropes. Each time Raschid returned he shook my hand and grinned, looking up at me with his dark eyes. 'Is OK Meesta Reesha.' He was reassuring me, and I felt very touched. I felt responsible for him. He had come out on this seemingly foolhardy trip only because of me. I had to look after him and get him back safely. And he felt exactly the same. It was a strange but very real bond that had sprung up between us. I had always been a loner, even at school – especially at school. My interest in life was going off on my own to observe and share the natural life around me. I didn't want anyone else around. I had always been self-sufficient, and only really happy when left on my own. Suddenly here I was in a very hostile situation, and very glad of and dependent upon the company of a young lad whose language I did not speak. It was a strange feeling.

I wanted to find the other two, or at least know where they were, for his sake as well as my own. Smiling at Raschid with a confidence I did not really feel, and returning his greeting of 'OK OK', I thought suddenly how alike our names were. I held him briefly by the shoulders, then pointed at him, 'Raschid', then to myself, 'Reeshard', then back at him 'Reeshard' and myself 'Raschid', making the sounds as similar as possible. He grinned and put his thumb up in the air. He had understood, and when I went off again was happily muttering the two names to himself.

I trudged back into the blizzard and made another fifty-yard life-line track for the others. This brought me to the ledge they had made for, above a steep valley. The snow had been well trampled here. I could see they had been lying down and wriggling along but the snow was already covering everything, and there was no sign of the two men. Where the hell were they? I could just see that their track had swerved sideways on and away from the lip of the precipice, so presumably there had been nothing there, no ibex for a shot.

There was nothing for it but to return to the yaks and wait. I was within a few yards of Raschid before I saw him, which was a bit worrying. He was overjoyed to see me, and kept shaking my hand. We stood next to the warm animals and waited. A half-hour passed. The snow had eased but we were getting dangerously cold. I showed him how to do cabby-warms round each other. My warmth was exchanged with his warmth. We took it in turns to trudge up and down and half-running on the spot – anything to keep the blood moving. The yaks waited patiently, just shuffling about behind a rocky shelter and nosing the snow. I doubted if they needed holding but dared not risk leaving them. If they had decided to wander away we would have been doomed.

Then the snow stopped, and the icy fog that had been with it lifted also. Although there was no sign of the sky we could suddenly see a hundred yards. All we could see around us were smooth slopes of white, with the vaguest blue shadow trace of the track we had made. Then the icy vapour rose even more, and thinned, and to our joyous relief a pure pale blue of sky began to appear above. The track became a more obvious deep blue shadow in the white surround.

We had heard no shot and there was no sign of the two hunters. We were totally alone, two humans and three yaks, just small dots in the snowy vastness. Everywhere was ominously quiet. Raschid must have found the silence oppressive too, for he suddenly shouted and then, I suppose imitating me from the previous evening, let out a howl like a wolf, which echoed all around us and rebounded off the mountain walls. The sound seemed to frighten him, for he stopped abruptly and clapped his hands over his mouth. He looked at me, and put his arms up in imitation of aiming a rifle, and then put his hands back over his mouth, shaking his head. I understood. We were supposed to keep quiet, and he was worried that he might have ruined a stalk at the very moment the American was going to take a shot at an ibex. That would get him into a lot of trouble.

But after a few moments there came back an answering shout from way over to our left. Thank God, I thought. They are all right, not lost, and the hunt is over, they are coming back – and we are not lost either. But I knew Pete would not be in a good mood. He hadn't got the prize ibex he wanted, nor had he shot anything for everyone to eat. Almost two feet of snow had fallen during the hours we had been out.

The two men eventually appeared, struggling up to us, looking weary. They had seen nothing. It seemed that the snow had driven the ibex from their usual valley. Ahmaddin said they would have gone to shelter in a big valley on the Russian border. He knew where, but now we had to get back. I thought that this would have been 'my' valley, but kept quiet.

'Is soon very bad, too much snow. Getting dangerous.'

Pete nodded, he seemed surprisingly cheerful for a man who had been thwarted of his goal. 'Yep, we need to get out, Rich. Ahmaddin says the snow will get worse now and the last herders are leaving tomorrow. That's the end of this trip. I would have liked to get that ibex, but I know when to quit. Still, it's not been a bad trip. I see you've been busy while we've been gone. Surprised you didn't build yourselves a snow-house.'

There was no sign of the track we had come out by, and I was wondering how we would find our way back. Looking directly up into the sky above us, it was like one of the blue mountain lakes with snow-white shores, but upside down. Weird sheets of icy vapour hung down almost like curtains from thousands of feet above, mingled together, then parted, opening and shutting, and sometimes briefly shimmering as their ice crystals caught all the rainbow colours from the sun. The effect was like a mirage, almost hallucinatory – very beautiful, very strange. I thought the aurora borealis must be similar, but even more intense. I noticed that Ahmaddin also looked up and across at a mountain in the distance. Then I saw he was holding a small compass, and realised he had plotted a course during the small space of time that everything was visible. He caught my eye and grinned, but didn't speak as he swung himself up on to his yak.

Raschid caught my hand as I offered him a lift into the space behind me, and we trundled together back to the camp. The snow held off, and we could see where we were going, but the yaks found it hard work. I noticed Pete went to sleep for most of the way. The old campaigner knew how to pace himself.

17

We got back into camp at about 10 a.m., seven hours after starting out, but there was hardly time to breakfast, and certainly not to rest. Because of the threat of heavy snow we were moving out straight away. The Afghanis had been busy striking camp and packing everything up. There was a great deal of noise and shouting. I stuffed my few belongings into my kitbag. Pia confirmed that the Sargass Pass was already closed, and we would use the route that Ahmaddin had come in by. I tried to close my mind to what that could mean. But visions of being stuck out there, unable to move, with miles of snow drifts and hardly any provisions, were dominant, and I felt a sudden apprehension. Pete however was philosophical.

'I guess these guys have this kind of trouble all the time, and know what to do,' he said when I mentioned my fears. 'I've been in trouble in many parts of the world, and found the locals knew exactly how to sort things out. You just have to trust the pilot knows more than you.' He thought for a while, then with a wry look added: 'They are more attuned to dying than we are anyway. They kinda accept that's how it is.'

I didn't find that very reassuring and didn't think he was right anyway. Yes, perhaps they accepted death more easily than we westerners did in some ways, but they didn't want to die any more than we did. But I did have faith in the pilot: our guides had proved that they knew exactly what they were doing. The panic in my mind subsided. Everything was going to be all right.

We made hasty farewells to those few, Petocz included, who were staying on for another couple of days. There wasn't enough transport for everyone, and they would have to wait for the yaks to return and collect them. But Petocz didn't seem at all worried. I think he was such a loner that he was relieved he didn't have to travel with the rest of us. And because he had been there all summer, he had a lot more gear than the others. Pete was taking up quite a lot of space with his rifle and trophy heads. I gave tips to the singing cook, the boy soldier, the dish-washer, the bread-maker, and a couple of others whom I had got to know. Five hundred afghanis each, no doubt rather small by their ideas, but rather large by mine; my small reserve of cash seemed alarmingly low. I asked Pia to explain that I was not rich like the Americans, that I was a worker like themselves. I think they had understood that anyway.

Everyone was very happy that it was all over. They had had enough and were going home. For them, 'Allah be praised, all had gone well.' I did not share this feeling. For me the mountains were a very special place, giving a sense of grandeur and might; something I had previously only experienced in my mind from reading, and I knew it was a once in a lifetime experience. My time in the deserts of the Middle East had given me a similar feeling on the occasions I had got away into their vastness, but nowhere near the intensity found here. Great music or literature or art had the same ability, but they had to be exchanged for the humdrum of life only too soon. Life up here in the permanently sharp air, with the towering white crests all around, was on a totally different plane and had a feeling of eternity. It had always been like this and it always would be. I was lost in my thoughts, and suddenly became aware I was being shouted at, and so with Raschid's help clambered up on to the burdened yak.

There was no room now for the boy to ride behind me.

This bothered me, as he had been on the move half the night, but the yaks were laden with all the kit from the camp as well as with everyone's personal luggage. They were fully burdened with bedding, cooking pots, empty oxygen flasks, Pete's rifle, a couple of ibex horns and the Marco Polo head and skin.

Raschid had to trudge along beside me, his skinny little legs often sinking into the deep snow. I had given him a sweater and a pair of my old long woollen socks over which he wore the inadequate rubber-tyre shoes, and he had tied some bits of felt over his trousers, with the tatty blanket tied over his head and shoulders, so he was more or less protected. Luckily, as I was towards the back, a bit of a track had appeared for us to follow, which made it easier for him. He seemed happy enough holding on to the ropes that held everything in place, so he was half-supported and half-pulled along, and from time to time he grinned up at me.

The sky cleared completely, and there was blinding light from a suddenly hot sun and, checking my trusty Swedish thermometer, I found the air temperature had soared up to 80°F. The snow crust melted very slightly and the crystals slid together, quickly freezing again in places into a hard and solid layer of jagged ice. The going became very slippery and difficult. Raschid moved behind the yak so he could walk in the holes made by its feet, clutching its fur to keep his balance and help him along. The ice formed prisms, and the sunlight was split into continuously shifting, piercingly glittering spectrums of red and yellow and green and blue. The Afghans had all tied pieces of black yak-hair rope around their eyes to prevent snow-blindness. It reminded me of the oryx in the Arabian desert, which have black eye stripes that reduce the blinding effect of the sun. Raschid was trying to bury his face in the yak's fur, so I shouted to Khasem to get one of the men to give him some rope. I had on my RAF sunglasses. They had been perfectly adequate in the Iraq and Jordanian deserts, but here, despite them, my eyes were screwed up tight against the glare. Our noses started to burn, not just we two westerners and the three Kabul staff, but those of the Wakhis too. Now they tied more black rope round their cheeks and chins as well. I pulled my balaclava and anorak hood even tighter round my face, protecting most of it.

Five vultures were circling around the corpse of a dead animal three hundred metres away, and one lammergeier was already down. I could see that it was a horse, and wondered where it could have come from. Most of the small herd of horses from the camp had long since been returned to the foothills, with just two left to help with our exodus. They were a couple of youngsters and very fit, but goodness knows how they had survived the past week of snow. They had been foraging by themselves, but had not wandered away from the camp and the ground flora was practically nothing but a tight rug of pale brown showing between the drifts of snow.

Raschid tugged at my foot, and pointed to a track in the snow to my left. He said what had made the track in his language, and I could see it was that of a fox. He was excited about that, and laughed gleefully to himself, pointing at the track and then himself and shaking his finger at me. He had spotted that before me, even though I had a better view. I gave him a grin and a thumbs-up. We understood each other despite the lack of a common language.

As we travelled on, I could no longer orient myself as to where we were. There was nothing to relate to, and we were using a different route to the one we had come in by. But Ahmaddin was in the lead, and knew what he was doing and where we were going. It crossed my mind that if anything happened to him there would be a big problem, but quickly pushed such thoughts away. What was really surprising was that I noticed Driver Ahmed was striding along on foot, more or less ahead of everybody. He was a young man of course, but he must have been very fit.

Eventually, at about 1600 hours, we arrived at a Wakhi nomad camp on a flat stony valley floor between high white peaks all around. Pia explained that this was the summer home of a group of Wakhi pastoralists, who tended their herds of sheep and goats on the Pamir Mountains for five months of the year. They were waiting to leave, and had only stayed on to accommodate our caravan on its own exit, bribed heavily to do so by arrangement through Pia and Ahmaddin. I marvelled at the means of communication that went on without we westerners being aware of it. The organisation behind the scenes was as good as it could be, and in these circumstances quite amazing. I said so to Pete, and he just stared at me and grunted. I realised he had no idea of what happened as long as things went well. He would soon have noticed had there been a problem.

We were to spend the night with these shepherds. There were only three yurts, which in effect were now felt igloos: thick yak-felt blanket-like coverings tied down on to stick frames. The walls were a kind of lattice work criss-crossed for strength like the geodetic designs of Wellington bombers in Second World War. The roof covering was resting on long slender ribs of willow sticks that had been curved at the bottoms by steam and heat, so forming a tight junction between roof slope and wall. It all looked very snug. And so it was, despite two problems, one of which we discovered in the morning. The first problem became evident quite soon after we crawled inside.

A small fire of twigs and dried yak dung was smouldering away in the centre of the yurt, surrounded by a semi-circular low mud wall. Rice and mutton were bubbling away in the saucepan perched on an iron trivet. At the apex of the roof there was a hole for the smoke to escape. When the door flap of felt and splines of wood was lowered, that hole in the roof was the only chink in the otherwise airtight capsule. This was a superb design against the elements: it kept out the cold and the wind. Wind chill is the killer in the mountains. However, due to the smallness of the 'chimney' hole, all the smoke wasn't escaping, and it hung well below at head height in a dense stratum of deep blue. The only defence was to sit down on the ground on ancient rugs, to keep below the smoke zone. The herdsman and his heavily covered wife lived here with their daughter, a very pretty but very grubby little tot of about three years. Pia introduced the herdsman, but I didn't quite catch his name. The wife, who kept her face averted from us, kept in the shadows at the back and was not introduced, and it would not have been polite to ask. More than impolite – it would have created hostility.

Pete settled himself down, and as the tot sidled up to him he took her on his knee. I remembered he had done this when we stopped somewhere on the way up. The child did not protest, and seemed entirely happy as she stared at the flames now rising around the pan. Pete explained that he had grand-children back home. The father smiled and said something in return. Pete felt in an inner pocket and got out his bundle of photographs and showed the man his own wife and children. The herdsman spoke to his wife, and moving across, showed her the photographs. She darted a look at Pete and gave him an invisible smile, handing the photographs back and then bending to busy herself with some dishes. The man returned to Pete and, giving back the photos, slapped him on the shoulder and spoke at some length, Pete nodding as if he understood. Both men spoke and smiled – neither understanding the words of the other, but each happy that contact had been made. I found the exchange interesting. Pete had pretty much ignored the men at the camp, and had certainly not made any attempt to be sociable or friendly. I wondered if he was relieved that we were on our way out and whether the pressure he put on himself to achieve his ambitions blinded him to the niceties of life. He was quite a complex character, far more so than Don. I wondered how he was now, and was about to mention this but the smoke began to wrack my lungs and, cold though it was, I went outside to get some fresh air.

Two teenage girls, dressed in black with red shawls and with their heads covered in black, immediately fled at the sight of the feranji in their midst. They shouted to some younger girls who also hid themselves. They had been rounding up the goats for milking. I counted about fifty or so milling around, the kids taking the chance to suckle the nannies, wagging their tails like metronomes out of control. An enormous brown and yellow dog came bounding across the yard, snarling and barking, showing fangs like a polar bear. It stopped two feet from me. One of the men shouted at it and hurled a rock as big as a cricket ball, hitting the dog on the ankle. It cowered down, and ran off howling into a corner between boulders.

The yaks were groaning and grunting away to themselves on the outer edge of the camp. I could see young Raschid moving among them. He saw me and waved, and I put my hand up in return, but two men spoke sharply to him and he turned back to his work. He had been put back in his place within the social order of the camp. Fraternisation wasn't allowed.

A transparent, vaporous moon was rising above the snowy peaks in the last of the blue afternoon sky, all the storm clouds having faded away. I noticed that some of the men still working away in the yard were wearing a semblance of traditional clothes of the oatmeal-coloured felt. These were mainly overcoats. Their trousers were hitched up and tied at the knee with string so that they resembled plus fours. That was how the farm workers of my youth had hitched their clothes up, to stop the irritation of cloth dragging in the wet

262

herbage – here it was deep snow that was a constant problem. The nomads' jackets were mostly any shape or colour. I had already heard from our guides how hunters in the past had handed over jackets to men looking after them. It was even rumoured that one lucky guide had been given the alpine jacket of King George V, while another thought his grandfather had got Roosevelt's jacket after the president had been hunting here. It was too cold to keep standing around doing nothing, so I went back into the smoky but warm yurt, and a plate of hot rice and lumps of meat.

The yurt stayed warm all night, and for the first time in weeks my toes stayed warm all night too. Sleeping on the ground meant our noses and mouths were in the smoke-free zone which was a relief. Dogs barked intermittently all through the night, presumably at wolves prowling nearby, while once there had been a tremendous rumble from a rock fall which shook the ground beneath us. I had gone out for a pee then, and found the snow peaks glistening above huge dark shadows, like corridors of clouds lit by bright moonlight. It was almost surreal, and I felt quite light-headed in the intensely cold air.

Everyone stirred early. Breakfast was tea in glass tumblers and some naan bread that had been baked the previous evening. Pete gave the herdsman 500 afghanis, although they had been officially paid by Pia on behalf of the Afghan Tourist Authority.

'A sweetener,' he said to me. I offered to chip in. 'No, Rich, that's OK. I've plenty to spare, and I know you're only Rich by name – your pocket is pretty poor I guess.'

He handed a coin to the little girl, who squeaked with delight and then hid her face in her mother's skirt. The woman's face was visible this morning and I saw the harsh wrinkles of her face briefly vanish as she smiled quite sweetly. She was quite handsome, in her late twenties probably, but showed lines of experience gained from her nether world of hardship. She noticed me watching her, and immediately pulled her headscarf across her face and turned away, busying herself with stacking pots and pans. They were also going to leave as soon as they were ready.

Our yaks had been unloaded for the night, and were now being loaded up again. Raschid was hard at work helping the men. I knew he was coming with us as far as Sargass, where he had relatives who would take him in. When all was ready he came running through the flock of goats and sheep, looking very happy and chattering away. Pia laughed and tousled his hair. I asked what he had said.

'Oh, Ahmaddin has told him where he saw the snow leopard as he came through on his way up, and the boy is going to watch out to show it to you. I doubt it will still be there though.'

I caught my breath. Raschid's excitement was infectious, but I hardly dared think that there was any possibility of it happening. It was a last chance but very unlikely. But Ahmaddin had seen one, a clear view, and only a few days before. I would need to keep very alert.

We left at seven a.m. in blinding sunlight. I noticed Ahmed, our original driver, set off on foot again at a fast pace ahead of our main party, and soon disappeared. I thought this more than a little foolhardy. I asked Pia what he was doing. Pia shrugged. 'He proves he is strong man. He says he knows better way than we go. I wash my hands.'

Out in the wide valley beyond the camp, yesterday's blizzard had drifted into one vastness about a mile wide and two miles long. It was about a metre deep. It seemed the snow had not settled on the mountains, but had blown into this enormous funnel. That was not good. I had just enough film left to take some pictures of the yaks forcing their way through it all, like steam trains in the alps. They kept stopping and looking round, as if to see how their companions were faring, which I found quite comical. The going was very difficult, and they seemed to be getting exhausted with the heavy loads on their backs.

Raschid ploughed doggedly behind me. He also soon began to look tired, despite hanging on to the ropes. I was worried about his stamina, and shouted to Pia to ask the boy if he was all right. The lad shook his head and said 'OK OK,' and looking up at me, 'OK Meesta Reesha,' his only words of English.

After five hours of ploughing on, we came to a steep valley leading down off the plateau. I had no idea where we were. It was of course a completely different route from the one we had come up by. But I thought we might be coming to the area that Ahmaddin had told me about, where he had seen the snow leopard earlier in the week.

Cliffs began to rise high around us as we began the descent through a steep narrow gorge, whose walls soon towered to a great height above our heads. This had sheltered the track from the snow, so it was now easier going. I couldn't really tell how high, but it seemed about a mile, perhaps even more. Green beards of ice hung down in layers of about five feet between fissures of rock, where flowing water had frozen solid. Our passage down into the gloom of the canyon echoed with the clatter of our movement, and there was also an almost silent hum of deep sound that must have been the air circulating and bouncing. It was a bit unnerving. After a while Ahmaddin sent back a message to say we were going to make a stop here, but not to make any unnecessary noise. I understood that he meant me to realise that this was the place he had seen the snow leopard. I raised my arm to show him I was aware.

There, to my total surprise, we found Ahmed. He was standing on a wide bare platform of rock in a triumphant pose. Once he knew we had seen him, he knelt on the ground and started to pray. He was obviously establishing to Allah how superior he was in strength and in piety. Others joined him. Others tethered the laden animals to boulders with their nose ropes and added to the murmuring chant. Raschid tagged on behind. The rest of us dismounted, and I was very glad to stretch and get my limbs moving. Having got my circulation going, I looked around at the extraordinary deep canyon which had so brutally been carved into this ragged gap in the earth's crust. I had never seen anything remotely like it before. It was as if a gigantic axe had been swung down and cleaved the land in two. I presumed that it had been formed by a massive earthquake, perhaps even comparatively recently, as it seemed the colossal sides of this ravine were only just hanging on and would surely crash down at any moment. It was a frightening, almost terrifying, but at the same time absolutely thrilling place to be. I was very much on the alert for any sign of animal life.

Suddenly I noticed a movement high above us right on the edge of the precipice, almost, it seemed, hanging out into space. It must be an eagle or a vulture, I thought, flapping its wings as it stayed still in the same spot. I got my binoculars out of the deep pocket I kept them in, and impatiently waited while the mist cleared off the lenses. Once I had got them focussed I was amazed to see that it was an ibex, a huge male with curving horns touching its back. It did not seem possible that it could balance where it was. It was not right at the top, on what could have been flat land, but on what must have been a ledge about fifty yards below. There was no sign of any such ledge however, just smooth pale maroon- or brown-coloured sheer wall. It appeared to be standing on air, and it stood completely still. So, perhaps it was trapped and about to fall. To my total amazement I then saw that another animal of equal size was approaching it from the left.

Pete heard me exclaim and asked what I had seen.

'Have a look,' I said, handing him the glasses. 'I can't believe it. That is impossible. There's nothing for them to stand on.'

Pete drew in his breath with an audible hiss. 'Jesus! That is two of the best heads I've ever seen. And the damn animals are out of range.'

'You can't shoot here anyway,' I reminded him. 'You are away from the licenced area. This is protected – and you would almost certainly start a massive rock fall.'

'Yeh, I know all that. Very tempting though. Either of them would do. That is the head I was after. That would have been the prize.' He handed the binoculars back to me. 'They look as if they're going to clash – you'd better watch for yourself. These mountain goats do impossible things. I've seen that sort of thing before, but maybe not quite so good as this.' And he moved off to check his bounty was still safely strapped on.

He was right. They did clash. The two giants gave the ultimate performance of male confrontation, banging their heads together as they seemingly floated in space. The ledge they were on could only have been just wide enough for their bodies. There was no room for error, seemingly no room even for movement. They were fighting on a tight-rope. This could surely only resolve itself in one, perhaps even both, falling to its death. At that moment thin vapours of new-born clouds began to appear high above, and soon whitened out the thin strip of blue sky above the canyon, very quickly dragging moisture lower down into condensation. Patchy snow began to drift across high up, making a rainbow dust as the sun briefly twisted the crystals through this prism. It was a strange phenomenon, rather like a thin multi-coloured quilt floating along in the air.

Raschid appeared at my side, holding on to my sleeve,

staring at the cliffs everywhere around us. Suddenly he tugged my arm and whispered 'OK OK.' He pointed upward and looked at me excitedly. 'Meesta Reesha, OK OK,' and continued in rapid Pashto which I could not understand. With a thump in my heart, I wondered whether this was the moment. I could see nothing. He was silent for a moment standing up on his toes, tense and dead still, but I could feel him shaking, then he whispered again, 'OK OK,' and tugged at my binoculars and pointed up to the top of the precipice, about two hundred metres to the left of the ibex.

I stared at everything through the glasses very carefully, but could see nothing but the clouds and the cliffs behind them, the whole pattern of white and brown changing all the time as drags of cloud moved across. Something flashed across my tunnel of vision, and swinging to the left I caught up with the white outline of an Egyptian vulture. I followed this as it glided high above, but Raschid pulled at my arm and pointed again at the first place. I carefully swept the glasses where he was pointing, but could see nothing other than rock. The boy was getting quite agitated, and jabbed his finger repeatedly towards the same place.

I heard the others return from their prayers. Pia noticed Raschid's excitement, and came over to us. There was a brief exchange between the two Afghanis, then Pia said, 'He say snow leopard up there. Maybe, maybe not.' He seemed to remonstrate with the lad, who looked upset and nodded his head vigorously and pointed again. The cloud was increasing and the brown gaps between them, showing the mountain walls, slid silently along. My heart was thumping away, and my eyes had begun to stream tears from the wind as I stared.

I asked Pia to see if the boy could explain more exactly where the place was, and impatiently waited, still staring up while information was exchanged.

'The snow leopard is sitting upright. It is looking towards

the ibex. It is underneath a place where the rock above it is a dark colour. You must see a small patch of snow shaped like a goat near to it and at the same height – but to the right.'

Then suddenly I could see the snow shape of the goat as the gap in the clouds opened briefly, and I followed the gap along as the clouds moved, and there, under the dark overhang, was the snow leopard, sitting on its haunches, dead still, its coat no more than the mottled colour of the rocks. It was hardly more than a shadow in the clouds, but for me at that moment it was the most exciting and important thing that had ever happened. For a few moments I stared hard, but as I watched the cloud came over again, and when it had cleared the animal had disappeared.

I turned to Raschid and grabbed his hand. 'Thank you. Thank you, Raschid. That was incredible, thank you.'

'OK OK,' was his grinning reply.

Pia interrupted. 'Be careful. Ahmaddin does not want the others to know about the animal. They might come back and kill.' And turning to Raschid he spoke sharply, obviously warning the boy of the danger for the animal. Raschid sobered immediately. I said, 'OK, Raschid, OK,' and turning to Pia asked him to tell the boy that I thought he had been very clever, and had explained very well the position of the fabulous animal, and that I would remember this moment all my life.

It was a good moment. Apart from finally achieving my dream, I felt equally good about the bond that had sprung up between Raschid and myself, and indeed I hoped with some of the others. I felt that I wasn't just another westerner, out for his own selfish ends, but someone they might remember and talk about. I was sure that the bond of the mountain ghost would remain between Raschid and myself. It certainly would for me, and I liked to think it would for Raschid.

While we had been engaged in our own drama the men

had made tea and handed round naan bread and some cheese. Then we set off again. We got to Sargass in the early evening. Raschid would be stopping here, so after the evening meal I managed to get him alone and offered him a generous handful of money. He hesitated and hid his face. I realised he felt that I was his friend, that he was my equal, and this was not necessary, almost an insult, so I called Pia over and explained.

'Tell him it is a prize – like winning a race on a horse or at buzkashi,' I said. 'I was planning to give a prize to anyone who found me a snow leopard.'

This seemed to satisfy him. His smile returned and he cheerfully gave me his usual 'OK OK.'

I also sought out Ahmaddin and thanked him for making the opportunity for achieving my dream, and told him how much I admired his skill. He shrugged. 'I earn my living. That is all. But I know I am good at my work.' I didn't give him a tip. I knew Pete had been generous, and that was sufficient. We shook hands and he disappeared back to his own home.

That night, in bed with the fleas again in Sargass village, I went over again and again that moment of seeing the mountain ghost, before it vanished for ever behind the curtain of clouds. I was amazed the boy had been able to see the leopard without binoculars, but realised he was young and had very keen eyesight, while my eyes had been very sore from the strong sunlight and the wind in the canyon the previous day. I had been the same at his age.

In the morning I saw that the harvest scene that I had watched as we came up was well over. A man was ploughing the one-acre field with an ox and a wooden plough that one might have seen in England in early Victorian days. The Wakhis saddled our horses for the long ride out. The yaks were being gathered up amid a great deal of noise. As we were about to leave I looked around for Raschid. He came forward from the doorway of a hut, holding something carefully, as if it would break into a thousand pieces if he dropped it. He handed this treasure to me. It was the tip of a Marco Polo horn he had picked up somewhere in the Tulabai valley.

'Meesta Reesha, Meesta Reesha,' he said, 'OK OK.'

I took it with the care and gravity with which he handed it to me, and made a great show of placing it carefully in an inside pocket, patting it gently afterwards. I shook his hand, and his smile has become as bright a memory as the snow leopard that he found for me so long ago.

Postscript

The BBC did not attempt to film my story. The logistics of sustained high-altitude work on such elusive subjects, together with the almost impossibility of travel with enough equipment, was at that time (remember, this was the early 1970s) beyond their resources. Then the situation in Afghanistan itself meant the project became totally impossible. For shortly after my adventure, trouble erupted in the country from within its own government: basically, a coup by the communist faction, but complicated by other factions also wanting power. In due course this unrest enabled the Russians to invade the country, ostensibly to restore calm. This meant the whole area was 'out of bounds' for many years. Even today the Chinese have not reopened their border.

I lost touch with Dr Petocz, who had to move out of the country. But much of the Wakhan has today become an area of protection for the rare animals living there, though hunting continues in bordering Russian territory. I did however remain in contact with Pete Serafin to the very end of his life. Every Christmas we exchanged brief news with our cards. His adventures continued right across the world, with many more impossible escapes, and finally he told his story to a friend who published the book privately, a copy of which was sent to me. Pete said the Afghan adventure was the pinnacle of all his adventures.

When I returned to Sussex and my family, and went back to work at the Kingley Vale National Nature Reserve I was rather taken aback to see how very small the 820-foot-high

South Downs hill now seemed, when standing in the valley looking up at it. It was just a small hillock which I could run up with not the slightest breathlessness! Today it has resumed its stature as one of the grandest 'green mountains' of the South Down chain, with its high aerial overview of the English Channel.

But far back in my mind, the world's greatest peaks still sit massively stern and everlastingly shining white in memory, together with that reminder of fabled animals that I was so privileged to see almost as shadows hidden from the human mind, in one of the last sanctuaries of the planet.